MOVING
OF
MOUNTAINS

THE REMARKABLE STORY OF
THE ÅGASTYA INTERNATIONAL FOUNDATION

ADHIRATH SETHI

Published by
LID Publishing
An imprint of LID Business Media Ltd.
LABS House, 15-19 Bloomsbury Way,
London, WC1A 2TH, UK

info@lidpublishing.com
www.lidpublishing.com

A member of:

businesspublishersroundtable.com

Impact stories contributed by Avya Gupta via interviews with Agastya students

Agastya ecosystem illustration based on an original design contributed by Sheetal Kataria

Printed by Severn, Gloucester
ISBN: 978-1-911687-44-3
ISBN: 978-1-911687-45-0 (ebook)

Cover and page design: Caroline Li

THE MOVING *OF* MOUNTAINS

THE REMARKABLE STORY OF
THE ÅGASTYA INTERNATIONAL FOUNDATION

ADHIRATH SETHI

MADRID | MEXICO CITY | LONDON
BUENOS AIRES | BOGOTA | SHANGHAI

CONTENTS

20+ YEARS OF AGASTYA
A TIMELINE OF HIGHLIGHTS

The ITPL
brainstorming
session

First teacher
training sessions

First science fair

Agastya formally
registered

1999

First employees join

Ecological work
starts on campus

2001

J. N. Tata
Auditorium speech

First meeting
with Rakesh
Jhunjhunwala

First meeting with
President Kalam

Pivoting from
school to a school
for schools

2003

1994

2000

Land acquired
in Gudupalle

Birth of the
Young Instructor
programme

First meeting
with Alok Oberoi

2002

First buildings
on campus

First mobile
science lab

First art
workshop on
campus

2004

National Centre
for Biological
Sciences (NCBS)
brainstorming
session

Work starts on
Jhunjhunwala
Discovery Centre

1994-1999

Creating the
philosophy

Core leadership
team develops

2007-2009

First mega-
science fairs

2009-2011

Expansion in
North Karnataka
begins with
government
support

Support from
the Deshpande
Foundation

Scaling up of the
Young Instructor
Leader programme

First science
centre (Koppal)

2005

2007

2009

2011

2006

2008

2010

Memorandum of
Understanding
signed with R.
Jhunjhunwala
Foundation

President Kalam
visits Agastya
Mobile Lab in
Bangalore

Ramji asked
to join the
National
Knowledge
Commission

2009-2010

Operation
Vasantha begins

Core team
expands

2012-2013

CSR Bill comes
into effect

Agastya's mobile
lab is recognized
among top
100 global
innovations by
The Rockefeller
Foundation

Art /
Media Art
outreach

2011

2013

2015

2012

Former
President Kalam
visits campus

2011-2013

Expansion
in Karnataka
via core
science
activity
centres
(CSACS)

Start of
the training
and quality
assurance (TQA)
programme

Guru Gruha
Astronomy
Centre and
VisionWorks
inaugurated

2014

Support from the
Infosys Science
Foundation

Expansion in
North India begins

Books launched:
*Wisdom of Agastya,
Rise of the Fireflies,*
and *Blazing Fireflies*

'Dung Beetle'
auditorium on campus
inaugurated

Agastya's TechLa
Bike wins Google
Global Impact
Challenge award

2016

IIM-B model
developed for
impact analysis

Agastya
wins Marico
Innovation for
India Award

Jhunjhunwala commits funding for next 10 years

Sarga Samvad programme launched, supported by the Oberoi Family Foundation

The Ramanujan Math Park inaugurated

Bio-discovery Centre and Innovation Hub on campus

2017

Formation of the Navam Foundation

2020-2022

Butterflies of Agastya book launched

Inspirational Indians programme launched

Agastya awarded the Andhra Pradesh State Green Award

2019

Development and launch of ActiLearn 1.0

2021

Expansion in North-East India (Bodoland)

2022-2023

2023

2018

2020

2022

Launch of Agastya 2.0

Launch of Agastya Virtual School

Clinton Global Initiative felicitates Ramji Raghavan and Agastya

T-SAT Design Thinking programme

2020-2021

Covid Lockdown innovations: Explore, Play, Learn (EPL), Smart TV, Home Lab Kit, WeLearn app

2014-2018

Innovations: Lab on a Bike, TechLaBike, Lab in a Box, i-Mobile Lab, Lab on a Tab, Maja Box

THE AGASTYA ECOSYSTEM
A DISCOVERY-DRIVEN ENTERPRISE MOVEMENT

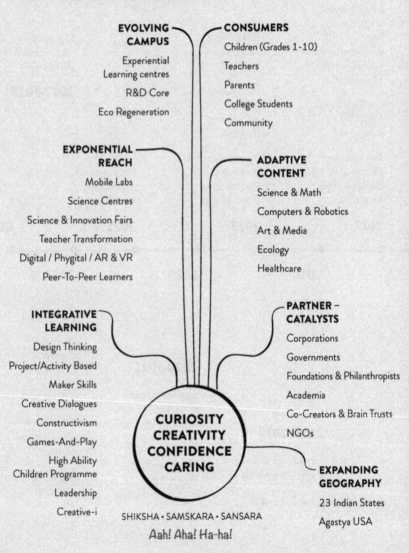

EVOLVING CAMPUS
Experiential Learning centres
R&D Core
Eco Regeneration

CONSUMERS
Children (Grades 1-10)
Teachers
Parents
College Students
Community

EXPONENTIAL REACH
Mobile Labs
Science Centres
Science & Innovation Fairs
Teacher Transformation
Digital / Phygital / AR & VR
Peer-To-Peer Learners

ADAPTIVE CONTENT
Science & Math
Computers & Robotics
Art & Media
Ecology
Healthcare

INTEGRATIVE LEARNING
Design Thinking
Project/Activity Based
Maker Skills
Creative Dialogues
Constructivism
Games-And-Play
High Ability Children Programme
Leadership
Creative-i

PARTNER – CATALYSTS
Corporations
Governments
Foundations & Philanthropists
Academia
Co-Creators & Brain Trusts
NGOs

CURIOSITY CREATIVITY CONFIDENCE CARING

EXPANDING GEOGRAPHY
23 Indian States
Agastya USA

SHIKSHA • SAMSKARA • SANSARA
Aah! Aha! Ha-ha!

x

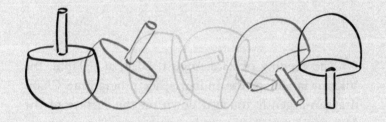

FOREWORD

A.S. KIRAN KUMAR,
FORMER CHAIRMAN, INDIAN SPACE RESEARCH ORGANISATION

On the evening of 23rd August, 2023, at 6:04pm, the Vikram lander of the Indian space programme Chandrayaan-3 gently touched down on the surface of the Moon in a region close to its south pole. The event was witnessed live on small and large screens across India by the extensive Indian diaspora across the globe, and the world at large applauded what was a crowning achievement. The landing was followed by the Pragyan rover coming out of the lander to carry out observations of the lunar surface. The success of Chandrayan-3 resulted in a feeling of immense joy and pride for the entire nation, as it demonstrated India's ability to explore the surface of our closest celestial neighbour, a daring technological feat. A few days later, I met my grandnephew, who had only just learnt to speak. "I saw the moon landing!" he happily exclaimed to me, giving me pause to think just how deep the success of Chandrayaan-3 had seeped into the Indian psyche.

However, the event also brought back memories of 7th September, 2019. On that day, the entire nation experienced the agony of defeat, as the lander of Chandrayaan-2 failed to perform a soft landing on the lunar surface.

And yet, I believe that it is this ability of being able to learn from the inadequacies of unsuccessful attempts and build capabilities to overcome limitations that sets successful explorers apart. Much like the Mars Orbiter Mission in 2014, where India became the first country to successfully insert, in its maiden attempt, a satellite around Mars that had travelled about 600 million kilometres over 10 months, the Chandrayan-3 mission demonstrates the process initiated by Dr Vikram Sarabhai to harness India's evolving technological capabilities into putting objects into space.

In 1957 when Russia put the first man-made object into space, India was a fledgling democracy, emerging from centuries of colonial rule and struggling to provide its citizens with a better life. India's use of space technology was only to provide an effective means of linking the nation through broadcasting, communication, navigation and disaster mitigation, apart from providing observational information to aid in governance and in the planning and monitoring of resources. Today, India is among only a handful of countries with an end-to-end capability of building satellites for various applications and launching them into space using our own rockets. A process initiated in the early sixties, with the dedicated efforts of generations of Indians graduating from diverse institutions across the country, has shown that through purposeful perseverance, teamwork and innovation, it is possible to overcome the limitations of resource constraints and technology denials, and beat seemingly insurmountable odds.

Humans have an intrinsic quality to explore and make sense of what is around them. They are curious about nature, trying to imitate and mimic things, building tools to extend our ability to observe beyond the five sensory organs, and to perform activities beyond the physical limits of the functional organs. In this process, the exploration of the external world beyond the self and an internal exploration of the self are both involved.

Every child, as soon as it emerges from the womb of its mother, begins its journey of exploring the world around it. This journey is a relentless process that continues throughout its existence. How this journey transpires depends on a host of conditions that the child has no say in, during the initial periods of its life. In this journey, by making use of the sensory organs that it is endowed with, the child learns to receive inputs from the world surrounding it. It learns to imitate and mimic the behaviour of people and other living beings around it. The child's ability to observe, be curious and make sense of the world is enormous and boundless. However, the child's environment and the people responsible for its survival and growth also have a significant impact on the child. A weak environment can result in many intrinsic abilities of the child remaining unutilized, and can lead to an inability to make complete use of the capabilities it is endowed with.

India, a land of seekers, had once studied methods of bringing awareness to individuals and had evolved into a prosperous society. However, following multiple invasions, India went through long periods of external rule that not only affected the living conditions of its people but also impacted its education system. Centuries of external subjugation forced India into a predicament wherein it was unable to provide its children an environment conducive to becoming aware of their intrinsic abilities.

Following Independence in 1947, India went through a challenging period as it worked to improve the living conditions of its citizens. It had to ensure that that its people were not just provided with opportunities to develop skills and improve their own abilities to negotiate life, but also to contribute meaningfully to society so that future generations might live with dignity, comfort and the freedom to determine the course of their own journeys. This required every child to be provided the opportunity to explore the world. It required bringing awareness to children about their intrinsic abilities, the use of their sensory organs and actuators, and the intelligence they are endowed with.

It is in dealing with how to enable a child to successfully negotiate the limitations of its environment that one encounters a challenge of Himalayan magnitude. India, with its diversity of living conditions and social practices, poses huge difficulties when one attempts to bring any awareness to the child and enable the child to retain its curiosity to explore, build confidence, and creatively deal with the situations it encounters.

However, in this endeavour the Agastya International Foundation has demonstrated something unique. They have shown that it is possible to make a difference to the pursuit of bringing awareness to the child through the process of experiential learning. Agastya has found the formula needed to ignite the child's mind, to help the child explore the process of comprehension and to allow the child to develop the ability to use such learning to creatively solve problems.

The Moving of Mountains captures the saga of how a banker changed his life's course, established a world-class cause and contributed to changing the lives of millions of children across India. It vividly brings out the arduous task he undertook, and the process of growing an institution that dealt with various hurdles to pursue its objectives. It captures the amazing innovative abilities of many individuals involved in building an institution that has had a far-reaching impact on India's most disadvantaged children. The narrative brings out the relentless efforts, changing contours, and the numerous approaches and strategies that evolved during Agastya's two-decade journey. In fact, it could be said that Agastya's journey is one of discovery and exploration despite facing many hurdles, much like that of Chandrayaan-3.

Today, India has entered a new phase of development as it aims to provide its citizens with living conditions that are conducive for exploring both internal and external "space." Indeed, each such triumph of Indian space exploration boosts the interest of education in science and technology and drives forward creativity learning in general.

As the undue struggle for basic necessities becomes less pronounced, our task shifts to enabling the next generation to deal with the issues they face in a world where changes occur at an ever-increasing pace.

Understating the importance of an environment that allows for this calls for not just an appreciation of the efforts of the Agastya International Foundation, but also the support and encouragement needed for Agastya to continue their relentless efforts to reach millions of lives and allow them to experience the magic of 'Aah! Aha! and HaHa!' moments.

I am sure the efforts of the author in bringing out the journey of the Agastya International Foundation will strike a chord in the reader, and not only inspire them but also enable their own efforts to make a difference to the lives of people across the world.

PREFACE

Summers in the south of India have a way of thinning the will of even the most resolute of individuals. In the state of Andhra Pradesh – where temperatures often exceed 40 degrees Celsius – a typical heat wave can comfortably claim the lives of dozens of people each year. Even the shade barely offers any solace from the dry, sapping heat, which writhes its way under one's clothes and settles there like a layer of gross discomfort.

Holding nothing but black umbrellas to shield them from the afternoon heat, three men stood atop a small hill. Their last vestiges of energy were draining away under the sun's brutal glare. The ground around them was stony and coarse for as far as they could see, the dead soil hospitable to nothing but the hardiest, thorniest shrubs. In the distance was the remnant of an old lake, reduced to little more than a large muddy swamp, breathing its last as it too struggled to survive the summer. The sky was cloudless, no birds sang, and the wind, when it chose to blow, only brought with it another torrent of viscous, hot air that blurred and distorted anything seen from a distance.

As uncomfortable as the men were, the heat was far from the largest of their problems. The land may have been rocky and lifeless, but it was all they had. The same government that had once bought into their vision and alloted the land to them was now demanding results and pressuring them to show some visible signs of progress.

One of the men looked wistfully at the 172 acres that he had so painstakingly acquired. He mused over his dream of building a world-class educational institution and it pained him to think that after five years of toil, the funds he had raised had yielded nothing more than a few sheds. In his mind, he could already see the buildings he had dreamed of and the scores of children that would come each day to be educated and inspired within them. But the reality was far removed from this. He needed more time and was searching for a way to somehow pro-tect this land while he hunted for the money required to develop it.

He looked across to the two men with him, hoping for some answers. One of the men – Yellappa Reddy – was an ecologist who had been called in to help revive vegetation in the barren land. The other – Dr. Venkatshamaiah – was a practitioner of Ayurveda, the ancient Indian sys-tem of natural medicine. Neither man had any expertise in construction.

"We have no money," Ramji Raghavan declared matter-of-factly, "and the government has said that unless we start showing some activity, they will need to repurpose the land."

He pointed to another, smaller hill across from where they stood.

"Is there anything we can do with that hill that will showcase that we are making use of this land?"

For a few minutes, the two men stayed silent. It was an absurd request. What could they possibly do overnight with neither money nor resources?

"Anything will do," Ramji reiterated. "I just need something cheap that makes it look like there is some activity on the campus."

Then, through a desperation no doubt catalysed by the searing heat itself, Yellappa spoke.

"We could make a *mulika vana*," he suggested, looking to Dr. Venkatshamaiah, who smiled and nodded in support.

"What is that?" Ramji asked.

"We collect large stones, paint them white and use the stones to make an outline of a man, a woman, and a child across the face of the hill. Then we grow medicinal plants and herbs that pertain to each part of the human body in the corresponding points on the outlines."

He stopped and gauged whether he was making sense. Dr. Venkatshamaiah chimed in now:

"So, we would grow *haldi* at the joints, as it is anti-inflammatory, and *tulsi*, at the head, since it helps soothe migraines and sore throats. It would be an exciting way for children to learn about the benefits of various plant species." (*Haldi* is turmeric and *tulsi* is Indian basil.)

"Would it cost a lot to do?" Ramji was intrigued.

"Nothing more than a few cans of white paint and a trip to a nursery. We could hire some men to paint and place the stones and have the whole thing done for a few thousand rupees."

It was enough. The *mulika vana* – although inexpensive – was eye catching and did its job of suggesting that the land was in use. It was a low-cost, high-impact solution that delivered exactly what was required – a little more breathing space.

In the years that followed, the Agastya International Foundation was able to sell its vision for transformative education. Donors came forth with the necessary funds and the campus flourished. Even as new buildings peppered the once forlorn land, the three white outlines stood like watchful guardians. They rarely escaped the notice of visitors, who marvelled at the concept and took walks on the hill to familiarize themselves with the herbs and their benefits. Few understood, however, that the *mulika vana* had been formed out of pure creativity in the face of near certain defeat.

Today, standing at the same spot the three men once stood at, one might struggle to believe that the campus was once a barren wasteland. Ecological initiatives – started by Yellappa and his team not long after the *mulika vana* was made – infused life into the campus, bringing back key species of plants and spurring the repopulation of fauna. The new buildings that were erected each had their own purpose. Here too, the use of low-cost, natural materials, unique cooling methods and distinctive design allowed each building to have its own story to tell.

Such is the story of Agastya, where creativity and innovation are not just taglines sold to further the cause of education but forged into the very DNA of the organization itself. Whether we look at the way in which the foundation fought for survival or the way it developed its unique model of delivery and distribution, or indeed its unorthodox approach to pedagogy, the common thread has always been creativity.

As is the case with most organizations that have thrived, Agastya's story is far from linear. Like a river that meanders towards the ocean, the foundation has allowed its path to change, so long as it never lost sight of its destination. The goal was, and remains, to grow into a movement – to take hard-learned concepts and disseminate them across the nation so no child should stay detached from the significance of creativity and innovation in education. Agastya aims to answer that most vital of all questions: how does one reach the child that cannot be reached?

The Moving of Mountains is the remarkable story of the Agastya International Foundation. It plots the inception of the foundation from an idea to revolutionize education in India to a towering beacon of inspiration, reaching millions of children a year. It charts the struggles of an organization whose mission to spark curiosity across a nation overcame numerous obstacles, both philosophical and financial. It follows the pedagogical learnings of Agastya and lands at the thrilling concept of 'Aah! Aha! Ha-ha!': an idea – like so many spawned by Agastya – that is rooted in simplicity but powerfully profound. It outlines the birth of an institution as committed to infusing the joy of discovery into its own DNA as it is to bringing the same to generations of underprivileged children.

Finally, it illustrates that most important message – that with creativity and innovation, no child need be bound by the circumstances to which they were born.

CHAPTER 1

THE PRIDE OF GUDUPALLE

For the otherwise uninformed, there is nothing very remarkable about the town of Kuppam. About a two-hour drive from Bangalore, it has a railway station, a few broad roads, schools, marketplaces and an assortment of other everyday establishments that one might expect of a small municipality in South India. The weather is dry for most of the year and the air is often dusty. Like so many towns that were once villages, it displays the tell-tale hallmarks of a rural landscape struggling to develop into something more metropolitan. Here and there, mud paths have mutated into semi-cobbled pavements. Crumbling shop fronts have been given a second wind with hastily installed glassy exteriors. Hoardings – that most obvious signal of urbanization – pepper the tops of buildings in almost every direction.

Kuppam sits on a point of confluence at the borders of three South Indian states: Karnataka, Tamil Nadu and Andhra Pradesh. It is perhaps this location that lends Kuppam – whose name in the local language literally translates to 'a meeting place or convergence' – an element of uniqueness. But state borders in South India seldom have any importance for travellers moving across them. Most will spill over from one state to another without even realizing as much. The roads leading into and out of Kuppam all look much the same and the scenery, while certainly picturesque, does not do enough on its own to tempt a traveller to stop and consider where they might be.

But something that started two decades ago just outside the town has taken Kuppam's name along with it on a rather incredible journey.

Hidden near the village of Gudupalle, the Agastya campus is a 25-minute drive from the main town. Given the obscurity of the rural landscape and the narrow country roads that branch out in all directions, GPS does not always fare well in these parts. As a first-time visitor, you would do well to lower your car window, choose any passer-by and ask, "Agastya?"

The name will invariably invoke an immediate air of recognition in the pedestrian. And then, if you are paying attention, you will notice something altogether different in their expression: pride.

"Agastya!" – the name is repeated with a mingling of reverence, affection and even ownership, as you are guided on the roads you need to take.

The entrance to Agastya's main campus isn't particularly grand. The board that heralds it is small and, but for the burst of Agastya's trademark orange lettering and logo, it might easily be missed.

You sense a change when you pass the board, turning off the narrow, gravelled highway and into the long, clean avenue that leads into the campus. The weather seems cooler and the surroundings greener; there is an intangible buzz around you that cannot be ignored. Your lungs are infused with oxygen-rich air, tinged with the mingled scents of unknown flowers and herbs. If it happens to have rained recently, the deep, red soil throws in its own aromas to delight the senses.

As the road winds to the right, an old, brightly coloured vehicle emerges, perched on a pillar, standing proudly atop a muddy elevation. You are told that it was the original 'mobile science lab,' now retired, and serving to pay homage to one of Agastya's most successful programmes in science education.

Perhaps the first thing to catch your eye as you approach the main campus gate is an image on the left of the avenue: a white sculpture of a cricketer – a batter in mid-pose after having struck the ball.

Only, as you drive further, the batter falls apart. You realize that it was never one figure. It is several fragmented pieces positioned at different distances and aligned in such a way as to look as one when viewed from the entrance. Depth perception creates the image of the cricketer. Already, your mind is being teased by the creativity that awaits within.

You see the words 'Aah! Aha! Ha-ha!' on a board welcoming you to Agastya. You will later be informed that this forms the core of Agastya's philosophy on education. They are the three stages of learning, starting with the question (Aah!), moving to the answer (Aha!) and culminating with the joy in playing with the knowledge acquired (Ha-ha!).

As the campus road ends, you are confronted by a black stone statue basking under a gazebo-like structure[1] – another sculpture, only this one is whole and made in the image of a squat, potbellied man who offers a beatific smile to his visitors. The man, you come to learn, is the venerated Maharishi Agastya, a sage and scholar of ancient times. Revered for his immense wisdom and knowledge, Maharishi Agastya is said to have committed himself to the spread of education across the Indian subcontinent. It is something that the foundation – his namesake – now emulates admirably.

From this point on, having offered you a sufficient taste of what to expect, the campus bursts alive in all directions.

To describe Agastya's campus is not an easy task. Many have attempted to paint a picture of what might await a first-time visitor only to find that their descriptions fell immensely short of setting the right expectations.

"You told us it was beautiful, but we didn't realize it was *this* beautiful," newcomers often exclaim. Others lament that they wish they had had access to a campus like this while growing up.

Those who schedule day trips often protest that there is not enough time to fully explore the various labs, buildings and parks peppered across the landscape.

But beauty is only a part of what the campus offers. Environmental initiatives – driven passionately for over 20 years – have helped transform the surroundings from a once arid wasteland into an oasis. The trees planted in the earliest days of the foundation have started to throw down dividends of flowers and fruit, as well as cool, welcome shade. Herbs and shrubs have been grown with a deep understanding of which species of plants form synergies with the native flora. Reforestation efforts and water-harvesting initiatives – including strategically placed reservoirs for rainwater – allow the campus to stay green even during the inevitable dry spells so common in the area. The revival of plant life has brought back the fauna. Plants draw in insects (such as new species of butterflies and moths), insects have brought back geckos, and geckos have brought back the birds. Even as you are told this, a peacock can be heard cooing in the distance as if offering a testament to the authenticity of the environment's burgeoning richness.

Then, as though to underline the vibrancy of life on campus, you are told about the deer, the snakes and the wild boar that visit at night. Even herds of elephants, known to have lost their traditional path through the erstwhile jungles that were consumed by the surrounding towns and villages, use the campus's green cover to migrate undetected.

In addition to its natural beauty, the campus's transformation into a veritable theme park of creativity and innovation can be experienced as you continue along the arterial road that loops around it. From the simpler, earlier structures nearer to the entrance, you start to notice larger, more ingenious buildings as you proceed further: the massive auditorium, made to resemble a dung beetle; an astronomy centre, which houses the world's largest model of the solar system; a bio-discovery centre, made in the form of a termite hill; the lizard-shaped art and innovation centre; and the Jhunjhunwala Discovery Centre – made to emulate the San Francisco Exploratorium.

In total the campus has nearly 30 buildings, each more ambitious than the next. Each one of these architectural marvels dedicates itself to a certain specialization of art or science. Each comes with its own story and imparts its own learnings. Eco-friendly techniques have been employed to ensure both the use of local materials and a synchronicity with nature that allows the buildings to stay cool even at the height of summer.

Experiencing the campus requires a minimum of two days, if not more. In truth, the campus is so infused with science that even after multiple visits, you might find something new that you missed earlier. Little titbits of wonder are sprinkled inconspicuously to be discovered by anyone who cares to go deeper. A stray globe labelled 'Mars' may catch your eye. It appears completely misplaced until you are informed that each of the first four planets have been positioned deliberately around the campus. If we consider the astronomy centre as the sun, then each planet's model is placed at a distance proportional to where it would be in the actual solar system (for the remaining planets, they have been placed further out on campus, but not quite to scale, as this would require positioning them many kilometers outside campus!). Elsewhere, in the maths park, dedicated to the genius mathematician Srinivasa Ramanujan, you might see a stray set of seemingly random numbers painted along the pathway. You follow the numbers to their source only to realize that they are the decimal values of pi, extending across the campus.

While science was the beginning of Agastya's journey, the arts have started to take hold as well, evidenced by the myriad murals and sculptures across the campus, and by plays, art classes and dance recitals conducted in the auditorium.

The energy on this 172-acre campus is intriguing, revolving around these throwaway nods to learning. They can make any adult long for another shot at their youth and wishing they could be reintroduced to academia in this engaging manner. But the mission was never about the adults.

The Agastya International Foundation is a charity with the bold ambition of sparking curiosity, nurturing creativity and instilling confidence and caring for all the underprivileged children of India. This most arduous of tasks involved pushing against a tide that had waylaid Indian education, turning it into a rote-based, syllabus-obsessed and exam-centric system.

At the turn of the 21st century, and with the help of some of the world's foremost scientists and educationalists, Agastya mapped a plan to take hands-on learning to the remotest parts of rural India. The campus was originally envisioned as a school, but it eventually became the hub of a highly fragmented delivery system that spreads across India, taking science education to every corner. The mobile science lab – Agastya's award-winning delivery mechanism – became the key element of this system. Fed by strategically placed science centres across the country, the mobile labs go from school to school along with an Agastya instructor (or 'igniter' as they are informally known) armed with close to 100 curated low-cost experiments.

The instructor's mandate: to make learning joyful and to show children science in action. This is science they can hold and experience and even break. Science that had hitherto been trapped between mundane lines in their textbooks.

The mobile science labs themselves are always being upgraded, with new experiments added as the instructors work tirelessly to adapt to Agastya's ever-evolving teaching methods. Brightly painted with Agastya's trademark cartoon figures, the labs are – both literally and figuratively – the burst of colour that any dreary school day needs.

As the popularity of the mobile labs grew, new and innovative programmes were launched to complement them. The Lab-on-a-Bike, Lab-in-a-Box, Lab-on-a-Tab, media labs and the Gifted Children programme all added to Agastya's ever-expanding repertoire. In 2013, Agastya's mobile science labs featured in the gallery of the top 20 global innovations in education in the Rockefeller Foundation's NextCentury Awards. Agastya's TechLaBike won the Google Global Impact Challenge award in 2014.

Meanwhile, a dedicated focus on teacher training allows under-funded government schools access to methods designed to increase the effectiveness of their own teaching staff. Agastya's Teacher Training Centre offers a rigorous programme. Teachers trained here wear their upskilled status like a badge of honour, sometimes referring to themselves as 'Kuppam returned' – a playful twist on the idea that IT engineers trained in America would often say that they were 'US Returned.'

Within a few years of its foundation, Agastya was drawing interest from the Indian government. School attendance rates had started to rise, and the quality of teaching was improving in those areas where Agastya was operating. With the help of government partnerships and the support of private donors who believe in Agastya's mission, the foundation has scaled rapidly, now reaching five million children each year. Cumulatively, Agastya has reached an incredible 25 million children[2] and over 200,000 government schoolteachers since inception.

All the while, Agastya's campus in South India has developed into a world-class centre for learning – an R&D home base where new concepts are ideated, tested and then prepared for dissemination across the country. While it does not function as a school, it offers children in other schools access to science learning that would otherwise be far out of their reach. Each morning Agastya buses head out from the campus, returning with over 600 students from surrounding schools who get to experience Agastya's unique learning methods. Trained instructors (or igniters) help the children better unravel the science and explore beyond the basic concepts they may have learnt in school. Children showing an aptitude and an inclination for learning are encouraged to delve deeper into their subjects, while even the government schools' teachers are offered training to make them more effective once they are back in their classrooms.

To understand the true effect of Agastya, however, you need only to speak with the children that Agastya reaches. As the story goes, a young girl named Uma was once asked what impact her visits to the Agastya campus had had on her. It was expected that she might say she had learned a lot of science and that her test scores at school had improved. Instead, she looked up confidently and said, "Sir, I am not afraid to speak any more." This may seem trivial in the developed world, but in India, where girls were often discouraged – even forbidden – from getting an education, it speaks volumes.

Uma was the first girl in her village to attend engineering college, inspiring other girls after her to have similar aspirations.

As the philosopher Jiddu Krishnamurti once said, "It is the function of education to eliminate fear."[3] The Agastya International Foundation, while rooted in learning, has opened a world of possibilities for underprivileged children. It allows them to be their most unbridled, creative selves, without the fear that might otherwise hinder them or the doubts that might prevent them from exploring what could be.

As the foundation continues to scale and take hands-on education into the quietest corners of India, other initiatives are constantly being deployed to engage children and further the cause of sparking curiosity. Science fairs across the country draw in tens of thousands of children within the span of a few days. Night schools utilize Agastya's models to keep rural children from mischief while their parents return from the fields. Educationalists from around the world, both inspired by and drawn to Agastya's methods, conduct workshops on campus and in science centres. The book *Acti-Learn 1.0* – containing hands-on activities and experiments for children to try at home – helped rural children restricted by the pandemic to still taste the joys of science before becoming a vehicle for fun, origami-based science learning. Initiatives abound within the organization, driven by teams that remain as hungry to learn and explore as the children that Agastya reaches.[4] With Agastya's over 1,500 staff and over 5,000 volunteers, it is no wonder that new innovations are constantly being dreamed up and rolled out.

But, like all great institutions, Agastya did not happen overnight. Disparate events, people and ideas needed to collide and find harmony before the journey could truly begin. And, as unlikely as it seems today, 25 years ago, Agastya was little more than the musings of a disgruntled banker and the three wise men he approached to ease his quandary.

1. The structure is actually an open temple, specially constructed in the Pallava style of architecture.

2. Agastya calculates its reach using internal models that incorporate the number of interactions, the frequency of these interactions, and the intensity of the interactions.

3. Jiddu Krishnamurti, *Krishnamurti on Education*

4. See https://www.agastya.org/acti-learn-1

CHAPTER 2

THE BANKER, THE BROKER AND THE THREE WISE MEN

For the architects of illustrious institutions, predictability is rarely an ally. Indeed, if there is such a thing as a common thread linking organizations that have stood apart, it is that they have all encountered numerous unknown unknowns. Success is most often forged from a willingness to tear down hard-held beliefs, to recalibrate assumptions, and to pivot wildly and without hesitation when the moment calls for it. Being constantly stymied in any attempts to move forward becomes a way of life. It serves as a sort of teasing reminder that to create genuine impact, one cannot expect to stroll unhindered with the aid of some well-intentioned roadmap.

The effect of this is that great leaders must, by necessity, stay unattached to the path they choose to bring their vision to life. On the matter of the vision itself, however, there is often little room for negotiation.

The initial concept for Agastya and the foundation that eventually emerged were two vastly different entities. In trying to influence meaningful change, Agastya constantly deviated from its original plan, zigzagging like a wandering brook as it felt its way across unfamiliar terrain. External factors, and indeed a willingness to evolve its own understanding, forced the organization to stay adaptable. Yet, the conviction that education and learning could be better served by its mission formed the core of a philosophy that was held in statis, even as the methods, models and metrics used to achieve it remained in a constant state of flux. The origin of that philosophy lay in a rather peculiar ambition that one of Agastya's founders, Ramji Raghavan, grew up imagining.

When he was younger, Ramji often dreamed of living in Shangri-La, the mythical Himalayan kingdom in James Hilton's novel *Lost Horizon* (1933). It was a stray ambition that would keep coming back to him: a school tucked away in the mountains amid gurgling springs and fruit orchards, overlooking majestic snow-capped mountains. A school for creative boys and girls who would one day lead India and change the world.

The image of such a school was not without substance. As a student at the Rishi Valley School, Ramji had grown up in an institution steeped in the tenet that education needed to be a transformative experience for a child, and not merely a transfer of knowledge. Founded by Jiddu Krishnamurti, Rishi Valley – nestled among the unquestionably picturesque Horsley Hills in Andhra Pradesh – was something of a utopia. A certain oneness with nature and a clarity of thought when it came to education were both carved into the minds of its students. Ramji, who joined the school as a boarder at only age five, benefitted not only from the 11 formative years he spent there but also from his father's own association with Krishnamurti.

A former student of Rishi Valley himself, Ramji's father – K. V. Raghavan – had frequently interacted with the great philosopher. A true captain of industry, K. V. Raghavan would end his career having headed some of India's largest institutions, including Imperial Chemical Industries (ICI), EID Parry and Engineers India Limited (EIL). As chair of EIL, he was at the helm of India's biggest engineering consulting company, overseeing ambitious, nationally important projects in the manufacturing space, and expanding the company into global markets. While at ICI, he had hosted Krishnamurti at his company house in Kolkata's upmarket Alipore.

"My father had regaled me with many personal conversations that he had had with Krishnamurti," says Ramji. "During one such conversation Krishnamurti recounted the story of a young high court judge. A Cambridge

University graduate, he was all set to reach the highest office in his profession. One day he sat down and thought deeply about his life, decided it was not what he wanted for himself and walked away from it all. 'Think of the courage of the man, Sir,' Krishnamurti told my father."

This was a statement that would resonate with Ramji's own decision, albeit much later in life. The ability to stare down his life's achievements and turn away towards something more enriching would not only define Ramji but also inspire those who would choose to walk with him on Agastya's journey.

In addition to Krishnamurti, the senior Raghavan had developed a close bond with the then principal of Rishi Valley, Dr. S. Balasundaram. Their conversations, in which Ramji frequently partook as he grew older, delved deeply into education. The discussions often centred around India's inability to develop quickly enough to ensure that a majority of its citizens had a reasonable standard of living. It was here that the first seeds of Agastya were planted, in the idea that by nurturing curiosity and creativity in the young, and by giving teachers the tools to transform education, India might someday begin to turn the tides in its favour.

So, despite the farfetched and somewhat fantastical nature of Ramji's original dream, his concepts around education were rooted in a philosophy that had been wrought in some of the most brilliant educational minds and tested to immense success across some of the greatest schools.

In the years following Rishi Valley, however, Ramji would tread a fairly well-beaten path. Graduating from Delhi University, he would go on to complete his MBA at the London Business School (LBS) and eventually find success within the world of finance.

Nonetheless, the tendency to seek an adventurous outlet was something that he frequently explored, if sometimes to the point of absurdity. After graduating from LBS, he visited the Cuban embassy at Hyde Park in London. His request: whether he might be able to get a job on a sugarcane plantation in Cuba. He had always romanticized the life of a farmer and imagined that doing farming someplace exotic would be a fascinating experience. However, this was at the height of the Cold War and the woman at the embassy understandably looked at him as though he might be mad. She quickly concluded the meeting, telling him that his request could not be entertained in any way whatsoever.

Returning to India after graduating from LBS, Ramji considered joining an LBS colleague working on a social initiative in rural Bihar. His father, mindful of the comfortable existence that his own success had allowed his son to enjoy, reminded him that if that was what he wanted to do, he needed to understand that there was no money in the path he had chosen. When his friend walked out of the initiative, Ramji dropped the plan and instead joined a management consulting firm in Delhi. While these anecdotes may seem disparate, they represent an inner conflict that Ramji was perhaps not yet willing to fully confront. Like a diver who backs away from the board a few times to steel himself, Ramji was testing his own resolve – peeking over the edge to garner courage before taking that final plunge into the unknown.

"I didn't have the courage to cross the bridge," Ramji reflects of this time in his life.

By 1996, Ramji was enjoying what many might consider a most enviable lifestyle. Having committed himself to finance, he had risen to the top of his field. After working his way up to vice president at Citibank in

New York, he had recently moved to London. Here, as a senior executive living in upmarket Kensington, he had clients all over the world and was hugely well paid even by the standards of the banking industry. A few years prior, he had met his wife, Monica, and the two of them were embracing the comforts that wealth invariably provides. The bonus of welcoming their daughter, Jeena, meant that life was good, and Ramji had little cause for concern. Any ambitions of building his school would need to wait, as both prudence and desire coincided at this time to suggest that his best course of action was to continue to build wealth for his family.

However, his inclination toward social entrepreneurship, while dormant, was in no way fully subdued. Frequent conversations with an old friend from LBS – Gopi Warrier – had Ramji starting to question his purpose.

In one of their discussions, Gopi reflected on a story that Ramji had himself narrated many years ago. It was about Krishnamurti helping a frail old woman to carry a heavy head-load of firewood to her home near Rishi Valley.

"Do you know why he did it?" Gopi asked. Ramji replied that he could not answer the question, as he would be speaking from his mind and not his heart.

"He did it because he felt her pain," Gopi concluded, adding, "The problem with you, old boy, is that you do not feel the other person's pain."

Ramji recalls that Gopi's words felt like a knife going through his heart. However, by his own admission, he could not truthfully oppose them.

"Gopi gave me the confidence, the spiritual fuel to make the leap," Ramji affirms. "But he also cautioned me that I was merely a delivery vehicle for whatever cause I chose to pursue, and that ego should play no part in my journey forward."

The pleasant equilibrium that Ramji had begun to take for granted was slowly unravelling. Money, career and status were quickly losing their charm. Thoughts of his original vision of a school were once again taking precedence and a life in finance was feeling increasingly mundane and tedious.

Ramji had often discussed his dream with Monica when they first met and had found her supportive. Now, on the precipice of a life-altering decision, he brought the topic up again and learned that her stance had not changed. She encouraged him to follow his heart.

So, in early 1998, Ramji Raghavan quit his high-paying job and began to work on plans to build his school. While he initially kept his base in London, he eventually relocated his family to Bangalore, where his father was settled.

The resulting impact on Ramji's lifestyle was not insignificant. By Ramji's own estimate, he forsook around 90% of his potential lifetime earnings when he decided to leave the corporate life. Speaking about the years that followed his move to India, he recalls three main facets of change. The first was the scaling back of comforts. With the tap shut on his income, nearly every expenditure was suddenly under scrutiny. The second was the social impact. His phone no longer rang with the same frequency and his social interactions – including those at work that usually help to balance the stress of a corporate life – ceased almost completely. Finally, there was the loss in status. It would be many years before his achievements with Agastya would overshadow those of his banking career. Until that time, new introductions were hardwon and even close friends remained somewhat sceptical about what appeared a most foolhardy purpose.

The fact that Ramji had no real experience as an educator was something that needed to be remedied before he could embark on his journey. As is so often the case, success in one field affords us the confidence that we will translate that success into anything else that we do. The meticulousness that comes with working in finance ensured that Ramji's first step – like any good project in a corporate setting – would be to evaluate the landscape and understand the finer nuances of running an educational institution. He approached an old teacher from Rishi Valley – M. V. Prasad, who was now the principal of Daly College in Indore.

"Managing a school is more complex than managing a business. If you let the standards go down, you will find it extremely difficult to bring them back up," Prasad advised.

Through his connections, Ramji spent the next year studying different systems of education and visiting institutions that had stood the test of time. In addition to Daly College, he visited the Atomic Energy School in Mumbai, which educated the children of India's elite scientists, and the famous Doon School in Dehradun, which had produced many exceptional leaders in business and government. Outside India he visited Eton College in the UK, the Phillips Academy in Andover, near Boston, Stuyvesant High School in New York, and the Teachers College, Columbia University, New York. Discussions with various educators – however, whenever and wherever he could find them – threw up more insights.

The deeper he went into education, the more glaringly he understood a simple truth: that the kind of schooling that he had experienced as a child, and indeed that the more privileged enjoyed, was far removed from the model being followed in the bulk of Indian schools. A rote-based, exam-oriented system had driven children and teachers to eschew critical thinking. 'Answerism,' or knowing the right answer, had all but eliminated original thought and enquiry. As one Indian educator told him, education for the middle classes in India was "like a hundred-metre race on steroids." Young Indians were being taught 'what to think' not 'how to think.'

These findings were regularly taken back to the senior Raghavan and to Balasundaram. These two wise men pressed him to dig deeper and understand the fundamental challenges to education before making any attempts to remedy them.

During this time, Ramji's father suggested a meeting with P. K. Iyengar, the former chair of India's Atomic Energy Commission, who had also later reported directly to two prime ministers – Rajiv Gandhi and Narasimha Rao – in succession. As the head of one of India's most important scientific missions, Iyengar had worked with iconic scientific leaders such as Homi Bhabha and Vikram Sarabhai and had helped to develop and mould a new generation of scientific talent in India[1]. Iyengar and Ramji were related by marriage on Ramji's mother's side, although they had only ever met when Ramji was younger.

"I remembered him as an ambitious man, very driven, a nationalist who was proud of India's achievements in space and atomic energy. His devotion to making India an important player on the world's scientific stage was evident in everything he said," Ramji recalls.

In 1974, Iyengar was one of the leading members of the Smiling Buddha project, testing India's first nuclear bomb. He had interacted with Indira Gandhi during the time the first tests were being conducted near the village of Pokhran in Rajasthan. He recalled being asked by Gandhi, "Dr. Iyengar, what if this does not work?"

"In that case, Madam," Iyengar had replied, "the laws of physics have ceased to hold true."

Meeting after a gap of nearly ten years, Iyengar and Ramji instantly found they were on the same wavelength.

In May 1998, India, under Prime Minister A.B. Vajpayee, detonated five nuclear bombs in a series of tests known as Pokhran II. The intent of India to become a nuclear power was making headline news across the globe.

"It was somewhat grating to hear young news anchors on the world's TV channels talk angrily about India's nuclear tests," Ramji remembers of the time, "almost like teachers scolding a truant child. Pakistan raised the ante in retaliation by exploding six nuclear bombs. I asked the cabbie who drove me to Iyengar's home, in Saras Baug, Mumbai, what he thought of the nuclear explosions that India and Pakistan had just conducted. He had no idea what a nuclear bomb was and muttered some inanity. As I pressed the doorbell of Iyengar's home I smiled nervously at the cabbie's blissful ignorance of a portentous event and the irony of my imminent meeting with one of its architects."

A while later, a similar conversation ensued during a cab ride that Ramji and Iyengar took in London.

"On a taxi ride to my home in Kensington one night I got into a rather prickly argument with a cabbie who spoke somewhat judgementally about India's role in the Kargil War, with Pakistan. The conversation veered towards India's atom bomb, and I couldn't help but tell the cabbie that one of the creators of India's bomb was sitting next to me in the cab. The cabbie seemed dumbstruck for a moment. Not to be outdone, he declared that we would be passing the Iraqi embassy shortly. Suggesting that Iraq was always looking for more firepower, he asked me with a smile how much I thought the Iraqis might pay him if he were to drop Iyengar off at their embassy. Iyengar looked nervous and relaxed only after we reached my home without incident."

Iyengar's intense and energetic mind, combined with a global perspective on science and development, made the conversations between the two men stimulating and enlightening. Like Ramji, Iyengar believed that to achieve widespread social and economic development, India needed to create a pipeline of creative and innovative young minds that would apply themselves to solving social and economic problems.

"The Indian education system does not produce enough graduates who can think outside of the box," Iyengar said to Ramji, adding that while the importance of inculcating the scientific temperament was expressly mentioned in India's constitution, this had not translated into action or been disseminated to the masses. It was a sobering reality that Iyengar and his team were confronted with when seeking talent for their tests in the field of atomic research. Students had impressive degrees on paper, but they were just that: pieces of paper signifying book knowledge at best.

He attributed India's difficulty in developing to the lack of a spirit of enquiry in education, including an absence of 'cause-and-effect thinking.' This had created a growing cadre of youth without basic problem-solving skills. India's vast and highly touted reserves of human capital, it would appear, merely constituted quantity and not necessarily quality.

Iyengar was ready to support Ramji's project to build a school that would foster creativity in children and teachers. His involvement would give Agastya a crucial connection to the scientific community. His expansive network would open doors that allowed an invaluable influx of ideas, concepts and advisers, and the very designs for the models that Agastya would use to spread hands-on learning across India.

As Ramji continued his quest to acquire as much insight into education as he possibly could, Balasundaram suggested that the time was now right for him to find a partner, a co-founder. He suggested that Ramji meet with Mahavir Kataria.

A qualified chartered accountant and a former president of the Bangalore Stock Exchange, Mahavir, like Ramji, was an alumnus of Rishi Valley. He had an eclectic background, having been exposed to accounting, finance and industry. In addition to his brokerage in Bangalore, he had owned a manufacturing unit.

"I often used to go to see Dr. Balasundaram to talk about schools and education," Mahavir recalls. "My kids were of school-going age and we often spoke about what a good education meant and whether schools today were offering that. One day he asked me whether I remembered Ramji. I said, 'Yes, he was a couple of years my junior; we used to call him *chintu*. He was very mischievous.' So, 35 years after leaving school, Ramji and I reconnected for the first time."

It is a hallmark of great endeavours that there often exists a complementary relationship in the abilities of their key members. In this sense, Agastya was no exception. Ramji's drive, boldness and hunger to build a world-changing institution were commendable. However, his strengths lay in his formation of unique, often counter-intuitive concepts and visions, in his ability to build and nurture a vast network of thought leaders and funders, and in an immense talent for communication and public speaking that – while at this point still unexplored – would one day form a cornerstone of Agastya's incredible success in spreading its message.

In contrast, Mahavir understood operations and could implement real-world, on-the-ground solutions.

He also had a firm grasp of all the regulatory hurdles that would invariably present themselves, and he would pre-empt and resolve these to ensure that Agastya remained above board and complied with regulations. Eventually, he would be at the helm of most of the building projects that turned the Agastya campus into a truly distinctive educational playground.

"He does what he is good at, and I do what I am good at," Mahavir muses. "He would never ask me to give a speech, and I would not expect him to manage statutory regulations. From the beginning, we understood each other's strengths and weaknesses, else an organization of our size would have had some serious issues by now!"

From 1999, over the next seven years, the foundation was run from a single room in Kataria House, a herit-age (or 'protected') property owned by Mahavir's family, on Kamraj Road in Bangalore. Lunches were sent to the office by Mahavir's wife, Chandra. Even when the team grew, Chandra made sure that hot, homecooked food was always on offer, whether at the office or by ensuring everyone broke for lunch at Mahavir's home nearby.

In April 1999, Agastya was officially registered. The name itself was a product of yet another conversation between Ramji and Gopi Warrier. Over a pizza in London, Warrier suggested the name for its connection to education.

"I asked Gopi for a name. He closed his eyes for a few seconds and then said 'Agastya,'" Ramji remembers

Maharishi Agastya, the sage revered in so many ancient Indian texts, was notable for his contribution to grammar, medicine, science and the arts. He finds men-tion in all four *Vedas*, both the epics of the *Ramayana* and the *Mahabharata*, as well as in the *Puranas*.

In mythology, Agastya is said to have come upon the Vindhya mountains during his travels from the north of

India to the south. Seeing that the mountain range was growing much too fast, he asked it to lower itself so that he might pass over it. Agastya is then supposed to have requested the Vindhya to stay lowered until his journey back to the north of India. Since he never travelled north again, the mountains stayed lowered. One implication of this action was that humans and animals were always able to move freely between the north and south of India, thereby aiding the unity of the subcontinent.

Various etymologies exist around the meaning of Agastya. In some, the name denotes 'one who brightens,' relating to Agastya as the Indian name for the star Canopus. However, a verse in the *Ramayana* describes the name as a combination of *aga*, or 'mountain,' and *gam*, meaning 'to move.' Together they connote 'one who is the mover of mountains.'

The name resonated with Ramji. He told his father about it and was informed that there was a temple dedicated to Maharishi Agastya near their home in Bangalore that Ramji's mother, Lakshmi, used to visit. Ramji visited the temple and was delighted to see two marble statues of Maharishi Agastya and his wife, Lopamudra.

With the support and encouragement of K. V. Raghavan, P. K. Iyengar and S. Balasundaram, Ramji and Mahavir ploughed forward with zeal. The plans for building their school as well as the structure and approach to the pedagogy were crafted in parallel. It seemed sensible, at this time, to assemble a group to discuss these preliminary thoughts. With the help of the three wise men, the team began putting together a group that would partake in Agastya's first brainstorming session.

It was the turn of the century. The markets were buoyant, and liquidity was at an all-time high. With a well-established network in the world of finance – many of whom regarded Ramji's move as praiseworthy – funding did not look like it was going to be a challenge.

If there were storm clouds brewing in the distance, they were presently shrouded behind the euphoria of two men on a journey that would redefine them, and indeed make a rather pronounced impact on the world of education itself.

1. The exploits of India's atomic scientists, including P.K. Iyengar and India's former President Abdul Kalam, was made into a rather thrilling TV series called 'Rocket Boys'

CHAPTER 3

TAKING THE PLUNGE

There are no great works – only small works, done with great love.

If there is any truth to this axiom, it was certainly embodied by Agastya in the earliest days of its inception. Even as a fledgling foundation, Agastya behaved and functioned as though scale was pre-woven into its DNA. The founding team consisted only of two executives – with no background in education – and the three wise men of the previous chapter for guidance. However, Agastya's first brainstorming session was done in a manner akin to what might be expected of a much larger, professionally run organization.[1]

In April 1999, Bangalore was only just gaining recognition as an IT hub. The new Information Technology Park Limited (ITPL) was a gleaming symbol of the city's seriousness about garnering an international reputation that would propel it into the next century. Its mirrored exterior drew parallels with buildings in New York or London, and having office space there was a status symbol to which many companies were eager to subscribe.

Ramji managed to persuade Goh Kuak Hat, the young Singaporean head of ITPL, to let them use a conference room at no charge. This small act of generosity by the head of ITPL played a part in facilitating the beginning of important ideas that would shape the thinking and prospects of thousands of poor children and schoolteachers across India.

Gathered in the room were a disparate group cobbled together from the contacts of the founders and the three wise men. They comprised two professors (Dr. Khincha of the Indian Institute of Science and Mr. Prasad, the principal of Daly College), a college student, the head of a non-profit organization, two schoolteachers, a businessman and Ramji's wife, Monica. With them, as always, were K. V. Raghavan,

P. K. Iyengar and S Balasundaram. It was an intentionally unstructured group bringing together different personalities, viewpoints, and perspectives.

"I began the meeting with a question: 'What makes a person creative, innovative or a great problem-solver?'" says Ramji. "The question provoked Iyengar to describe the harmful effects of a lack of cause-and-effect thinking on society, saying that the school system did little to promote such thinking among its students. Schools needed to proactively create opportunities for children to learn cause-and-effect thinking. Prasad spoke about the importance of language and the arts, which led to a friendly debate on the relative importance of science and the arts in education."

"Rather than start with preconceived thoughts and premises, the brainstorming's unique and transformative value lay in its reliance on a series of fundamental and cascading questions, to build Agastya's mission statement. This emphasis on questioning vs. 'answerism' was to be a feature of future Agastya meetings leading to many surprising and unexpected ideas and innovations."

Stemming from the discussion were provocative questions: What is creativity? Is it something innate, or can one acquire the skill? Can you raise the speed limit of creativity in a nation like India? How effective are teacher training programmes and why has teaching become a profession of last resort in India? Can teacher and student mindsets be evolved? In so many schools, why is there an absence of joy in learning and how can this be reversed?

K. V. Raghavan made an astute observation. Taking inspiration from his own experience in training managers, he opined that teacher training programmes were ineffective because they were disconnected from the school classroom. Teacher training needed to inculcate interactive, hands-on and real-time learning methods to transform the process. Using an analogy, he described the symbiosis between a medical college and hospital to explain how more interactive and practical teacher training methods with direct links to the school class-room could raise retention, improve teachers' ability to learn and positively impact children's performance. At some point during the discussions, Iyengar – the consummate scientist – explained to Ramji: "If I give you a 100 counterintuitive science experiments to do, I guarantee that in a few weeks a non-science guy like you will look at the world very differently."

The intense, full-day session was concluded around four crucial observations. First, infusing a spirit of enquiry and a creative mindset in children would require a shift from rote-based, chalk-and-talk teaching methods to more hands-on experiential learning. Second, creativity could be nurtured by building learning environments that encouraged children and teachers to question, observe and experiment. Third, hands-on science, if aligned with the school curriculum, might be an effective way to spark curiosity in children and fill an important gap in education. Fourth, teacher training in experiential teaching-learning methods is essential to create a multiplier effect wherein each teacher goes on to train many more, thereby spreading the techniques exponentially. To do this effectively, teacher training centres would need to be co-located with schools.

The session culminated in what would be the cornerstone of Agastya's core mission: "To spark curiosity, nurture creativity, and instil confidence in children and teachers through hands-on learning."

The notion that teacher training was seminal to restoring creativity in the education ecosystem was a revelation for the two executives. In the non-government institutes where they had been educated – such as Rishi Valley – it was always taken for granted that teachers were capable and engaged by default.

For most teachers in government schools in India, however, this was far from the case.

Hence, the education of students, which had hitherto been the core focus of Agastya, would need to be done in tandem with the education of teachers. This was to be the first of many recalibrations that the founders would make.

In another sense, however, it was fortuitous that teacher training had now gained prominence within Agastya's mission. For one, the back-and-forth between the trainer and teacher allowed for more leeway as mistakes could be corrected and improvements could be made dynamically. Children are impressionable and their understanding could be impaired by employing untested methods of teaching. However, with adults, trial and error could be used to refine teaching methods and approaches before deploying these in schools. Additionally, through Iyengar, the foundation already had a connect with V. G. Gambhir of the Homi Bhabha Centre for Science Education (HBCSE), where considerable research on low-cost experiments had been conducted, leading to the development of several hands-on models. Gambhir, who was keen to expand the mission to educate teachers, agreed to run teacher training workshops for Agastya free of charge. An introduction was also made to Hari Parameshwaran, whose company, Dynam, produced hands-on learning kits for children and who likewise waived his fees. In June 1999, the two planned a pilot workshop for schoolteachers from a private school in Bangalore.

Gambhir's approach was not only a unique experience for the teachers but also for Ramji and Mahavir themselves. For the first time, they witnessed the impact that low-cost, hands-on learning can bring in a group that is hungry for knowledge. More importantly, they saw the power that simplicity has in drawing out and illustrating even the most complex of principles.

Gambhir started by asking the class to explain what burns when a candle is lit. It seemed an easy enough question; the answers were split between whether it is the wick or the wax that burns. To everyone's surprise, Gambhir was not convinced. He encouraged the teachers to dig deeper, and the ensuing debate animated the class instantly, as theories, reasonings and arguments now flowed freely. The same teachers who often insisted that expensive labs and equipment were crucial to propagate learning were having the time of their lives on a question around a simple candle.

The answer, of course, is that it is the air around the wick that burns. More specifically, the wax, pulled up through the wick as a liquid, is vaporized into a gas that ignites to form the flame. The principle of pyrolysis – which addresses states of matter, capillary action, combustion and energy – was wrapped up in one small experiment requiring no more than a lump of wax, a wick and something to light it with!

As Faraday[2] said, "There is no better, no more open door by which you can enter into the study of natural philosophy than by considering the physical phenomena of a candle."[3]

Notwithstanding the evident success of the pilot, the team was understandably nervous to take the workshop from private to government schools. By reputation at least, private school teachers were relatively well paid and more

motivated when compared with their government coun-
terparts. Getting government schoolteachers engaged
would be far more challenging. Even before starting, the
founders had been told to expect cynical, jaded teachers
who would see little benefit in any external intervention
or training from an unestablished foundation.

On a warm morning, Ramji and Mahavir, along with
Gambhir and Parameshwaran, waited for a group of
teachers at the entrance of a guest house in Kuppam.
The choice of Kuppam – like so many choices the foundation initially made – was merely a function of chance
and opportunity. A friend of Ramji's had made some
connections within the government of Andhra Pradesh,
and through these connections the foundation had
convinced the government to allow them to conduct
their workshops in spare spaces within government
schools and government-run auditoriums in and around
Kuppam. There wasn't much room for error, though, as
the teachers' feedback and responses would influence
whether Agastya would even be allowed to continue its
work in the area.

In the private school workshop, a single question was
enough to spark a debate and set the ball rolling. Here,
with government teachers, the trainers opted for a more
indirect approach. Using everyday objects such as paper,
candles, strings, coat hangers, balloons and rubber bands,
they began depicting simple experiments at first. Then,
almost seamlessly, they posed seemingly straightforward,
albeit deceptive questions for the teachers to answer, as
they handed over the materials, asking them to replicate
the experiments as they worked on their responses. The
action-based element to the class changed the mood
instantly. Already intrigued by how pedestrian objects
could be used to teach scientific principles, the teachers

now chuckled at their own attempts to make the rudimentary models. Engaging questions from the instructors soon facilitated debate, which was interspersed with
whoops of amazement and laughter from the teachers
as the energy levels rose. The two founders watched,
enthralled, as this allegedly disinterested group turned
their own beliefs about what constituted an invigorating
classroom session on its head.

The message that the teachers fed back to their
superiors was filled with positivity, leaving Ramji and
Mahavir with a sense of triumph. Over the next 12 to 18
months, Gambhir and Parameshwaran conducted sessions for over a thousand government teachers. Winning
their support would be a crucial step in proving the effectiveness of hands-on education. It would also cultivate a
reputation in and around Kuppam that would form the
very building blocks of Agastya's future endeavours.

As the teacher training workshops gained traction,
Agastya found itself with access to a steadily growing
pool of enthusiastic, trained instructors eager to showcase their newfound skills. With the help of HBCSE,
Agastya started conducting small science fairs in villages. This was a logical step, a bridge towards the kind
of student education that would be needed at the school,
the plans for which were still being drawn up in the
background at a frantic pace.

During this time, two more senior figures were persuaded by K. V. Raghavan to join Agastya's small but
hungry team. R. Krishnan, former director of the Gas
Turbine Research Establishment at the Defence Research
and Development Organisation (one of India's foremost
scientific bodies), was a highly respected name in the
scientific community. In addition to his wealth of knowledge, his involvement, like Iyengar's, would give the

foundation access to some of the most gifted minds in the country.[4] Key among these – although it would still be many years until that association was formed – would be Dr. A. P. J. Abdul Kalam, the president of India.

H. N. Srihari, a former colleague of K. V. Raghavan's from Imperial Chemical Industries, was also brought in. He would lend his expertise on team management to Agastya's growing cadre of volunteers, and he would eventually join Agastya's board of trustees.

"K. V. Raghavan had a special skill in picking people for certain specializations," says Srihari, who was considered because of work he had done in educating rural children while working in the remote town of Gomia, in Bihar. "In all my years, I had never seen him make a mistake on people management. We used to have meetings in his house in Bangalore and those discussions led to his suggesting my name for Agastya."

The science fairs were among Agastya's first outreach initiatives. They were usually held in any available open space – such as a large school classroom, auditorium or community hall. Models were lined up on desks, and visitors would go from desk to desk, interacting with them and posing questions to the volunteers. It was not unusual to see a gaggle of children huddled around a single science model, shooting questions non-stop at the instructor.

Numbering first only in tens and then in hundreds, children from surrounding schools and villages would walk or hitch rides on buses or even a friendly tractor to make it to the small fairs. Word had started to spread of a unique and exciting style of learning, with moving parts, flickering flames and colourful liquids. Concepts were patiently explained, rather than dictated, and questions could be asked without fear of rebuke or ridicule.

If Agastya needed any real-time validation of its core philosophy, it could be seen in the eager eyes of children who chose walking miles to reach a science fair over a day of mischief-making or lazing in the hot sun on a weekend. As predicted, hands-on learning was not only an enriching experience for the children but also allowed the teachers to fine-tune their skills. Like thespians who hone their craft with each weekly performance, the teachers were experiencing multiple iterations in a single afternoon, allowing them to catalyse their own methods of delivery for maximum impact. These same teachers would, on the following Monday, be teaching in their respective classrooms with a little more panache than they might have earlier cared to showcase. Agastya's multiplier effect had already started to take hold.

Whether Agastya's initial interventions had any measurable impact, we cannot really say. In the early days, Ramji once presented some statistics to his father showing a substantial improvement in student grades in the schools located near the campus. The senior Raghavan, always an astute observer of human nature, smiled and shook his head. He explained that it was too soon to directly attribute any such impact to Agastya's teaching methods. If grades had improved, it could be because Agastya's programmes had motivated children to study harder. Similar increases in school attendance rates were also observed, but again, Agastya's impact on this may have purely been from a motivational standpoint. This was not inconsequential, but nonetheless it was too premature to start heralding any tangible impact.

It stands to reason, however, that the waves that Agastya was creating were beginning to ripple across the countryside. The region was awakening to a whole new method of learning. With its science fairs and teacher training workshops clearly resonating with children and adults alike, the time had finally come to create a physical embodiment of Agastya.

Ramji's Shangri-La was ready to be built, although unsurprisingly it was a far cry from what he had first imagined, both physically and philosophically.

1. A film crew videotaped the brainstorming session for future reference and posterity. Alas, the tape was misplaced and lost. It deprived future Agastya stakeholders of an opportunity to witness the emergence of pivotal discussions that shaped and defined Agastya's future.

2. Considered the father of electricity, Faraday discovered the principles underlying electromagnetic induction, diamagnetism and electrolysis.

3. Michael Faraday and William Crookes, *A Course of Six Lectures: On the Chemical History of a Candle* (London: Griffin, Bohn, and Company, 1861).

4. Unfortunately, Dr. R. Krishnan passed away in 2021, before he could be interviewed for this book. However, his name echoed throughout nearly every interview conducted – a clear indicator of the monumental contributions he made in shaping Agastya.

CHAPTER 4

TAMING THE WILDERNESS

As you make the drive up from Bangalore to Gudupalle, you cross a town distinctive in its deeply colonial leanings. The structures stand out against the otherwise local architecture and rural setting – steeply pitched red-tiled roofs with dormer windows, gothic columns along broad open facades, and the inimitable pale-yellow exterior with which colonial bungalows in the south were often painted.

Once known as Little England, this mining town at the Kolar Gold Fields was among the richest settlements in India during its peak. The British took control of the gold mines in the late 1800s and – apart from sending a lot of gold over to England – built a self-sustaining haven for themselves, boasting hospitals, schools, a boating lake, a golf course, a swimming pool and a gymkhana.[1] It is also supposed that Little England was the first town in India to be fully electrified.

However, as the mines eventually ran dry and the wealth accordingly evaporated, the town slowly sank into relative obscurity, leaving only the structures to speak of what once was.[2] One dubious aspect of the town's legacy, however, lingered.

To serve the needs of the town, and indeed the larger needs of British settlements across the south of India, the area around the Kolar Gold Fields had been denuded of its trees. Around 100 square kilometres of forestland had been wiped out to fuel the insatiable fires of industry. Additionally, chemical effluents from the mining process had been allowed to slowly mingle with groundwater, causing a chain reaction of natural destruction. In later years, a botched attempt at revival saw the planting of copious amounts of acacia and eucalyptus, which – unbeknownst to the botanically challenged – were invasive species that only furthered the devastation.

The lush green belt – once replete with lakes, streams and a thriving ecosystem of both flora and fauna – was now little more than a barren wasteland.

Incredibly, it was within this wasteland that Ramji and Mahavir considered building their dream school.

In fairness, it was never their first choice. After initially scouting several locations closer to Bangalore with the help of his father and Dr. Balasundaram, Ramji had resigned himself to the fact that to get a meaningful enough portion of real estate, he would need to move further into the wilderness. One piece of guidance he received was that no matter what, he was not to accept land free of cost. However, land close to Bangalore would prove expensive and deplete most, if not all, of the funds that Ramji had managed to collect.

"The government's advice to Ramji was not to take the land free, but to buy it," says Dr. Kota Harinarayana, an eminent scientist and a friend of Agastya who is famous for having developed the Tejas, India's indigenous light combat aircraft, which has won many accolades. It was good advice as, legally speaking, it would allow Agastya a little more leeway in later years than if the land had been a government freebie.

With cost driving the decision, the proposal to find land near Kuppam was put forth. The foundation's activities in and around the area had done enough to convince the local government of its seriousness about building a world-class school. It also helped that Kuppam, located close to the three Indian states of Karnataka, Tamil Nadu and Andhra Pradesh, was logistically very convenient. Kuppam being only a two-hour drive from Bangalore also meant that the difficulty of finding good accommodation near the campus would be avoided, as day trips could frequently be made. Being on the rail route between Bangalore and Chennai, Kuppam station was an added attraction, as visitors could come from both these cities via train, if necessary.

The issue, of course, was the quality of land in and around Kuppam itself.

After being shown several tracts of real estate of varying shapes and sizes, the team zeroed in on the most suitable candidate: a dry, arid, rocky and notably desolate area. Standing on the lifeless, undulating terrain, Ramji felt rather hopeless at first. The air was warm, still and dusty. It was scarcely possible to breathe deeply without feeling its dryness in the lungs. The heat, radiating off large, obstinate-looking granite and shale rock boulders, was enough to sap energy and enthusiasm from anyone that lingered too long. A few goats loitering nearby seemed unimpressed by the meagre offerings that the gravelled, lifeless ground had coughed up.

At the time, the proposed campus was also inaccessible by road. To reach it, you had to climb up steep steps built on the southwest corner for pilgrims walking to a nearby temple. Finally, the land's undulation meant that constructing buildings and playgrounds would be expensive and challenging.

"Agastya's future campus looked nothing like my idyllic dream of Shangri-La," recalls Ramji. "Seeing my disappointment, my father counselled me, 'Don't see the land as it is today. Imagine what it might become.' It was inspirational and prescient advice."

His father's encouragement lifted Ramji's downbeat mood and forced him to look for the positive. Immediately, he saw that the land's elevation gave it a breathtaking view of the surrounding countryside. Indeed, there was a point on the campus where you could see all three of the Indian states at once. Ramji imagined a library on the hilltop with a 360-degree view. A reservoir known as Mustrahalli Lake was visible in the distance. It suggested that while water was certainly scarce, it was not impossible to find.

Set on a tall hill in the distance stood an 800-year-old temple to Lord Shiva. It spoke of the age and character of the land – a land that had perhaps lost its way and was waiting for someone to infuse life back into it.

So, less than 12 months after the Information Technology Park Limited brainstorming session (see previous chapter), Agastya acquired a 172-acre parcel of land near the village of Gudupalle near Kuppam.

Enthused by the promise of what could be, the founders discovered yet another facet of their continual recalibration. They could not honestly preach excellence in education unless they imbibed the very values and virtues being disbursed. A world-class school could not boast facilities and methods alone. If Agastya wanted to walk the talk, ecological initiatives to revive the campus would need to be given as much importance as science education itself.

A few months after Agastya was conceived, on an Air India flight from London to New York, a young entrepreneur named Sandeep Tungare listened rapt as K. V. Raghavan described to him the dream that was Agastya. The two had only just met when seated next to each other, but by the end of the flight Tungare would give the senior Raghavan his card and ask him to pass it on to Ramji. Tungare and his partner, Ravi Reddy, impressed by their subsequent meeting with Ramji, agreed to fund a part of the campus's development. The two men would each give USD 100,000 to Agastya.

The initial development of the campus was a case study in resource management. Even with the seed money, funds were very scarce, requiring Ramji to shuttle between India, the UK and the US to try and bring in investors. This left Mahavir with the task of taking the raw, untamed, undulating land and hewing it into some semblance of form that would be flat enough to then be developed by an architect. It was trial by fire for Mahavir. Pulled into – quite literally – unfamiliar terrain, the former stockbroker would not only excel at this task but also acquire a taste for project management that would see him supervise the development of ever more audacious buildings as the campus evolved.

In the early days, however, the work was tedious, and it became clear that help with the essential legwork was needed.

The Tirupati Tirumala Devasthanam (or TTD) guesthouse – the same one where Agastya had done its very first training workshop with government teachers – was the only decent lodging within a 30-minute drive of the campus. For many years, until the foundation was able to build suitable accommodation of its own, the guesthouse remained the resting point for anyone who needed to stay overnight at, or near, the campus for Agastya-related work.

It was here that Koppala Balaram, a young man working at the TTD guesthouse, became curious as to the comings and goings of the two founders. He approached R. Kesavan, another regular at the guest house and a consultant to Agastya. He was informed that an international school was coming up in Gudupalle and he was intrigued.

When he pressed Mahavir for details, Balaram was delighted to learn that there was some short-term work on offer. At the time, Balaram was doing an LLB (law) course via correspondence; any extra money he could make was certainly welcome and the opportunity to help a school made it seem like it would be interesting work.

The primary challenge facing Agastya was that, as mentioned, the campus offered very little flat land on which to build. Despite dreams of multiple labs, hostels, an auditorium, a library and living quarters for staff, there was barely enough of a plateau on which to rest even a table. Given the expense and inaccessibility of earth-moving equipment, Mahavir visited the factory of Bharat Earth Movers Limited (BEML), fortuitously located just 30-odd minutes from Agastya's campus. After explaining the foundation's mission, Mahavir was able to convince BEML to loan Agastya a single bulldozer for the period of one month. Agastya would need to fuel the vehicle, but they had unlimited use of it for 30 days.

If an organization's first employee is an indication of those that will follow, Agastya could not have asked for a better start than Balaram. Along with Kesavan,[3] Mahavir, and a few more hired workers, he worked tirelessly to shape the campus in those 30 days. Driving a tractor hired from Kuppam town, he shuttled men, tools, and fuel back and forth from campus.

"There was nothing on campus, not even enough shade to keep a water bottle cool," muses Balaram, adding proudly that the sapling for a rain tree that today stands grandly at the entrance to the campus was brought in his pocket.

"After completing the earthworks, I had to go to Kuppam in the evening and bring diesel for the next day. I had never driven a tractor before and now I was driving one all over the place."

With the use of the bulldozer, the main approach road to the campus was carved out, along with the arterial road that would wind its way past so many labs and buildings in the years to come. Key areas were flattened, keeping in mind the long-term ambition, even if the funds did not yet exist to raise any structures.

Working the land was arduous, done under the glare of a merciless sun that clearly cared little for Agastya's noble mission. Nonetheless, with a timeline hanging over their heads, the team pushed forward relentlessly. By the time the deadline to return the bulldozer arrived, the iron-saturated earth had been chewed out of the dull, rocky surface, and dark red cuts streaked across the campus. If seen from above, they might have resembled the first, seemingly haphazard yet deliberate, strokes of an artist on a blank canvas – a canvas destined to become nothing short of a masterpiece.

Agastya's boldness was always something that enticed anyone who chose to affiliate with the foundation. From the beginning, staff, well-wishers and donors alike marvelled at the sheer audacity with which plans were charted, even when the resources to execute those plans eluded Agastya at the time. The conviction that means would unfailingly follow purpose was always the natural state of functioning for both the founders and those that later joined them.

While the land itself had been miraculously reshaped over the manic 30 days, no new infusion of funding had presented itself during the same period. Still, Ramji had shared his plan with many a potential donor and was positive that something would come through very shortly. Having no liquidity to woo any architects with, the founders decided nonetheless that the time was right to step out and find someone to build their school.

The response was unexpectedly overwhelming.

To paint a picture of the campus and explain the purpose of the school that might one day dwell there,

Mahavir wrote a brief that was sent to several well-known architectural firms. The brief described the land as well as possible and then included two restrictions: the first, that no building constructed should obstruct the view of the land beyond the campus, and second, that there should be a common thread, or theme, connecting the buildings. This simple write-up was powerful enough to pull many name-brand architects forward, each one as eager as the next to work with Agastya. The founders were somewhat stunned by the enthusiasm.

"I got a call from Germany," recalls Mahavir. "The person spoke with me for an hour and a half. He compared the land's undulations to Scotland and said that the letter I had sent brought the image to life in his mind. He wanted more time to make his presentation. I told him, 'Take more time, but we want it to be an iconic project.'"

The fervour of the architects was not unfounded. It was increasingly rare for a plot of this size to be offered up for development in such a unique manner. The kind of school that Agastya had envisaged was no longer being built anywhere. The campus's 170-odd acres were untouched, and therefore primed for something magnificent. For any architect, the opportunity to imprint their creativity on such a vast expanse was nothing short of a dream project.

Ultimately, four firms were shortlisted and came forward to make presentations. Of these, three had built miniature mock-ups of the school they proposed. Each of them wanted the project so badly that they even agreed to waive their fees. It was as though Agastya's campus was a magnum opus that would define whomsoever was fortunate enough to be given the chance to create it.

One architect, however, connected with the founders on a more emotional level. It seemed that while

Sharukh Mistry was certainly excited to build Agastya's dream school, Agastya's cause also resonated deeply with him.

When Mahavir's daughter, Sheetal, spotted Sharukh staring wistfully across the land, she joked and asked him whether he was already imagining where each building might go.[4] Sharukh smiled and replied that he wasn't. He was instead envisioning how he might preserve the beauty of the land.

Sharukh's aim for the campus was to exploit 'biophilia' – an idea suggesting that we all have an innate connection with nature and other living beings.

"We wanted to use the lay of the land – we wanted to use the water movement," he says, remembering his first impression of the campus. "We stood on the land and we saw how the water flowed, we saw how the sun rose and moved across the sky. We wanted to engage the children and have them ask questions about things around them, about the buildings. We didn't want buildings that stood alone and screamed, but that came across as part of the land."

As daring as the founders were, Sharukh and his team matched their passion with equal zeal. Plans were drawn up for this most monumental of undertakings. Plans to create buildings that would throb with the very energy of the ground that appeared to have birthed them. Plans to take the barren wasteland and turn it into an oasis of joy and learning. Plans to create a school like none before.

The excitement, however, was short lived. Soon after Sharukh's selection, both founders and architect would need to put things on hold.

Most of the funding commitments that Ramji had anticipated for the project were quickly being withdrawn. It was the poorly timed arrival of the dotcom bust, and the easy money that had appeared to sway generously in Agastya's favour had dried up practically overnight. Newly minted paper millionaires, whose hubris had extended into foolhardy charitable commitments, were suddenly penniless. Even old money, sensing the threat of those most uncertain of times, retreated into its fortified enclaves to wait for the markets to improve. The two social entrepreneurs would find that in a battle of consequence, the nobility of a cause rarely supersedes the preservation of prosperity.

It would be many years before Ramji would find the critical mass of financial infusions needed to build Agastya in a manner akin to how it was originally intended. For now, a period of intense reflection and extreme scarcity would follow. It would be these hard knocks, interestingly, that would push Agastya down the path that would ultimately define it. The founders, so intent on building their dream school, would instead find that etched in their struggles lay the markings of a movement that would alter the landscape of education itself.

1. A sporting and social club. Gymkhanas around India today continue the colonial tradition of such members-only clubs.

2. Despite this somewhat grim representation of the present state of the town, the Kolar Gold Fields Golf Course remains popular to this day.

3. Sadly, Kesavan passed away in 2021, before he could be interviewed for this book. He continued to be closely associated with Agastya until his death. His contributions included laying much of the piping and cabling around the campus to ensure water and electricity distribution. At one point, he was the only person who knew the exact layout of the piping across the campus. You could not have dug a hole on campus without first checking with him.

4. An extremely talented designer, Sheetal would go on to create much of the Agastya artwork that became such an integral part of the foundation's message of fun in learning.

CHAPTER 5

THE BLESSINGS OF SCARCITY

It is a premise well-examined that innovation is often drawn from the tangled mess of crisis. However, to assume causality between the two is to undermine the discipline and tenacity that allow original thought to thrive even when an endeavour is mired in adversity. Despite the romanticism around stealing victory from the depths of defeat, the product of hardship is most commonly failure. Success is reserved for those precious few that persistently counter the uniqueness of their predicaments with equally unusual, if sometimes desperate, resolutions.

With funding having all but evaporated, Agastya's founders knew that in the current scenario, banging harder on their begging bowls was an endeavour steeped in futility. World markets were in turmoil and portents of doom were showing no signs of changing their tunes. Instead of looking outward, Agastya's team used this time to introspect and delve deeper into refining the concepts that had thus far been developed.

"I began to read a wide range of books on education, science, history and religion – a luxury that I'd had little time to indulge in as a banker," Ramji recounts. "Indeed, this period of constructive laziness became one of the most intellectually fertile periods of my life."

With the benefit of hindsight, it is now clear that there were three primary advantages driving Agastya's unlikely resilience in its first six or seven years despite the myriad stumbling blocks it encountered.

The first was the composition of the team. Other than Balasundaram, none of the others had any background or experience in education. This eclectic mix – a banker, a stockbroker, a scientist, a corporate CEO and a school principal – formed the core of Agastya's founding members. It brought together what proponents of design thinking refer to as 'non-domain experts' – namely, masters in their own field who bring structured thought and hard-won perspectives into a completely new arena, allowing a kind of cross-pollination in thought processes.

This unfamiliarity with education meant that ideas were limitless, unrestrained by any previously entrenched beliefs.

"Because we came from diverse backgrounds, we were forced to ask questions rather than develop answers," says Ramji. "When you approach something through inquiry, the results do tend to be better."

The Indian system of teaching had been put in place during British rule to churn out an army of clerks and yes-men to support their colonial overlords. The Lancastrian system of education – also called the Monitorial System or Madras system – was developed to mass-educate students in a factory-style environment. Interestingly, the motto of its innovator, Joseph Lancaster, was "Qui docet, discit" – "He who teaches, learns." This was a precursor of peer-to-peer learning, which somehow got lost in the Indian education space, leaving behind only the rote-learning system that most institutions seemed content with.

All members of the founding team had had a chance to step away from this system at some point and see the potential in an alternative. Unencumbered by the factory-style, exam-centric version of education, Agastya shamelessly explored avenues that any traditional models of learning might have balked at. It opened possibilities that challenged the status quo and allowed originality and purpose to take centre stage.

The second advantage Agastya had was a pre-installed attitude for expansive thinking among the founding team. K. V. Raghavan had helmed huge projects while at Engineers India Limited and Imperial Chemical Industries, and P. K. Iyengar had spearheaded India's enormously audacious march into nuclear energy. Ramji himself was a product of a banking system somewhat infamous for a culture of insatiability and over-the-top thinking. An ingrained comfort with large numbers ensured that Agastya's wild ambitions were rarely tempered by its unequivocally contrasting and limited early reach. Large-scale plans were allowed to remain in the mix, meaning that when the resources did arrive, the pieces to set these plans in motion were already in place.

The final advantage, although it scarcely would have seemed as such at the turn of the century, was the paucity of funds. It is almost certain that had Agastya had access to the investments it needed at the time, the foundation would have moved along a very different narrative. Tepid funding forced the founders to employ design thinking elements, squeezing more from less in an effort to stretch every resource to its limit. It also dictated a readjustment in perspective with regard to the field in which they had chosen to focus their energies.

Unlike, say, food or healthcare, education did not carry the same sense of urgency within the charitable space. A hungry or sick child might immediately evoke sympathy and coax a donor to loosen their purse strings. But Agastya would find that the same emotions could not be tapped into to further their cause. The schooling system was churning out millions each year ill-equipped with the tools needed to succeed on a world stage. However, streamlining education was still seen as non-critical in India, where poverty, understandably, takes centre stage.

Complicating this further was the fact that Agastya was looking to revamp what it believed to be a broken system. To borrow an analogy from nature, water cannot easily infiltrate compact soil, but it will quickly seep through fallowed soils with open spaces between the grains. Similarly, in a business or a social venture, the speed of dissemination of new thoughts and their funding depends on the openness and porosity of the environment. New theories take longer to infiltrate a closed environment than an open and absorbent one. The inability to raise funds stemmed from the fact that most investors were unable to buy into the gravity of the situation that Agastya was outlining. Many agreed that the system was flawed, but few saw it as a problem that should or could be easily addressed, especially when money was scarce and so many other issues required more immediate attention.

The saying "abundance makes you poor" could not have found a better example than Agastya in those first seven years. The methods, and indeed the culture, that would spill out of this need to constantly overcome financial constraints would set the foundation on a route untried and untested. The ability to question, adapt and discover new pathways became a vital skill of the Agastya team and allowed the foundation to start developing the tools required to set it on a new trajectory altogether.

While grand plans to build an extraordinary campus were being formulated, discussed, celebrated, and then sadly deferred, Agastya's early initiatives had continued gathering steam in the background. Along with the teacher training workshops, the village science fairs had gained an appreciable amount of traction around Kuppam. The Agastya ethos had started to infiltrate people's minds, even if no one was quite sure what Agastya did, other than it being somehow connected with science. With a crisis of identity within Agastya itself, this slender yet definite connection to education was as good as could be hoped for.

Gambhir's team was using the synergies between teacher training and science fairs so that trained teachers were then demonstrating their knowledge at the fairs. However, the imbalance between the number of teachers trained and the number of children keen to visit the fairs was placing a constraint on any efforts to magnify reach.[1] Considering there was no money to pay additional teachers to partake in the fairs, the existing model could only manage a few hundred students at a time. Furthermore, barring a few exceptions, teachers were unwilling to devote their time over the weekends to be trained for an activity that was not strictly needed as per their school curricula.

In February 2000, with the help of six staff from the Homi Bhabha Centre for Science Education (HBCSE) and eight passionate local schoolteachers, Agastya conducted science fairs for more than 13,000 children over six days. Children flocked in from all corners, using any mode of transport they could find. The surging crowds made people management an issue and made teaching a huge challenge. Local police needed to be called in. It was exhausting work, made more so by searing temperatures.

The fair was a runaway success, leading to an almost immediate surge in demand for more such science demonstrations. The pressure on the team, however, had started to show. It didn't seem like they would be able to sustain the pace much longer, given that the numbers were only going up. It all came to the fore a few months later when, while planning for a science fair for 500 students, the team was suddenly informed that they might need to brace for close to 5,000. The number was, quite simply, unfathomable. It was only two days before the fair; calling the whole thing off would have risked a considerable loss of face for Agastya. With neither time nor resources, the team was stunned into momentary stupor.

Seemingly out of nowhere, a few young girls approached them. With smiling faces radiating both mischief and quiet confidence, they declared that they would be happy to volunteer as instructors if the team agreed to train them. It was a suggestion fraught with risks. How would these children fare under the pressure of questions from their peers? Would they even be taken seriously? How would their involvement impact perceptions of Agastya? With such limited time, would any training given to the children be effective at all?

Despite these reservations, with the clock ticking and no alternatives having presented themselves, the team accepted the girls' proposal. They spent the next two days training nearly 100 student volunteers.

On the day of the fair, the Agastya team waited apprehensively for the first batch of visiting students to arrive. With them, the student-teachers also stood nervously as they waited behind their models. The large room was brightly lit, with colourful banners all around. Within it were many rows of tables, each staffed by a young student checking and rechecking their models to ensure everything was in place. The morning heat had started to fold into the arena, adding to the tense discomfort that comes with bracing for the unknown. The entire scene was taut with anticipation coupled with a genuine curiosity as to how the visitors would first react when they came upon their peers waiting to teach them science.

The time finally arrived. A grumble of gathering footsteps was followed by a brief, somewhat confused silence. Then, a delighted murmur flitted through the crowd. Word began to spread across the arriving throng and move like a giddy current through the queue that had formed outside. Students, not teachers, would be conducting the fair.

It could be said that Agastya's first brush with peer-to peer learning was a result of pure happenstance – a reckless gamble born of a foolhardy purpose to somehow move forward at all costs that could have easily backfired. And yet, 5,000 was a large enough number to convince the team. They had stumbled upon something spectacular.

Students were suddenly less afraid to ask probing, even audacious questions to someone of their own age group. The student-teachers were not only building confidence with each demonstration of their respective models, but also ironing out their own doubts and refining their understanding. The process of teaching was allowing them to engage, debate and revisit the very topics they were explaining. If a student-teacher stumbled, they could accept the assistance of an adult teacher or, even more heart-warmingly, the help of a peer who may have had a better handle on the topic. Most encouraging was that the students, rather than mock a student-teacher who was struggling, were egging them on, even working with them to decipher the answers together.

Friendships were being formed, theories were being shared and at the heart of all this was an aspiration from the arriving students that they too could soon become student-teachers.

News of this unconventional fair that was being administered by children reached as far as the surrounding towns and villages. Curious parents and community members now stepped in to see for themselves what all the fuss was about. However, excitement tends to carry with it a customary smattering of drama.

Like so many things in India, progress can rarely march forward until those foreboding gatekeepers, tradition and custom, have had their say. In an attempt to overcome the heat, and indeed to allow them to better explain their models, two Muslim girls had removed their veils to teach. Word of this reached their parents, who rushed into the fair seeking an explanation and were no doubt armed with choice rebukes for the two girls. But anger and concern suddenly transformed into proud smiles when they saw their daughters animatedly teaching science to their peers. It was a moment where the rigidity of what should be was spontaneously softened by the possibility of what could be. The incident would live on in the minds and hearts of the founders and often serves as a reminder of what they themselves stood for.

This conversion of a hopeless, do-or-die predicament into a success was more than a one-off victory. It laid the foundation for Agastya's peer-to-peer teaching programmes. Eight years later, India's National Knowledge Commission would recommend these programmes for nationwide dissemination.

The bright girls who had stepped forward to diffuse the crisis were applauded for their ingenuity and courage. They would form the first batch of a very elite cadre that Agastya would go on to call the Young Instructor Leaders (YILs). In years to come, scores of gifted, driven children would be supported and trained in Agastya's methods, their numbers growing into the tens of thousands. Young Instructor Leaders would, time and again, emerge victorious at the IRIS (Initiative for Research and Innovation in STEM) national science awards, consistently besting the brightest children from India's top schools. Each of these victories was a glowing vindication that Agastya's methods not only sparked curiosity but were also carving out world-beating excellence.

Despite these hard-won victories and although the team remained focused, this period was not without friction. Emails shared between Mahavir and Ramji tell of mounting tensions. Mahavir believed that Ramji might have sold an untenable vision and did not have the investor base to turn their ideas into reality. Ramji insisted that Mahavir's attempts to scale things down were not going to result in the world-changing impact that they had set out to have.

Encouraged by the success of their existing programmes, the founders resolved to continue studying different models of education. Even with the looming undeniability of funding issues, the drive remained to acquire as much know-how as possible to help them develop the campus and channel what little money was raised into areas where impact could be maximized.

"You could ask me what kept me going those first five or six years," muses Ramji. "There was not much to show for it. The reason I managed was because for me, Agastya was a romance. It was an idea and a dream and when such a thing possesses you, you tend to forget other stuff. You get obsessed." Indeed, there could be little else to explain why the two executives, that had built otherwise prosperous lives for themselves were willing to rough it out in the searing forty-degree heat, driving to campus and back in an un-air-conditioned Ambassador vehicle[2], staying at cheap establishments, eating questionable food at roadside eateries, or waiting hours on end at a government official's office.

Even as the acquisition of the land was being hailed as a victory by well wishers, the lack of funds meant nothing could be built on it in the first two years. Ramji describes the tension he felt each day waking up and dreading the phone call inquiring whether construction had begun on the land. Short of more money, something dramatic needed to happen to propel Agastya forward.

The idea of a mobile science lab originated in 2002 during a dialogue between Ramji, Mahavir and K. V. Raghavan. They were on a car journey to the Chinmaya International Residential School in Coimbatore – a fact-finding mission to understand the costs involved in building an international school.

The discussion began with a question: if they didn't have the money to build a school to attract children and teachers, would it not be cheaper and just as effective to take education into the villages instead? The impact of the science fairs had already shown that students were eager to learn. Considering the portability of the models, would a mobile lab not be able to bridge the present gap between Agastya and the children it needed to reach?

The revelation that they could take the mountain to Mohammed immediately threw up a slew of potential benefits. With greater reach, the cost per child would fall substantially with a mobile lab as compared with a lab on the campus. A mobile lab could also be far more dynamic, moving at will to those areas where it was most needed or where schools were most supportive. Visually, it would enhance Agastya's community engagement. Its synergy with the science fairs was also undeniable.

As electrifying as the prospect was, it would also mean a dramatic shift in focus. From developing the campus, Agastya would now be working more towards serving rural societies. And, while the science fairs were certainly popular, there was little guarantee that the mobile lab – which would most likely need to impose itself on a regular school day – would receive the same acceptance from schools and teachers.

It was in no way a frictionless decision. Many had their hearts set on a physical campus and convincing those that had given their efforts to the cause that the script was being rewritten was not easy. For the founders, it asked of a seismic shift in both focus and prioritization.

The team decided to press ahead with the mobile science lab initiative after weighing the obvious positives against potential hidden pitfalls. But another more human reason persisted for their decision.

"Agastya had engaged the time and attention of important people like Dr. P. K. Iyengar, Dr. R. Krishnan and my father," says Ramji. "Showing progress was vital to keep their interest and enthusiasm in Agastya alive. The mobile lab would demonstrate a positive movement, albeit in a direction that no one had anticipated."

A former classmate of Ramji's – S. Vasudevan – was a vice president at Hindustan Motors. With his support, Agastya was able to get a second-hand rural transport vehicle.[3] Additionally, the HBCSE in Mumbai gifted Agastya a trunk containing numerous low-cost science experiments. This collection of models was the result of extensive research by HBCSE and mirrored – by design – those that were being demonstrated at the science fairs.

With the hardware in place, the team now needed that most crucial element: a willing teacher. However, a peculiarity of Indian culture would present itself almost immediately when the hunt for an instructor began. It would be something of an encumbrance for a while to come but would eventually result in a solution of award-winning proportions.

The issue the team faced was in finding a teacher who would be willing to drive a van.

India's class and caste system often ensures that certain functions rarely mingled. Teaching is seen as a profession of high repute. Driving a van, considerably less so. To ask a teacher to drive a van would be to suggest the unthinkable.

Given budget constraints, the move to recruit a teacher also meant that Balaram's role would be made redundant. Despondent over losing a job he had come to love, Balaram trudged home to inform his wife that he would soon be unemployed. She was having none of it. On her insistence, Balaram made a spirited pitch to be trained as a science teacher. It was a tempting prospect, not least because it would mean holding on to a colleague that the team had come to value. It also addressed the issue of getting a teacher to drive a van, as Balaram had no qualms about the same, given that he had been manning a tractor thus far!

However, Balaram's qualifications posed a problem. He had a liberal arts degree and no teaching experience whatsoever. Deciding he was worth the risk, the founders asked the HBCSE team to interview him. As expected, they were impressed with his enthusiasm and agreed to train him further.

On 15 August 2002, the 55th anniversary of India's independence, Agastya launched its very first mobile science lab in a village near Kuppam. Balaram, the curious young man who had worked at the TTD guesthouse, would be the very first instructor.

"At that time, there was no artwork," states Balaram. "It was only a white van. Kids would run away, scared, thinking it was an ambulance coming to give vaccines. But once they saw what was inside, I used to be cheered. They used to call me 'Agastya Balaram.' Some people would bring their mobile phones to the van to be repaired; I had to explain to them that we were not that kind of mobile lab!"

With help from Gambhir, Balaram slowly adapted to and then thrived in the role he had grabbed out of sheer desperation. The feedback he brought from the field was promising. Children loved the experiments and teachers considered the van's arrival as a welcome and productive break to the school day. The founders egged Balaram on to continue performing what they called his "village magic" until they came up with more money or a better idea.

The novelty of the mobile science lab, and its positive reception in the villages around Gudupalle, energized Agastya and brought some much-needed visibility to the foundation. In October 2002 the *Times of India* carried an article on Agastya's mobile science lab titled "Kuppam's Newton Becomes Villagers' Driving Force." It showed a smiling and animated Balaram teaching village children, with Agastya's mobile science lab in the background. The *Times*'s coverage captured the attention of the Karnataka government, which requested Agastya to launch a similar lab in their state. The lab consequently began making trips to schools in nearby Kolar.

Despite government support and the friendly attitude of schools in welcoming Agastya's mobile labs, roving through uncharted tracts to reach smaller villages was not for the faint of heart. While working in the Paderu tribal areas, about 20 hours away from campus, Balaram and his team were approached one night by a band of Naxalites[4]. It was a nerve-racking experience as the armed men inspected the van and made their own assessments on whether the Agastya team posed any kind of threat. In the end, the Naxalites praised the good work being done by Agastya, complimented the team's efforts, and disappeared into the forests in peace.

The mobile science lab was a striking example of an innovation that emerged from quick and innovative thinking under pressure. It was in no way the first of its kind. Others before Agastya had explored and even implemented similar mobile labs. However, Agastya saw the potential to combine three disparate elements in a way that had not commonly been done before. They melded mobility, hands-on learning and low-cost models into a single force of relevant, scalable science for a mass audience. In doing so, the mobile science lab became an instrument to take not just the 'what' and the 'why' but also the 'how' of science into the minds of the least privileged.

You could certainly spark curiosity with a computer, or an expensive microscope, or a state-of-the-art model of a fighter jet. But the interaction would be mostly one way. Agastya's models, in contrast, were designed to be played with, dismantled and even broken. They allowed children to delve not only into the theory of science but also to dissect it, build it back up again and even replicate it at home using everyday objects.

Within a few years Agastya would become the largest operator of mobile science labs in the world. CNN would feature Agastya's efforts in a 2017 piece titled "Einstein in the Village," and the Rockefeller Foundation's Next Century Awards would name the Agastya mobile lab in its gallery of the top hundred global innovations of 2013.

On a summer's afternoon in 2000, Ramji sat in the waiting room of Goldman Sachs's plush London office. He wasn't quite sure what to expect of the man he had come to meet. Alok Oberoi, a Cornell-educated financier, had been introduced to Ramji via a common friend and Ramji, being in the sort of position where no stone could be left unturned, had called on Oberoi in the hope that he might support Agastya.

Oberoi, the head of international private wealth management at Goldman Sachs, was similarly unsure of the man he had agreed to meet. Like so many, Oberoi was intrigued by the story of this former banker who had apparently given it all up at the prime of his career to become a social entrepreneur. If nothing else, the interaction alone might be worth the time he was giving to Ramji.

But Oberoi had also been thinking about philanthropy more seriously of late and had begun considering how he might start giving back to India.

According to Oberoi, his meeting with Ramji was severely delayed. When Ramji finally did enter his office, Oberoi apologized and declared that as it was well past lunchtime, he would have his assistant send up some sandwiches. The food arrived and, as the two men continued their discussion, Oberoi began eating while Ramji made his pitch. It was a while before Oberoi, midway through a ham sandwich, inquired as to why Ramji was not eating anything. Politely, Ramji stated that he was a vegetarian.

His composure stuck a thunderous chord with Oberoi.

"First, I made him wait. Then I gave him ham sandwiches and then I realized he was vegetarian. I was so taken by his calmness that I was sold on him instantly and offered to put in money," Oberoi reveals.

While the incident sold Oberoi on Ramji, Agastya's work was what really impressed the financier. He liked the rural focus of the science fairs and quite literally bought into the philosophy.

"It goes to the basic principle of investing," he explains. "If we put a dollar into something, we knew that it would have massive dividends in rural India. We also knew that India's rote learning was not offering creativity. We had someone here that was looking at it from first principles and wanting to infuse creativity back into the system. To me, whether it was going to work or not, I had no idea, but we had to try."

After their first meeting, Oberoi signed a cheque for $10,000. Months later, this was followed up with another cheque for $20,000.

The following year, Oberoi would quit Goldman Sachs and start his own investment firm, ACPI Investments Limited, and lay the groundwork for his own charitable venture, the Oberoi Family Foundation. ACPI's and the foundation's contributions towards Agastya would go towards constructing the first buildings on campus – a physics lab and four small classrooms. Over the succeeding years the Oberoi Family Foundation's donations helped to build the Oberoi Centre, launch several mobile science labs, train hundreds of teachers and helped launch Sarga Samvad – Agastya's arts and innovation initiative.

Oberoi would also join Agastya's board of trustees in 2007. As a beacon of clarity and good judgement, he would bring his dynamic, forward-thinking style to board meetings. His involvement was crucial in propelling Agastya's expansion over the next decade.

Like the first sprinklings of water on a parched patch of earth, the infusion of funds was absorbed by the foundation as quickly as it came. After laying stagnant for over a year, the campus was finally seeing some activity. It would be fair to say that these were the humblest of beginnings, but first steps are often the toughest.

In addition to the early buildings made possible by the Oberoi Foundation, a biology lab, funded by the Dr. Reddy's Foundation, was also constructed. Anji Reddy – a pioneer of India's pharmaceutical industry – heard Ramji speak for 15 minutes before agreeing to fund the lab.

"The Agastya model has the potential to transform rural India and there is great potential for it to be disseminated to all parts of the country. I am happy to be jump-starting this revolution," he said in an interview at the time, showing incredible foresight about Agastya's future.[5]

The campus's early, low-cost structures compensated for their simplicity by housing a plethora of science models and experiments to delight any school-going child. The buildings, rudimentary by design when compared with those that came later, were nonetheless an immense source of pride for the Agastya team. They alone knew the hardships, the countless rejections and the numerous hurdles that had been surmounted to bring these labs and classrooms into being.

Without yet having money to build residences for any fee-paying students, the foundation invited local village kids to come and use the labs. Each day, about two dozen children from government schools within walking distance would visit the campus. The footfall was scarcely enough to adequately utilize even the modest facilities. It would lead visitors to politely remark that "Agastya needed more traction" and that "the foundation was still in its early stages." So vacant did the campus seem that prior to bringing a prospective donor, Ramji would call ahead to the campus manager and ask him to quickly invite more children to create the illusion of activity.

Agastya began conducting more teacher training workshops both on and off campus. Professors S. V. Subramanyam and H. L. Bhat, from the Indian Institute of Science (IISc) in Bangalore, led these workshops. Unlike the workshops conducted by Gambhir and Parameshwaran, those by Subramanyam and Bhat focused on teaching science content. Local schoolteachers appreciated the rare opportunity to attend lectures by IISc professors.

It was around this time that the founders – after having crunched many a number and taken a cold hard stare at the reality they were up against – decided they needed a new mode of approach. Studying other schools and colleges had told them that the figure they needed to build their residential school was in the region of $5 to $8 million. It contrasted rather humiliatingly with the $250,000-odd they had managed to raise thus far.

More importantly, the mobile science lab and science fairs were drawing the engagement of thousands of children. The number of interactions was many orders of magnitude greater than what they might have had with a static school. In terms of sheer impact, it appeared that a wider net cast across the less privileged strata would be a far more enriching and soul-rewarding endeavour than a school that might reach only a few thousand children at most.

These considerations gave pause to the Agastya team and resulted in them asking that most crucial of questions: "Would we rather fill a glass to the brim, or would we rather raise the level of the ocean by one millimetre?"

It was a pertinent and thought-provoking trade-off. Rather than build a school and use the methods developed by Agastya to benefit an elite few, the foundation could instead be a 'school for schools' impacting the neglected millions across the country.

They had opened a door to new possibilities. A school for schools would reach and benefit many more children and teachers than a stand-alone school could. It would free Agastya from the burden of an exam-pandering syllabus and from being constantly accountable to education officials and parents for grades. The foundation would have the freedom to experiment and create new content and approaches to learning. With the campus as the R&D hub, this new system had far more flexibility in terms of financing. Lower fixed costs implied that scale and reach could expand or contract depending on the availability of funds. There was also no pressing need to fully develop the campus all at once; it too could grow, evolve and flourish as the foundation's activities did.

To pivot in the manner that Agastya did took remarkable courage and a substantial clarity of purpose. Along with the focus on science fairs and the mobile science labs, the decision to abandon the original plan for a school was a seminal step in Agastya's journey. This capacity to innovate under pressure became a hallmark of Agastya, while the determination to act when needed became one of its defining qualities. There would be other course corrections, naturally. But none would be as definitive as the decision to remap the very core of the organization's activities.

Ramji began to understand that his vision of Shangri-La needed to be reimagined. It was never meant to be a haven, tucked away for only the fortunate few to enjoy. It was a gift that needed to permeate the furthest reaches of the country, to ignite young minds and to wrest a whole generation into an era of creativity. However, the manner in which the campus would eventually come alive would surpass even his wildest boyhood aspirations.

1.   In another sense, this also reflects the glaringly high student–teacher ratio in government schools in India, where a single teacher may be required to teach a class of over 100 students.

2.   Initially, the team used K. V. Raghavan's car for the commute. However, this hardly seemed fair considering the number of trips needed and the harsh roads to and from campus. The Ambassador was a gift from S. Vasudevan of Hindustan Motors. Ramji and Mahavir paid out of pocket for fuel for many years until funding was more abundant and could cover these expenses or indeed allowed for a more comfortable vehicle.

3.   The very same vehicle that today stands on a pedestal on campus.

4.   Maoist rebels are often heavily armed. The Naxalites have been locked in a decades long battle with the Indian government over the rights of farmers, workers and tribals.

5.   Anantha Krishnan M., "Dr. Reddy, Agastya Will Take Science to Villages," *The Times of India*, last modified 23 October 2003, https://timesofindia. indiatimes.com/city/bengaluru/dr-reddy-agastya-will-take-science-to-villages/articleshow/247285.cms.

CHAPTER 6

BOLDLY INTO THE UNKNOWN

In the corporate world, a pivot is usually spoken about with shades of reverence. It signifies a never-say-die approach, a survivalist mindset, and a versatility in both operations and management. These three aspects do not often coincide when needed most. Management books wax lyrical over global brands that spun themselves around crucial inflection points to sustain or even surpass their erstwhile business models. Nintendo made noodles, Play-Doh manufactured wall cleaners and Wrigley's jumped from soap to baking powder before eventually settling on chewing gum.

Agastya's move was far less drastic, so you might have expected things to be much easier from here on out. However, a pivot brings no guarantees. Like a ship that alters course to let its sails inhale new headwinds, an organization may find itself dashed against rocks just as easily as it might race into the nearest available sunset.

The surety that Agastya had made the right decision came from the reasoning that it happened organically. To the best of their abilities, the team had stayed true to the purpose of sparking creativity and nurturing innovation. A combination of factors from both within and without had resulted in what eventually seemed like a very natural progression to becoming a school for schools.

As such, the change brought with it a host of advantages that enthused the founders and gave them more control over their own narrative. And yet, complications remained.

Financial constraints had not miraculously come undone. Indeed, convincing a donor to invest in a school was possibly easier than selling something that was untried and untested beyond Agastya's very local sphere of operations. Further, the very fabric of the organization would need to be unravelled and respun, keeping the new approach in mind. Rather than expensive buildings and state-of-the-art facilities, the focus would need to shift to mobile labs outfitted with highly replicable, low-cost equipment. Rather than recruiting from an elite teaching pool, Agastya would need to build a team of young, enthusiastic, unproven foot soldiers willing to traverse the inner reaches of rural India.

Despite these issues, Ramji was positive that they had made the right call. His numerous discussions with potential donors had shown him enough to know this. While Agastya was still not an easy sell, the right donor would see it for what value and impact it could have on a national scale. Agastya didn't need to persuade everyone to give a little; it only needed a few wealthy visionaries that would put their weight behind it. Ramji was convinced that if he could only create a brand around Agastya, he could bring such benefactors in.

But to begin building a brand, you sometimes need the support of a far bigger one.

In the early 1980s, Ramji had been recruited by Antonio Riera to work in Citibank's Puerto Rico office. Riera, who had a PhD in computer and systems engineering, saw a lot of potential in Ramji and had indeed previously failed to poach Ramji to come work for him.

"He was very bright, very articulate, and was not afraid at all to voice an opinion," Riera describes. "He was so different from the people I saw over there [in his team at Puerto Rico] that I felt if I could have him in my team, it would be good."

Riera and Ramji worked together for many years, during which time Ramji moved from San Juan to New York and eventually London. Like so many in Ramji's circle, Riera was shocked to hear that Ramji was quitting and heading back to India.

They kept in touch and in 2003 Ramji reached out to his friend, now a senior partner at Boston Consulting Group (BCG), to see if he could help give his brand a much-needed boost. Riera connected Agastya to Janmejaya Sinha, who headed BCG in India at the time. With his help, a report was written on the Indian education space.

The BCG report objectively mapped India's education landscape in a similar vein to how Agastya had been trying to express it thus far. With the benefit of BCG's enormous knowledge database and analytical rigour, the report brought clarity to the picture that Agastya had been trying to paint. Charts around high dropout rates, low engagement and the crippling shortage of quality teaching staff at the government school level[1] were all laid out in trademark BCG colours. The figures constructed a quantitative moat around Agastya's more instinctive, on-the-ground, and anecdotal experiences to complete the argument that Agastya was selling.

The study acted as a supporting document to help Agastya validate its approach. It forced potential donors to take the foundation's cause more seriously and view its mission around hands-on learning as a viable antidote to a now tangible national-level problem.

With some funds trickling in and activity levels rising, it was suggested that the founders employ someone to manage operations on the ground. Balasundaram recommended B. Subramanyam for the position of administrative head. Subbu, as he was called, had worked with Balasundaram at the Valley School in Bangalore, where he had also assisted in reforestation drives around the school's 200-acre campus.

Hesitant to take on any full-time staff due to the unpredictable nature of funding, the founders initially dragged their feet. A short while later, Ramji by chance met a man during another school visit. Impressed at first by his manner, Ramji was then pleased to learn that this man was the same Subbu who had been recommended to him. He invited Subbu over for dinner and described his plans for Agastya.

Ramji offered Subbu a salary of 13,000 rupees a month (about $250 dollars at the time) and said that he could personally guarantee the same for a period of two years. Beyond that, it would depend entirely on whether Agastya even existed. The salary was not substantial, but Subbu was keen to take the job anyway.

When Ramji probed further as to his true motivations, Subbu replied: "Because I believe Agastya is creating a large canvas, and I would like to paint on it." This would not be the last time that the founders were taken somewhat aback by the unbridled passion with which Agastya's employees viewed their roles.

Subbu was a resourceful self-starter who took on all tasks willingly at any hour of the day or night. His skill in dealing with people from a wide variety of backgrounds and across the chain of command was evident from the beginning. Even when Agastya was still unknown and it was difficult to attract staff, Subbu successfully recruited from the local towns and villages. Over the next year, using only word of mouth, he managed to recruit nearly 50 young science graduates.

As the issue of getting staff became less dire, the bigger problem of training, mentoring and most importantly motivating them became imperative.

Creating a team of result-focussed individuals who would proactively carry Agastya's mission forward was something of a challenge. Neither of the founders had previously trained young staff, let alone a diverse group with small-town or rural backgrounds. There was little doubt that the new joiners were keen to learn. However, two anxieties persisted among them. The first was a genuine concern around the question of how long Agastya would even last. The second was a hesitation about speaking up or voicing concerns in the presence of their seniors. The founders knew there was presently not much they could do to address the first concern. The second, however, was something they decided they needed to set right.

The reason for the employees' reticence was understandable. Like the children that Agastya was trying to engage, the young graduates being enlisted were from backgrounds where lessons were dictated and debate was discouraged. The belief that a teacher taught and a student listened had been hardwired into them. It didn't help that India's deep-rooted system of hierarchies led to a perception that any disagreement or conflict with a superior could lead to punishment, if not a termination in employment.

Ramji and Mahavir, through their actions, needed to demonstrate that fresh opinions and differing points of view would be welcomed, rather than suppressed. The solution, unsurprisingly, was already in their midst.

The same hands-on learning methods being used to educate children could have an equally positive impact on the instructors. It lowered their inhibitions, stimulated them to think and question, and improved communication. Teaching became fun, interesting and highly interactive. As the teachers began to draw on their experiences in the field, they began to suggest improvements to the models and experiments. Staff meetings soon became hotbeds of discussion and deliberation as instructors gained confidence in their own points of view and demanded recognition.

The effect of these changes was a heightened spirit of camaraderie and productive innovation within Agastya. The awareness that the techniques the foundation was propagating needed to also be absorbed internally was beginning to take hold. Agastya's employees began to see that they had to be curious themselves in order to spark curiosity in children. Evidence of their proactivity was showcased when an Agastya employee would proudly demonstrate a new model or experiment that they had created or adapted.

As Agastya eventually grew, the drive and eagerness of these new recruits would be a defining factor in ensuring that quality and scale did not feed off one another. Eventually, the lack of availability of enough fresh graduates would force the foundation to employ even dropouts, as long as they had the right attitude. In coining a belief system around this, Ramji would go on to declare that the only degree that he was interested in was a BEE degree: a 'bachelor of energy and enthusiasm.' This somewhat playful but very apt classification was encouraging because it allowed even non-graduates to make a difference within a system that was striving to be completely meritocratic. For their part, the founders themselves imbibed this ethos with such fervour that you could just as well have accused them of having doctorates in energy and enthusiasm.

This all made for a very heathy environment of back-and-forth dialogues that laid the framework for the culture of egalitarianism for which Agastya became known.

The intense on-the-job training was seen as a rite of passage and became a pillar of Agastya's ability to expand without diluting the talent pool. New hires understood that this was a nascent organization that didn't necessarily have the resources to support them in every way.

Yet, the vision that Agastya was painting was inspiring enough to instil a sense of ownership and entrepreneurial drive in the instructors themselves.

Dilip Kumar Gowda, who joined in 2006, recollects some of the hardships that early instructors willingly embraced: "In those days there were no guest houses or hotels available to us. If we wanted to eat a good meal, we needed to have a good session with the community so we would get invited for dinner! Every day we were going to a different village. We had to spend the night in the vehicle or in the school or the panchayat.[2] Now there is a guest house for every location, but earlier, when we joined, we would get a backpack with a jumper, a sheet and a pillow. It was understood that some nights, you would need to sleep in the van."

Another candidate, Subramanyam Naik, arrived for his interview in a suit and tie. Naik was shocked when he was told that his job might entail cleaning tables or even toilets, setting up experiments and physically maintaining the mobile lab. Naik declared that he had not earned a college degree to do manual work. He changed his mind and joined Agastya when he heard that his seniors – including Ramji – regularly performed such tasks to advance Agastya's mission. It is a common joke that Naik has not been seen in a suit since his interview. Instead, he progressed to become one of Agastya's most competent regional heads.

To further manage Agastya's growing team, the founders approached Balachandra Warrier. Bala was the brother of Ramji's friend Gopi Warrier and had recently retired as the vice president of operations at the TI Group in Chennai. Ramji had met Bala a few years prior in London and had heard that Bala was looking to do some non-profit work following his retirement.

As chief operating officer, Bala was entrusted with managing the growing pains that any organization invariably experiences. "I really liked the keyword 'curiosity,'" says Bala. "The campus, it was wilderness. I had to put down processes, go down to the nuts and bolts."

Bala joined in 2005, by which time there were still only five mobile labs in the areas surrounding the campus. Even with his wealth of experience in administration, the unfamiliarity of building the foundation from the ground up meant there was a lot of learning to be done on the job. His 2.5-odd years with Agastya would see a steep rise in activity that he is credited with having helmed.

———————

Although Subbu was performing his role in managing the campus to great effect, he was not an educator in the strictest sense of the word. His knowledge of flora and fauna, however, was impressive and this led to his contribution to perhaps one of Agastya's most celebrated initiatives. There was an understanding among the team early on that even with strained resources, the ecological recovery of the campus should not stagnate. Everyone agreed that those precious 172 acres of arid, lifeless land would need to experience a renaissance.

As former students of Rishi Valley, both Ramji and Mahavir had witnessed, first hand, the possibilities of a revival at a scale matching what the Agastya campus required. Situated on a belt recognized as drought-prone, Rishi Valley had rejuvenated its land despite constant and often prolonged rainless spells. Decades of water-harvesting and conservation efforts had built some measure of security, such that even one good bout of rain every two years was sufficient to recharge the groundwater and keep the valley thriving. Reforestation stimulated vegetation so that birds began to return to the valley: an impact so pronounced that by the early 1990s, the valley had been officially declared a bird sanctuary.[3]

Students at Rishi Valley played a major role in driving such initiatives forward, resulting in a genuine respect for the environment. Tree planting, ecological projects, and even desilting and cleaning around the percolation tanks were as much a part of a student's life as academia. As a result, Agastya's founders – like many others that passed through Rishi Valley – were aware of the allure of learning while being nestled in greenery. Scientific principles had been embedded in their surroundings, and they carried a oneness with their ecosystem with them long after their formal education concluded.

In this way, having themselves felt the profound impact of an education coupled with nature, the founders were determined that Agastya's children should experience the same. Moreover, if Agastya wanted to showcase that creativity and innovation were more than mere taglines, there existed no better way to illustrate this than by bringing vivacious, vital life back to the campus.

Subbu's work on reforestation around the Valley School campus in Bangalore had brought him in touch with various people within the Karnataka government's environmental department. One of them was Dr. Yellappa Reddy, a former chief conservator of forests and environment secretary of Karnataka.

When Subbu brought Reddy to see the campus, the latter was excited by the possibility of revitalizing the land.

"The land has been degraded," he told Ramji, "but I believe I can bring it back to its natural state."

He described the land's normal state as a semi-deciduous shrub forest. Ramji welcomed his verve but confessed that he could not afford to pay him a salary.

"Don't worry about my salary," Reddy reassured him. "I am going to do this for my soul."

Reddy referred to his long-term strategy for regeneration as 'gentle manipulation.' In an interview for a short film on Agastya made in 2012, he expounds his theory on the biotic stress inflicted on the land due to years of deforestation, over-grazing, and the use of harsh artificial pesticides. He illustrates that fertile, mineral-rich topsoil, which usually takes hundreds of years to properly form, had been allowed to wash away within a few decades, leaving the land devoid of the ingredients needed to adequately nurture vegetation.

Reddy's first act was to protect the campus from cattle, which he did by fencing the boundary.[4] He wanted to observe how the land would respond to this action before meddling with the soil or adding new plants.

His next move involved planting certain keystone species to encourage biodiversity. Several experimental herb gardens were created with the aim of understanding which flora might naturally thrive even in the poor-quality soil of the campus. These gardens included a *mulika vana*, which was created out of sheer desperation to keep the land from being reacquired by the government when Agastya's building activities had stalled (as described in the preface). Created on a hill face that overlooked the campus, three giant 100-metre outlines of a man, woman and child were formed using white stones. Herbs specific to the body parts whose ailments they addressed were planted along the outlines. Such herb gardens were a great attraction to children and adults alike, who would walk through them on

campus tours to learn more about the medicinal properties of plants.

Reddy was also a keen believer that introducing certain varieties of spider could, within months, start to
naturally control the pest population and allow nascent
life in the ground to start blooming. "There are several
endemic species in the earth that will soon begin to
express themselves," he declared.

From 2002, over the next decade and a half, Reddy
would reshape the land entirely along with a home-
grown team of Agastya's environmental warriors.

Laksh Kumar and N. Lokanatham,[5] who both joined
Agastya around 2010, recall the numerous stages of
this rejuvenation.

"There is no such thing as barren land," Laksh states
emphatically. "You need to do the research. Loganatham
and I consulted a lot of people – we even got a technical
report from the Indian Institute of Science (IISc) and
used this to replant and further study the ecology."

One major culprit impacting plant life was the over-
population of acacia. An invasive species native to Aus-
tralia, acacia is hardy enough that it can survive even
the harshest of summers. In this sense, its destructive
impact is more a result of it being able to propagate even
when other plants around it are dying or in stasis for
lack of water. Lantana was another unwelcome species
that the team went about trying to eliminate. Brought to
India as an ornamental plant by the British in the early
1800s, the shrub has run rampant across the south of
the country. With its offering of black berries that birds
seem to love, its seeds get dispersed far and wide, leading to a proliferation that has many environmentalists
gravely concerned. The dried lantana provides a perfect
bed of fuel that, if ignited by an irresponsibly flicked

match or cigarette, can drum up a rousing forest fire. Such fires were common around the campus and were proving tougher to manage with each passing year.

The soil quality was another issue that could not easily be addressed. Analysis showed that the soil was rocky, with very low levels of nitrogen, potassium, and phosphorus. In some places the earth was white and chalky, suggesting that most of the organic matter and minerals had been stripped away. In other areas, the soil was a deep red, characterized by an overabundance of iron. Nether was conducive to thriving plant life.

Finally, there was that insurmountable issue of rainfall. Historical data showed the site had only 400 millimetres of rain a year. It was adequate. However, with the rocky, porous nature of the soil, most rainwater seeped right through the earth rather than collecting to recharge the groundwater on campus.

To push the land into something resembling self-sustainability, the team employed a three-pronged approach.

First, eradicating acacia and lantana became one of the cornerstone initiatives by Reddy's team. Even today, with close to 80% of the acacia having been eradicated, the species remains a threat. Residents of Agastya's campus have learned to spot tiny acacia saplings sprouting from the ground and will periodically bend down and pluck them out, almost by habit.

Soil revival would take a while, but the process was started by first planting indigenous trees such as neem, banyan, jamun, peepul, and flame of the forest around the campus. These saplings were heavily supported with organic fertilizers, manure, and water. Certain trees such as badam (Indian almond) were added to aid in composting. Unlike most other trees, which shed annually, the badam tree sheds its leaves completely every three months, providing a valuable, regular source of organic matter for compost.

In 2009, a highway project near the campus felled two banyan trees. Not to be outdone, Agastya had the enormous tree trunks brought to the campus and placed in an area now called the Sacred Grove. Given proper care, the trunks began sprouting their own saplings so that today a large banyan tree stands proudly by the two horizontal trunks. Agastya uses this example to show that life, if nurtured, can always find a way.

The reviving tree life allowed fauna, however miniscule, to slowly make its way back onto the land. As the trees grew taller and began to self-sustain, their falling leaves and fruits resuscitated dormant colonies of insects. Once the insects had repopulated, lizards and small birds started returning. With the arrival of birds, the ecosystem would shift gears entirely. Bird droppings are rich in the trifecta of plant nutrients – nitrogen, potassium and phosphorous, all of which the land desperately needed.

Birds also significantly increased the breadth of seed dispersal. Sandalwood, whose seeds only germinate after their fruit is eaten, digested and excreted by birds, experienced a burst of activity in later years. Saplings of both the regular and the much rarer red sandalwood, or red sander, could suddenly be spotted all over campus.[6]

Rainwater harvesting became the third area of focus. In total, 18 check dams (containment areas to restrict the flow of water) and 8 percolation tanks were created around the campus after studying the flow of water during heavy rains. The check dams ensure that water does not quickly flow away from the campus, while the tanks store rainwater, allowing it to gently permeate into the surrounding soil to ensure that moisture stays trapped in the earth. Another interesting innovation was the creation of semi-circular saucers on slopes and circular saucers around planted trees. The saucers hold about 10-30% of the rainwater that passes through them and over time have encouraged the growth of biomass. Now, the biomass roots aid in trapping more moisture, and allow the rainwater to seep to greater depths.

Aside from the thought and planning behind these strategies, the Agastya team's relentless and unwavering implementation was what truly made the difference. This pursuit of excellence allowed them to push back against a decline with centuries of momentum behind it and usher in an era of rich, self-propagating life.

In 2005, Reddy and Subbu were featured in a *Business World* article titled "Sons of the Soil,"[7] which commended their victories in bringing the Agastya campus back to life. In 2015, a team from the IISc studied and documented the campus's explosion of biodiversity. In 2019, Agastya was awarded the Andhra Pradesh State Green Award. These accolades underlined the exemplary job that Reddy and his team of successors did in bringing a green revolution to a once forsaken land.

As the years passed, it was just as likely for visiting faculty to come to Agastya to collaborate on education as it was for them to want to study the environmental metamorphosis. The view from the buildings, once an open expanse of nothingness, is now often obstructed by green sentinels. Teeming with vibrant life made evident by the cooing of birds across the land, Agastya's campus remains a case study in ecological endeavours and a source of immense pride for the foundation.

A book titled *The Roots of Creativity*, was published by Agastya in 2017 showcasing the extensive measures taken to revive the campus. It covers initiatives on ecology, water conservation, renewable energy, bio-parks, waste management and community engagement.

True to his father's words (*see Chapter 4*), the land that Ramji once surveyed with dismay was eventually transformed into a haven of creativity.

1. In India, government schools are the same as state schools. However, these are usually only attended by children from poorer families. Even middle-income households would usually send their children to private schools, which are more expensive, but still not prohibitively so.

2. Local municipality headquarters

3. These initiatives won Rishi Valley the Indira Priyadarshini Vrikshamitra Award for 1995. This national award is given for pioneering work in reforestation and wasteland development.

4. This was perhaps the only action by Agastya that was unpopular with the surrounding villages, and it generated some bad PR for the foundation at the time. Within a decade, regenerative efforts would create so much surplus grass that villages were invited to cut and take what they needed. The land, which at one time had barely had enough grass to feed a single cow, was generating in excess of 10 lakh rupees ($15,000) worth of grass a year, given freely to the villages.

5. Lokanatham, who left Agastya in 2020, was famous for his early morning eco walks at 6 am. His passion for Agastya's flora was such that, for him, each tree, shrub, sapling, and even weed had a meaning and a story behind it. Stopping at a seemingly random sapling, he would delve into its history, its impact on the surrounding ecology and its potential uses in medicine. As a result, he would barely make it 100 metres from his starting point in nearly 90 minutes!

6. Sandalwood also poses a security threat to the campus, as smugglers keep tabs on the growth of these trees and can plan heists to fell trees and steal the precious wood. The foundation understands this is something that needs to be addressed today to avoid problems once the trees reach maturity. They are working on developing an alarm system for sandalwood trees.

7. https://maitreyahc.wordpress.com/2011/02/11/agastya-foundation-land-restoration/

CHAPTER 7

WORTHY CAUSE, WORTHY PEOPLE

There is a paradox concerning altruistic undertakings that are done in the right spirit.

On the one hand, the non-profit nature of the venture places very stringent limits on how resources can be allocated. Spare funds are unavailable for lavish get-togethers, for bold marketing campaigns or for hiring from the cream of the crop. Members of such organizations would never be seen at five-star events handing out flashy brochures, or on recruitment days at top business schools pitching to eager graduates.

Even networking – which could be argued to be essential for the growth of any enterprise – requires carefully weighing the potential benefits of a meeting against a shoestring budget for travel and entertainment.

And yet, if the cause is just and the vision is worth selling, taking the charitable route often opens up a remarkable number of possibilities inaccessible to others.

Even with its operations still nascent, Agastya never failed to impress anyone who cared to understand what the foundation was trying to achieve. Its honest attempts to reshape learning resonated with some of the largest academic establishments, throwing open doors that may have otherwise taken far longer and far more persuasion to even squeeze through. The sheer scale of the mission astounded even the boldest institution builders, and the fact that the team seemed capable enough to pull it off forced them to take Agastya seriously.

Early on, the founding team developed a significant number of contacts on an almost semi-personal level, with help from immediate friends and family. Ramji will often credit his wife, Monica, for her ability to win people over and make them see the vision that was Agastya. She would frequently reach out to friends and family, pushing them to donate to Agastya in any way they could. With a steadfast determination to stay in touch and grab the slimmest chances to connect, Monica's irrepressible manner reignited many an opportunity that Ramji would have otherwise thought lost. An unabashed champion of Agastya's cause, Monica once approached an Army General in Bangalore airport and engaged him in a conversation about the foundation's struggles to expand in the border states of Rajasthan and Gujarat. The meeting resulted in Agastya getting the army's collaboration in spreading education among village children in the border areas of Rajasthan.

As a Bangalore-based foundation with a focus on STEM education, Agastya also cultivated many well-wishers within local scientific fraternities over the years. The partnerships and collaborations thus created would help Agastya tremendously, as brilliant minds would selflessly offer their services to further Agastya's efforts.

In addition to the scientists from the Homi Bhabha Centre for Science Education (HBCSE), Agastya usually found help in nearly every corner it asked for it.

If you were to apply Maslow's hierarchy to an organization, there is reason to suggest that entrepreneurs struggle because the basic requirement for growth – intellectual resources – is so hard to come by early on and indeed without significant cost. Agastya overcame that by approaching retired people and nurturing in them a belief that their time would be well spent furthering a cause that was worthwhile.

"They had all the knowledge and insight and we realized that there was a 'cognitive surplus' that no one was tapping into," says Ramji.

The seed of inspiration for this came from the three wise men themselves. Each highly respected in their own field, they selflessly gave many hundreds of hours to further Agastya's mission. As a result, when the call went out to other scientists, academics and corporates to contribute, the response was overwhelmingly positive. This sense of service became a part of Agastya's DNA. The example set by the three wise men was something that others saw as worthy of emulation.

Retired scientists from the Defence Research and Development Organisation (DRDO) and the National Aerospace Laboratories designed many of the models, experiments and exhibits that came to populate the Agastya learning system, along with the teaching manuals that went with them.

Professors from the Indian Institute of Science (IISc) ran many of the early science and math workshops for teachers. It was also a study done by the IISc in later years that helped the ecological restoration of the Agastya campus. Further, a team led by the IISc would establish a butterfly park on the campus that would later be studied by R. Bhanumati, leading to a 2019 book titled *Butterflies of Agastya*.

Scientists from the National Centre for Biological Sciences (NCBS) played an important advisory role and helped to establish Agastya's bio-discovery centre, which became a valuable addition to the campus.

These highly respected organizations were forward-thinking and saw Agastya's model as a way to ensure that future scientists were given the right platform on which to nurture their thirst for knowledge. For these academics, Agastya was an ideal conduit to convert their ideas into on-the-ground action and gauge their impact.

"What impresses me is that there are a lot of organizations that do that kind of work, but no one does it with this kind of scale, ambition, quality and passion," says K. VijayRaghavan, the former director of the NCBS, who also served as the principal scientific adviser to the government of India from 2018 to 2022. Ramji had been introduced to VijayRaghavan in 2004 by P. K. Iyengar and they stayed connected.

"In computer science, 'garbage in, garbage out' refers to faulty input producing faulty output," observes Ramji. "The obverse also is true. Success often reflects the quality of partnerships and collaborations that you build with individuals and organizations."

It might be tempting to think that mere phone calls or chance conversations created the myriad connections and collaborations that Agastya would eventually develop. In truth, the dream that was Agastya needed to be sold, repackaged and sold many times before the right individuals took notice. However, there was one watershed moment that took the foundation's name to the most relevant people at a time when it was most needed.

On a cool Bangalore morning in 2003, educationalists, scientists, policymakers and a host of other academics congregated in the J. N. Tata Auditorium to hear a series of lectures. Housed within the IISc's stunning campus, the hall could accommodate about 900 people. It was barely half full as Ramji took to the podium. People of varying eminence were set to speak that day and the audience thinned and swelled in accordance with the same. Having been invited to speak at the annual Rotary Governor's Meet, Ramji now looked unsure. The sparsely populated room stared back at him, the expressions of the audience a mingling of scepticism and a lack of recognition. Seated in the front row was K. V. Raghavan, whose presence gave Ramji a much-needed boost in confidence.

As he began his talk, some members of the audience continued conversing among themselves, as is sometimes the case when an unknown speaker tries to command a crowd.

Ramji Raghavan is not a large man, and his manner is generally unassuming. However, his unequivocal command over the English language is something that others take notice of nearly instantly. He has a polished accent that can be characterized as neither Indian nor British. He speaks at a calm, measured pace and places great importance on enunciation and the use of vivid imagery to engage anyone he converses with.

Despite the murmurs in the crowd, Ramji's opening words cut through the conversational undercurrent and people paused momentarily to focus on the podium.

Ramji's speech was specifically on education in India. Rather than put Indian education down, he decided instead to first chalk a rich history of India's accomplishments across various fields of study. For the next half an hour, he spoke about Aryabhata and the invention of the zero and of Srinivasa Ramanujan and his brand of mathematical genius, which the world still struggles to comprehend. He brought up C. V. Raman and S. N. Bose and their invaluable contributions to physics.[1] He addressed Chanakya and his treatise on political strategy, which was used to catapult the Maurya dynasty into power. He described the achievements of Ayurveda and India's astounding contributions to healthcare, where surgical procedures – including plastic surgery – were being conducted as early as the 7th century BCE. He discussed astronomy, metallurgy, music and architecture, and described how India was, at one time, a pioneer in virtually every one of these fields. He recognized Nalanda and Takshashila, India's key seats of learning in ancient times, revered the world over for the exemplary individuals who taught and studied there. He extolled Gandhi's period in South Africa and Sardar Patel's tackling of the floods in Gujarat. He echoed Patel's response at being asked to pen India's history: "We do not write history, we make history."[2]

At the core of it all, Ramji explained, were creativity and innovation. India had, at one time, built a civilization of insatiable curiosity that led it to relentlessly seek answers to everything around it. This was why, at its peak, India was considered a global superpower long before that phrase was even formally adopted or properly understood.

Sitting in the audience, you could sense each member swelling with pride. A few got up and left but returned to the hall shortly with more people in tow. The room was filling up as some stood in the aisles and along the sides of the auditorium, all enrapt at the speech, which wove a rich and intricate tapestry of India's greatest achievements.

Then, after luring the room into a sense of security, Ramji asked them to consider where India presently found itself. Was curiosity still being nurtured in young minds? Was an education based on marks alone churning out any more C. V. Ramans and Ramanujans? Did the audience truly believe that India's school system was doing justice to the centuries of excellence that preceded it?

Finally, Ramji talked about the importance of a return to cause–effect thinking; the need for energy, enthusiasm and passion; and the indispensability of quality in both thought and action.

He then described Agastya. He laid out its mission to reverse the apathy within education and release the potential of several untapped millions. He expressed unfettered hope that hands-on education could reignite curiosity and take India back to its former status as a cradle of global innovation.

It was a bit of a gamble to use the audience's patriotism to lift them high, only to let them come crashing down with a harsh prick of reality. For a moment, the room was quiet as pride morphed into pensive reflection.

Then a gentleman stood up. He appeared confrontational at first and it seemed he might accuse Ramji of being anti-national. Instead, he smiled and complimented Ramji on a wonderful speech, saying that it had given him much pause for thought. Another gentleman stood up and seconded this sentiment. Then a third stood up and shouted, "Sir! Everything you said is true. But you really made me proud to be an Indian!" The room erupted in agreement as Ramji was given a standing ovation that refused to die down quickly.

Although Ramji had hoped his talk would offer some much-needed exposure to Agastya in the right circles, he never expected his brand to explode in the manner it did that day. The speech at the J. N. Tata Auditorium instantly took Agastya's name to the kinds of scientists and thought leaders that it needed to connect with. It paved the way for the foundation to create the right introductions in both the private and the government sectors. Agastya would use these to delve deeper into the world of academia, which would become an essential support structure in the years to come.

In March 2004, about a year after the J. N. Tata Auditorium speech, Agastya would conduct another major brainstorming session. After the Information Technology Park Limited (ITPL) session over five years ago (see *Chapter 3*), this would be a fresh opportunity for Agastya to take stock of its efforts and goals by bringing together bright minds to weigh in on the foundation's approach. The event was held at the NCBS in Bangalore, where Dr. VijayRaghavan generously permitted Agastya to use the facilities for three days at no charge.

Unlike the ITPL meeting, where the group was far more diverse, the NCBS session was composed mainly of leading scientists. Aside from VijayRaghavan and his colleague Ubbaid Siddiqui, the group also included S. V. Subramanyam and K. P. Gopinathan from the IISc, V. G.

Gambhir of HBCSE, P. K. Iyengar, R. Krishnan, ex-Tata Institute of Fundamental Research professor Balu Venkataraman, Ramji and Mahavir. Rohini Nilekani, the author and founder of the Arghyam Foundation, was also present for the morning session.

The NCBS workshop produced a number of interesting recommendations. Among these was the suggestion that Agastya employ its own success with encouraging biodiversity on campus and link it to science learning for both teachers and children. Over three days of intense discussions, the group identified nine core concepts around which Agastya should focus and build its curriculum.[3]

Events such as the NCBS meeting were not only important for the direction they offered but also for the distillation of key ideas that Agastya's work was constantly churning out. They also proved to be an excellent way to match wavelengths among key contributors and consequently garner their support to further strengthen Agastya's standing. Finally, the process of debate that was followed in these interactions was a way to foster an internal culture of questioning in Agastya from the very beginning.

Both literally and figuratively, the foundation was in unchartered territory. It took the commitment of some very engaged and highly astute individuals, devoting what precious free time they had, to act as compasses to ensure that Agastya did not lose its way.

In addition to its invaluable contribution in structuring Agastya's early curriculum, the brainstorming session at NCBS culminated in the group making a presentation to V. K. Aatre, the head of the DRDO and the scientific adviser to the Minister of Defence. Aatre had heard of Ramji and of Agastya via Krishnan a few years prior. However, their meeting at the NCBS was what encouraged him to look more closely at what the team was doing.

"I studied in small government schools where two or three classes were combined," states Aatre plainly, revealing an astoundingly humble beginning for someone who would go on to win the Padma Vibhushan in 2016.[4] As head of the DRDO, he was Dr. Abdul Kalam's successor. "I never felt any teacher had had any great influence on me. This was something that Agastya was trying to change. What appealed to me was that Agastya's looked like a maverick approach."

Aatre agreed to build and loan Agastya a custom-built DRDO-registered mobile science lab. Unlike the other mobile science labs, this one would have a screen to show films. The van would be used to run science fairs for communities near the DRDO's operations in Ahmednagar, Maharashtra, where the van would also be built.

In August 2004, Dr. Aatre's tenure as the head of the DRDO would conclude and he would relocate to Bangalore, his hometown. Ramji asked him to become more involved with Agastya and offered him a seat on the board of trustees. After visiting the campus, Dr. Aatre agreed.

"I was convinced that Agastya was a transformational organization that India needed," he declares.

If Agastya's surefooted agenda was already turning heads in its favour and bringing in new contacts, Dr. Aatre's involvement would cut even deeper inroads into the scientific community. For a young foundation with no money for high-level networking, Agastya was being given the kind of access that no amount of funds could possibly buy. Eminent scientists such as K. Kasturirangan and Ramesh Mashelkar, heads of the Indian Space Research Organisation and the Council of Scientific and Industrial Research respectively, became friends of Agastya.

"I'm a great admirer of Ramji as an individual," says Mashelkar, "He has not only been a thought leader, but an action leader. There was a great need for what he was setting out to do. Creativity and innovation were critical needs. This kind of need had been felt across the country. Children must move from rote learning to learning by doing to learning by creating and learning by co-creating."

Apart from the DRDO – where Aatre's influence was substantial – other government institutions also became supporters. These included Bharat Electronics, which would sponsor solar streetlamps to light the campus at night. Finally, through his excellent relationships within the Karnataka government, Dr Aatre would eventually help to propel Agastya towards its most ambitious expansion across the state.

Whatever issues still persisted around funding, Agastya never lamented a paucity of intellectual capital as an obstacle to growth.

With access to world-class thinking, Agastya was not only casting a wide net but was also doing so at a quality level that even established, well-funded institutions might struggle to emulate. In a sense, this was a true Blue Ocean strategy in securing intellectual power. Over time, a training programme would kick in to encourage a kind of teaching talent osmosis from the high-level academics to Agastya's instructors. Early on, however, it was common to stumble into an Agastya teaching session and witness something truly amazing.

For Balu Venkatraman, teaching in villages and small towns was a unique experience. A former senior professor at India's prestigious Tata Institute of Fundamental Research, Venkatraman was a part of Agastya's brainstorming workshop at NCBS in 2004. The draw of Agastya was that it offered retired scientists such as him an opportunity to plunge back into teaching, albeit with far more raw and impressionable students than they had earlier been accustomed to.

"The teachers and children who attend my lecture-demonstrations have never been exposed to science concepts in this way. They have not seen experiments. It feels wonderful to know that you are making a real difference to the way people think about and perceive science," he says.

A typical class by Venkatraman would start at 10 am. The groundwork for the demonstrations was time-consuming. It could take up to two hours for Venkatraman and his assistants to set up the experiments. For lectures on colour and light, bed sheets would be draped over the window frames to dim the brightness in the dusty old room. Students waited expectantly, already anticipating that it would be no regular class.

Before he began his classes, Venkatraman would always urge his audience to participate. "You won't learn if you don't question," he often told his students. For six hours, interrupted by a one-hour lunch break, his students were held captivated by demonstrations of the properties of light, lasers and colour. Simple tools and techniques were used to illustrate the properties of light. An incense stick was burned, and a laser beam was passed through the smoke that curled upwards. Against the fog, the laser's presence was unmasked. His students would often sigh in wonder as they traced the red beam through the smoke. There were questions, interspersed with appreciative laughter at the beauty and simplicity of the experiment.

As one lecture drew to a close, Dr. Venkatraman filled a glass beaker with a solution of sodium thiosulphate. Into this he poured hydrochloric acid. Then, using an antiquated slide projector, he flashed light through the liquid mixture to create an image on the wall. A ball of light, very much resembling the sun in its gentle yellow glow, appeared in front of the class. Venkatraman explained that as the very fine sulphur deposited from the chemical reaction reached a critical size, it would begin to scatter blue light from the sides of the container and allow only red light to pass through. But as the sulphur particles grew further, they would no longer allow any light to pass through at all. The students sat mesmerized as the 'sun' gradually turned from yellow to orange and then darkened and faded away entirely.

"The sun has set, so it is time for me to go," Venkatraman declared to spontaneous applause.

As far as personnel went, Agastya's inability to offer anything resembling top dollar should have seen it scraping the bottom of the barrel for talent. But what the foundation was unable to offer in monetary benefits it compensated for by doling out in spades the kind of meaningful, soul-enriching work that was otherwise difficult to find. This may seem like a cliché in an era when companies are constantly trying to limit employee wage-hikes by offering more glamourous titles or positioning the work as rewarding. However, there is a marked difference between a corporation cutting costs on employees while celebrating burgeoning profits for its shareholders and a foundation whose selflessness is the only thing on display. Agastya would find – rather serendipitously – that the kind of people it attracted were those who were motivated by more than money and for whom the cause became an almost personal crusade.

In 2003, a young man named T. S. Suresh heard about Agastya through Mahavir's daughter, Sheetal. Intrigued by her description, he decided to visit the campus along with his wife, Hamsalatha K. Two years after this visit, Suresh was teaching at a private school in Bangalore, but found the work to be rather tedious. His mind went back to his experience at Agastya. He decided to reach out once more and he connected with Subbu.

"He was not sure how I could teach, as I am a diploma holder," Suresh says of his interaction with Subbu. Although Suresh was teaching in a private school, Subbu was not convinced that Suresh could effectively learn and communicate Agastya's teaching methods. "I told him that teaching is in my blood as I come from a family of teachers."

Subbu agreed to take Suresh on as an instructor for two weeks. Hamsalatha, or Hamsa as she is now known across the organization, agreed to accompany him. She had a diploma in computer science and was interested in the measurement metrics that Agastya was using to gauge impact. The caveat: there would be no pay. Both husband and wife agreed.

"We had only one mobile lab in Bangalore," Hamsa muses of this gruelling trial period. "The vehicle used to be parked in the Honeywell campus on Bannerghatta Road. We had to travel from Bangalore to Kanakapura. We used to get up at 4 am to get there by 9 am. We had to visit two schools where the mobile science lab was running. We looked forward to meeting the children and that used to keep us going."

At the end of the two weeks, impressed by their quiet, unflinching dedication to the task they were entrusted with, Subbu ended up hiring both Suresh and Hamsa.

It was an exciting period for Agastya. While the land and buildings slowly developed, it was also becoming clear to the core team that with the campus as the sole hub, their distribution model had limited range. Vans that operated in and around Gudupalle could return to campus at the end of the day, but Agastya had no bases beyond the campus for new vans to use. Relying on the kindness of corporates such as Honeywell to house their mobile labs was fine for the short term, but to really branch out, Agastya would need more hubs. The Koppal science project in North Karnataka[5] was the first step in translating this theory into action.

Funded by USAID, the science centre in Koppal was meant to emulate a mini-campus. Over the years, science centres would be located in spare spaces within government or corporate buildings.[6] Sizes would typically range from a thousand to a few thousand square feet. While these science centres could hardly replicate the size or the grandeur of the campus, they were integral if Agastya wanted to create a network spanning the breadth of the whole country. The plan was to strategically locate the science centres in the denser localities. They would be used as watering holes from where mobile labs could replenish their models and experiments before heading out into more rural regions. A typical mobile lab housed only about 100 models, but the science centres could store a larger selection. The mix in the mobile lab could then be curated to match the grade levels of the schools that were being visited on a given day. The science centres could also serve as a point of confluence for Agastya's staff and instructors, and nearby schools could even benefit from having their children visit. The hub-and-spoke model, which had been used so effectively for distribution in other industries, would now become the defining structure for Agastya moving forward.

However, when Suresh and Hamsa were packed off to Koppal with scarcely a few weeks of experience tucked in their pockets, this was still an unproven model. A city-bred boy, Suresh was apprehensive about doing a job that he was barely trained to do, especially as it was in a remote rural area with few educational or other facilities. The mandate seemed well above his level of expertise. Considering how important the project was, he could have been forgiven for wondering whether the team was punishing him for some mistake he might have unknowingly made.

"I felt like a person who has just learned how to swim and is taken and left in a boat in the middle of an ocean," he confesses.

He recalls Bala Warrier telling them, "You are the owners. The total responsibility of the programme rests with you. Just achieve the targets."

Ramji's comfort, and indeed confidence, in this decentralized management model stemmed from his experience with Citibank, where 'sink or swim' was a common initiation approach for new bankers. Agastya's ambition and the complexity of its task contrasted significantly with the kind of money it could offer. Identifying purpose-driven, high-energy, high-impact individuals early on was key to building the required momentum. As in any start-up, the first 10 or 20 people would drive the culture for years to come and Agastya needed them to be exemplary. Hence, the directive to Suresh and Hamsa was as much about succeeding in Koppal as it was about putting the new joiners through the wringer and seeing if they would emerge stronger for it.

The targets they were being asked to achieve were not insignificant. They included the establishment of a science centre, the deployment of two mobile science labs and the foundation of 20 bridge remedial schools. The remedial schools were a hybrid of academic and vocational training centres meant to allow school dropouts back into the system. The plan was to rehabilitate 200 school dropouts back into the school system over the next 18 months – a tall order indeed for two people with no background in running educational initiatives of any kind.

"The target was huge, the time was short and I had no experience," recalls Suresh. However, he was resolute in his ambition to make it a success. Egged on by Bala and the founders, Suresh and Hamsa began to think through their mission and formulate a plan.

Until the project, Agastya's only engagement in Koppal had involved sending a mobile lab for a few weeks on village community visits. The villagers had showed particular interest in watching the chemistry experiments and the general impression was that they had welcomed Agastya. Suresh decided to capitalize on the goodwill from these earlier mobile lab community visits and sought the help of local village teachers and community leaders to build a focused grassroots programme.

"I learned to embrace local customs, which included drinking the ultra-sweet jaggery flavoured tea that villagers would insist I drink. I learned the local dialect and actively engaged the government and community members in Agastya's plans for the district. Most important was Subbu's advice to me to use the two mobile lab drivers as my local bodyguards and intelligence gatherers!"

In order to feed their small team, they struck deals with local NGOs in the area that had food services already set up. In exchange for meals, Agastya would conduct free classes for them. It was an exercise in raw, opportunistic project management, stemming from the can-do spirits of Suresh and Hamsa.

Working around the clock seven days a week and running bridge schools at night by candlelight,[7] Suresh and Hamsa established Agastya's first hub-and-spoke operation in five months.

What drove a city-based couple to work in a remote and challenging environment like Koppal to create and launch an innovative education programme for rural children? Suresh explains his desire to make a positive difference to the poverty he witnessed among the village people of Koppal.

"Seeing how people struggled to survive on the most meagre resources, the negative effects of children dropping out of school and, above all, the warmth and humanity that I experienced with the community convinced me that I had both a role and a duty to help educate the children."

The Koppal project was not only an unequivocal success but also threw up a multitude of insights for the team to dwell on. Firstly, science centres were proven to gel well within Agastya's framework. Any further expansion of the mobile lab operations would need to work in tandem with the development of a complementary science centre network.

Secondly, Suresh and Hamsa had illustrated how Agastya could use synergies with local communities to catalyse growth. Their unconventional approach at Koppal became a yardstick against which future Agastya facilitators would gauge their success. Rather than wilt at the challenge, Agastya's employees would time and again demonstrate extraordinary resourcefulness in the presence of disheartening odds. Even when resources stabilized, Agastya's staff revelled in an almost guerrilla style of implementation when ready solutions eluded them.

Hamsa's work would also go on to form the backbone of Agastya's impact assessment studies. At the end of a teaching session, she would sit with the students and teachers and patiently interview them to gauge the positives and the negatives of their experience. This would be relayed back to the instructors to fine-tune their teaching approach and improve quality. Over time, her grasp on impact measurement would become a vital factor in managing donor expectations.

The Agastya bridge schools, however, failed to replicate in the manner in which the science centres did. Although a project a few years later attempted to duplicate the bridge schools on campus, the initiative never gained the required traction. But Suresh and Hamsa's night-school system indicated potential. It would take a few more years, but it would seed one of Agastya's most innovative and far-reaching programmes of all.

Agastya's impact in North Karnataka also drew the interest of the government. With the influence of Dr. Aatre, this brought the foundation its first major private–public partnership. The scale of this partnership would take the operations to a whole new level within Karnataka.

Before that, however, the foundation would finally find a supporter whose vision to scale hands-on learning across India would match Agastya's own untrammelled audacity.

1. C.V. Raman won the Nobel prize for his work in the field of light scattering. S.N. Bose is best known for his work on quantum mechanics, in developing the foundation for Bose-Einstein statistics and the theory of the Bose-Einstein condensate. The sub-atomic particle, the Boson, was named after him.

2. Balraj Krishna, *Sardar Vallabhabhai Patel India's Iron Man*

3. These were: (1) energy (physical, chemical and biological); (2) force, motion and machines (wave and periodic); (3) atoms, molecules and transformation; (4) light (colour and images); (5) living cells; (6) the human body, health, hygiene and animal life; (7) environment and ecology; (8) evolution of materials; and (9) mathematics. Each concept was assigned a leader (either from Agastya or a volunteer) and the curriculum was developed accordingly.

4. The Padma Vibhushan is India's second highest civilian honour, not to be confused with the Padma Bhushan, which is the country's third highest civilian honour and one that Dr. Aatre had already been awarded in 2000.

5. About 9 hours from Gudupalle and 6.5 hours from Bangalore by road.

6. As Agastya grew, space became less of an issue. Most older government buildings had plenty of spare room and the prestige of having an Agastya science centre on site often meant that Agastya was in a position to choose the space that suited it best.

7. The couple initially forgot to mention this to the team. On a trip to review the operations, Mahavir immediately had solar lights installed.

CHAPTER 8

THE BIG BULL

On a sunny afternoon in late 2005, in a boardroom overlooking a bay that leads to the Arabian Sea, Ramji Raghavan stood with his hands rather empty. The plush 15th-floor office in South Mumbai's Nariman Point had a breath-taking view, but this did little to allay Ramji's concerns at the moment. Behind him, a presentation illuminated the wall with Agastya's playful hues. In front of him, with his back to the view, the man to whom Ramji was presenting appeared to be losing interest.

The walls of the tastefully decorated boardroom were peppered with paintings and a few framed quotes by famous intellectuals.

"The markets can stay irrational for far longer than the rational man can stay solvent," read one attributed to John Maynard Keynes.

Across the room, an excerpt from Shakespeare's *Julius Caesar* stated, "There is a tide in the affairs of men, which taken at the flood, leads on to fortune. Omitted, all the voyage of their life is bound in shallows and in miseries."

Ramji had probably earlier walked into the room hopeful that his meeting with the brilliant stock market mogul Rakesh Jhunjhunwala (sometimes known as RJ) was indeed a sign of such a tide finally coming in for Agastya.

The table that stood between the two men had a scattering of figurines of various sizes. Each was similar to the others in that they were all statues of bulls – a collection of gifts given to Jhunjhunwala over the years in homage to his unofficial moniker as the 'Big Bull of India.' Indeed, beyond his reputation as one of India's most successful investors, Jhunjhunwala was known to be a fiery and energetic personality whose passion for debate forced anyone approaching him for money to come fully prepared for a brutal, if honest, dialogue.

And, although Ramji truly was ready for any line of questioning, he was understandably derailed by what was transpiring before him at that moment.

Jhunjhunwala, who had been attentive and engaged thus far, looked suddenly fatigued. His shoulders slumped, and there was a heaviness in his body language. Then, his head fell forward, and for a few seconds he went very quiet as his eyes seemed to shut.

The few others in the room, who were seated along the sides of the boardroom table, looked sheepish as Ramji, who had been animatedly presenting Agastya's case, stopped in mid-sentence, unsure of whether to proceed. However, in the next instant, Jhunjhunwala looked up, offering Ramji a kind smile. He apologized, saying it had been a very hectic few days, and suggested that the presentation continue.

Picking up where he had left off, Ramji tried his best to rally his arguments and regain his momentum. In his heart, however, he was all but convinced that he would not be leaving this meeting with any of the funds he so sorely needed for Agastya.

––––––––––

The meeting with Jhunjhunwala was the culmination of a few years of dialogue and effort. Ramji had first been introduced to the maverick investor in 2003 through Pankaj Talwar, a friend of Ramji's from London who had moved to Mumbai around the same time that Ramji had made his move to India. Pankaj, a former banker at Morgan Stanley, had met Ramji through a common friend and colleague, Guru Ramakrishnan. A man with an infectiously energetic personality, Pankaj was still immersed in the world of finance and had been supporting Agastya by making introductions to high-net-worth individuals in Mumbai. During one such meeting, it was proposed that they try to approach Jhunjhunwala. It was suggested that he might be the only man with the money and the foresight to support Agastya's grand plans for India.

Ramji recalls their first meeting, which happened in Jhunjhunwala's office near the Bombay Stock Exchange: "We described Agastya's vision to Jhunjhunwala. He listened closely and asked several questions. I could sense that he was assessing me. I described my background and aims for Agastya. He was curious to know why I had left my banking career in London to come and work for children in rural India. He was intrigued by the idea of a mobile science lab. Our meeting ended with his agreeing to fund a single mobile science lab. I was elated."

During this time, despite other victories, it was becoming increasingly apparent that the gap between Agastya's ambitions and the money available to fund them appeared to be unbridgeable. As the sole banker in the founding team, Ramji had been entrusted with bringing in donors and was feeling the pressure to deliver more than ever before. It did seem that in all other aspects, Agastya was blazing a trail. But it needed a regular infusion of funds to survive, and Ramji was finding it impossible to provide what was needed.

Frustrations, disappointments, and insecurities about the future were starting to show up in the work and the attitudes of some Agastya staff. The frequency of angry emails between Ramji and Mahavir had also picked up. Both men had not taken salaries for a long time and the mounting pressures were starting to crack Agastya's leadership. Even among the most ardent well-wishers, the impression was that Agastya had stalled in its tracks. Patience was starting to wear thin, as evidenced by a comment made by P. K. Iyengar to Ramji: "People are saying that Agastya does not have money to fund its ideas. We have been around for five years and have not even a brochure to show for it." The words were harsh, but not altogether untrue.

In his attempts to raise money, Ramji had explored every nook and cranny of the philanthropic world. He had received much the same response everywhere he asked. Larger family offices were interested in funding their own foundations and initiatives; smaller donors and corporates either did not buy into Agastya's vision or were already making charitable contributions to other causes. The little that the foundation did raise was barely enough to maintain the present operations, let alone finance a national-level initiative. Further, the money given was mostly tied to specific geographies and programmes. This meant that campus development was stunted and that those areas that most desperately needed Agastya's intervention could not be serviced, as corporate donors preferred the visibility provided by operations in more urban areas.

After his first meeting with Jhunjhunwala, Ramji left optimistic that he might finally have found someone that genuinely believed in Agastya's cause and had the means to help.

Around the time that they initially met, Jhunjhunwala was already something of a cult figure in the world of finance and investing. A self-made billionaire, he had spun unimaginable riches from a humble investment of some 5,000 rupees (less than $100) given to him by his father. Although he is often compared with Warren Buffett, Jhunjhunwala's track record suggests a staggering annual growth rate of about 67% a year over 30 years: an unapproachable record that is likely never to be matched.¹ It was no wonder that both fund managers and everyday investors hung on his every word.

Ramji met Jhunjhunwala a few times more over the next few months, during the course of which the latter made a commitment to fund two more mobile labs. Although he was supportive of Agastya, he urged Ramji to fund the bulk of his programmes using government partnerships.

Encouraged by the support, Ramji decided to pitch the idea for a building on campus. Walking into Jhunjhunwala's office one afternoon expecting good news, he was instead struck down. Jhunjhunwala firmly stated that he was already donating to many other charitable causes and had no plans to entertain any more requests for money from Agastya for the moment. It was a demoralizing moment for Ramji, who had begun to assume from their earlier interactions that he had found a steadfast ally who shared his hunger for growth.

Unsure of why his benefactor was suddenly displaying a change of heart, Ramji declared matter-of-factly that he was not asking for help, he was begging. Jhunjhunwala protested, saying that he had no intention to make another man beg. Ramji withdrew momentarily but collected himself to throw one final pitch. He asked Jhunjhunwala whether he knew who the chair of General Motors was. The investor shook his head. Then Ramji stated, "But you do know who John Harvard is."

The billionaire allowed himself a small smile. He understood where this was going. Ramji went on to elucidate the point further. In education, a person's name can last years, decades or even centuries. In terms of preserving a legacy, few endeavours could match the purity and longevity offered by education.

After hearing this, Jhunjhunwala relented and asked how much Agastya needed.

A few weeks after the meeting, Agastya began work on a new building: a computer lab with a couple of adjoining classrooms. As work commenced on the new structure, Ramji, while on a trip to the US, visited the Exploratorium in San Francisco. A veritable menagerie of large-scale science in action, the Exploratorium was an inspiration to Ramji. Conceived and created by Frank Oppenheimer[2] in 1969, the self-characterized scientific funhouse delights children and adults alike with its range of interactive models and displays. In addition, an on-site workshop that produced the exhibits made it unlike any museum or exhibition that Ramji had ever seen. It thrilled him to ponder whether something similar could be replicated by Agastya. He envisioned developing large-scale models that explained the fundamentals of science to children – contraptions whose insides could be seen so that the mystery behind the science that fuelled them could easily be unravelled and understood.

A short while later, back in Bombay, Ramji happened to bump into Jhunjhunwala once more while exiting a restaurant after dinner. Jhunjhunwala asked why Ramji had not called him and Ramji replied that he did not want to seem like he was pestering the investor for more money. They agreed to meet the following day, and Ramji described his obsession to build a 'rural exploratorium.' Jhunjhunwala leaped at the idea enthusiastically, offering to fund the first phase of the building. Just like that, one of the most significant investments in interactive learning in India was greenlit.

The conception, development and execution of the rural exploratorium were significant for Agastya for many reasons. Formally named the Jhunjhunwala Discovery Centre, it was the first truly large-scale project on campus. For its location, the team selected a hillside that overlooked the Mustrahalli Lake – a spectacular view for a building of great consequence. However, it was in populating the rural exploratorium that Agastya was forced to revisit the fundamentals of model-making and rediscover elements of both construction and scale. The team pushed itself to introduce the most outrageous experiments, intended to jog the imagination, force wonder and coax curiosity from even the most resistant of minds.

Using the San Fransisco Exploratorium "cookbooks" as reference, a list of 40 experiments was curated by a team that included R. Krishnan and M. A. Ramaswamy, a retired scientist formerly at the National Aerospace Laboratories. Among these, a pedal-powered buggy with four square wheels, would stand impudently by the entrance to the building, daring anyone to ride it. The vehicle – which could in fact be ridden over a specially made track – was virtually irresistible to visitors and an unforgettable experience for all. "How can something on square wheels roll forwards and backwards?" It was a question that instantly seized anyone that laid eyes on the unusual contraption for the first time. The answer was fairly simple: as long as the wheels stayed tangential to the track, the cycle could move along it. The track's specially made 'bumps' ensured that this condition was met. Anyone presented with this knowledge would now see motion in a completely different manner. It was this ability to repeatedly tease the mind with inquiry before rewarding it with reason that made interactions with Agastya a transformative experience for both children and inquisitive adults alike.

In order to build the models, the team approached a man named M. Shivkumar. The introduction was made by N. S. Leela, a former professor at MES College and a frequent and valued contributor to Agastya's in-house training programmes. A retired engineer, Shivkumar was also an amateur artist and had written two books on the history of clocks and bicycles. His passion for building models was infectious and he was keen to use his in-depth understanding of practical design and mechanics to make exhibits that could be used to teach children. For Shivkumar, Agastya was offering him the ideal platform to showcase and popularise his models among children.

"I used to go to campus and interact with the children," says Shivkumar. "It's not just about the functioning of the model, but the history of how such models have impacted humankind. I made a presentation on how simple machines were built – wheels, pulleys etc. – then described the more complex machines. The idea is to make the children understand how the engineering evolved."

Shivkumar co-opted a friend, Prakash, who had a fabrication workshop in Bangalore. Agastya offered Prakash the contract to build the exhibits and he agreed to develop them at a subsidized cost.[3]

This exercise in creating a dynamic library of outlandish, high-impact, interactive exhibits would be a tremendous success. For years to come, the Jhunjhunwala Discovery Centre would be the highlight of any child's trip to the Agastya campus. The large-scale models covered everything from optics to sound to fluid and wave dynamics. However, the pursuit of exceptional model designs also laid the seeds for Agastya's own model-making workshop – VisionWorks. Based on the workshop Ramji had seen at the San Francisco Exploratorium, VisionWorks would take close to another decade to set up. However, in time it would become the key ideation and R&D hub for models disseminated on a national scale.

When the Agastya team visited Jhunjhunwala to update him on the progress of the project, they took with them a tabletop model of the centre. Overjoyed by what he saw, the billionaire approved the second phase immediately. It was a proud moment for Ramji, who had brought his father along for the meeting. K. V. Raghavan, who was past 80 by this time, sat quietly in the corner, observing the interactions and saying nothing.

As he walked father and son back to the elevator, Jhunjhunwala stopped. A large man, he nonetheless made the effort to bend low and touch K. V. Raghavan's feet and asked him for his blessings. "Don't worry about money," he reassured them kindly, as the elevator doors closed between them.

This was an unusual and poignant act of humility for someone of Jhunjhunwala's stature and it would stay permanently etched in Ramji's memory.

Luck, as they say, favours the prepared. As work ploughed ahead on the Jhunjhunwala Discovery Centre, Agastya welcomed Alok Oberoi (of the Oberoi Family Foundation) and his family from London, who were enjoying a day on campus. While being taken through the under-construction Jhunjhunwala Discovery Centre Oberoi received a call from Jhunjhunwala. The oddity of the coincidence did not escape the two men, and Oberoi's glowing review of the manner in which Agastya had deployed Jhunjhunwala's money could not have had a more perfectly timed backdrop. Enthused by Oberoi's endorsement, Jhunjhunwala told Ramji that he was prepared to look at his involvement with Agastya more seriously. He deputed Manish Gupta, one of his senior aides, to help Agastya formulate a ten-year plan.

A graduate of the Indian Institute of Management, Ahmedabad, Manish had worked at Honeywell and The Boston Consulting Group before joining Jhunjhunwala's RARE Enterprises. He brought with him an impressive capacity for strategic thinking along with analytical rigour that would be invaluable to Agastya in the years to come. As a future member of Agastya's board of trustees, he had a deep understanding of Agastya's mission and what it would take to effectively accomplish it.

"RJ kept saying we need to do something big," recalls Manish of their early discussions around philanthropy. "We were starting to think that rather than give to many different causes, why not give more to fewer causes?"

Manish came down to meet the team in Bangalore and then visited the Agastya campus. He helped Ramji, Mahavir and Bala to chart the numbers from the ground up. They arrived at an outlay that would see Agastya potentially reach 3 million children and 100,000 teachers over the next decade. It was an impressive goal[4] that was underlined by an even more daring number. The ask – including both capital and operational expenditure – was estimated at 90 crore rupees ($20 million at the time).

Roughly three years after their first meeting, Ramji stood in the boardroom at Nariman Point to present his ten-year plan to Jhunjhunwala. However, contrary to all his expectations, the billionaire seemed uninterested. In his mind, Ramji thought that perhaps the number was far too large – that in their zeal, they had overestimated Jhunjhunwala's appetite and had put him off his meal altogether. Manish, who was sitting only a few feet away from Ramji, acknowledged the awkwardness but could only shrug his shoulders.

After apparently nodding off momentarily, Jhunjhunwala apologized: "I have been working round the clock."

"No problem. I am not in any rush," Ramji said placatingly.

They continued the discussion and, to everyone's surprise, Jhunjhunwala's head slumped forward again. There was silence, broken only by Jhunjhunwala's gentle snoring. Each passing second seemed to assure Ramji that he had truly reached the end of the line.

Suddenly, Jhunjhunwala was awake again, his eyes refreshed and his gaze sharp as he addressed Ramji.[5]

"How big is the plan?"

"Ninety crores over ten years," Ramji reaffirmed, taken aback by the sudden alertness.

"That's nine crores a year. I am afraid there's no one in India who will support that level of funding," Jhunjhunwala countered. He explained that charity in India still had a long way to go.

Staring down at rejection, Ramji was possessed with a wild idea. He told Jhunjhunwala that he was in the process of selling his house in Bangalore. He would give the entirety of the proceeds to Jhunjhunwala to invest on his behalf.

"Guarantee the return of my principal, and every year from the profits you generate on my money I will deduct my basic living expenses and give the balance to Agastya," Ramji suggested.

Jhunjhunwala looked bemused by this rather desperate and bizarre proposal.

"Why do you insult me?" he accused, albeit kindly. "Do you think I would call you to present a plan for Agastya and then have you sell your house to fund it? Besides, Ramji, it's not that easy to make money."

Ramji reasoned that it was merely his attempt to make the best of the impasse that they seemed to have reached and that he meant no disrespect.

Jhunjhunwala now turned to Manish and asked his opinion. Manish suggested that they should give Agastya a crore of rupees for the first year and raise the sum gradually based on Agastya's performance.

"No," the investor contradicted. "If we buy into Ramji's vision, we must ensure that he succeeds."

Manish then asked Jhunjhunwala what he proposed. There was a brief silence as Jhunjhunwala filed through the hard copy of the presentation that lay before him. He stared at the number for a few seconds and looked up at Ramji, who had sat down as he waited for Jhunjhunwala to make his decision.

"I will give you 50 crores," he declared plainly. "Are you happy?"

In Ramji's recollection of this meeting, he merely replied, "Yes, thank you!"

However, Manish's description adds an element of the true emotion that Ramji must have felt in seeing his life's great work finally taking shape. In Manish's telling, Ramji leaped from his seat, walked across to Jhunjhunwala, took both his hands warmly and shook them as he said a heartfelt thanks. A man not normally given to displays of emotion, Ramji's enormous relief was underlined by this spontaneity.

After seeing Ramji off at the elevator, Manish remembers rushing back to Jhunjhunwala to ask him why he had suddenly changed his mind.

"I went running back to the room," says Manish. "The moment he committed this number, I felt I was morally obligated. Ramji had made an impression on Jhunjhunwala. Jhunjhunwala felt Ramji was a man doing God's work and that backing him was the right thing to do."

Within a few months, a ten-year memorandum of understanding was signed between R. Jhunjhunwala

Foundation and Agastya. The funding was contingent on Agastya achieving the goals agreed with the foundation. Additionally, both Jhunjhunwala and Manish joined Agastya's board.

To say the money was put to good use was an understatement. Agastya's first order of business was to shore up key activities and ensure that under-serviced areas were immediately addressed. One unique aspect of the money from the R. Jhunjhunwala Foundation, as compared with other funds that Agastya typically raised, was the capital flexibility. The funds were fungible; they were not tied to any specific programmes, geographies or areas of study. This allowed Agastya to use the money as a gap-filler, ensuring that under-attended rural pockets received the same exposure to Agastya as more urban or well-populated areas. Over time, these funds would play a sort of gyroscopic role in balancing Agastya's activities. Programmes in localities where funding had suddenly been discontinued did not need to stop functioning but could rather be buttressed with the flexible capital and allowed to remain operational.

The other key use of the infusion was in developing Agastya's home base. The next few years would see an explosion of activity on campus, as new hostels and learning labs sprang up all over the once empty land. Sharukh Mistry and his talented team of dynamic young architects would finally have the opportunity to fully exercise the enthusiasm and creativity that had thus far been held in abeyance due to the shortage of funds. Their exploits would do nothing less than turn Agastya's once-barren campus into a wonderland of architectural marvels.

Finally, Jhunjhunwala's money allowed Agastya to go out looking for the kind of people who could help take the foundation to a whole new level. Much of the talent that would join in the coming years would form the mainstay of Agastya's unmitigated growth and unrelenting pursuit of excellence.

"There are those that fund programmes and there are those that fund the mission," Ramji says of Jhunjhunwala's contributions. "RJ was funding the mission. Without that, there would have simply been no way to scale in the way that we needed to."

It is interesting to note that the foundation, forged in frugality, never allowed the windfall to change its fundamental approach to expenditure. One necessary change was that both Ramji and Mahavir were finally able to draw salaries after each going seven years without one. However, Mahavir's tight control on finances ensured that overheads continued to be kept alarmingly low. It would be another few years before the team would deign to give up its makeshift office in an old bungalow in Bangalore and move to a better, larger, and admittedly more professional-looking location.

"I was never worried about the money being used frivolously," Manish quips. He had spent years on the board bemoaning the team's refusal to spend money on a proper office. "If anything, I was pushing for them to be paid more!"

After being a force for considerable good on the Agastya board for over a decade, Manish would relinquish his seat in 2017, when he branched out to found his own investment firm, Solidarity. He remains a valuable ally of Agastya to this day.

Utpal Sheth, who had helmed Jhunjhunwala's fund admirably over many years was appointed in his place. A highly respected figure in the field of finance and investment, Utpal would bring a unique blend of pragmatism, strategic thinking, analysis, and empathy in furthering Agastya's cause.

Jhunjhunwala's backing was in and of itself a massive boost for Agastya. But apart from the money, the mere fact that Agastya had been vetted and found worthy by a man known for his thoroughness and scrutiny on all matters pertaining to his investments had positive knock-on effects for the foundation. Ramji recalls the tone of a man whom he had called on for assistance a few months prior to that seminal meeting with Jhunjhunwala.

"He was brusque and practically slammed the phone down on me," recalls Ramji, who often muses that there is no better way to keep your ego in check than to run a charity and to try and ask people for money to fund it.

A few months later, Ramji called on him again and was shocked to hear the man constantly refer to him as "Ramji Sir." This was a short while after Jhunjhunwala had publicly started speaking about his collaboration with Agastya. Towards the end of the conversation, the man – now humble to a fault – sheepishly asked whether Ramji might arrange an audience with the billionaire investor, whom he considered as one of his heroes.

"I don't think he ever gave us any money," Ramji says with a smile. "But I was beginning to notice this sort of change in tone with whomever I spoke with."

Agastya's aura had been infused with significance. Whether they were offering help or not, both corporates and high-net-worth individuals could no longer ignore the foundation or write it off as just another charity.

In 2017, as the ten-year memorandum of understanding drew to a close, the R. Jhunjhunwala Foundation would agree to renew its partnership with Agastya. The decision was made without much deliberation on

Jhunjhunwala's part. In truth, he said during the meeting that he was very happy that Agastya had exceeded all his expectations, before then nodding off in the middle of the next presentation, waking up suddenly, and apologising. Ramji remarked "No problem, because every time you nod off, you come back with a big commitment," to which Jhunjhunwala smiled jovially. He had seen enough of Agastya's work to know that his funds were exactly where they needed to be.

In the markets, Jhunjhunwala had a reputation for being able to see beyond just the numbers. There was an inkling he got when interacting with a CEO or an entrepreneur that told him whether his investments would be well protected. According to Ramji, Jhunjhunwala had a unique gift that allowed him to see an undertaking through the eyes of the entrepreneur and gauge whether the person he was backing had what it took to take the route to success. It is possible that this approach allowed him to evaluate both Ramji and Agastya and conclude that his money would be treated with the respect it deserved, achieving what Ramji had promised it would.

Vidya Shah, CEO of the EdelGive Foundation, knew Jhunjhunwala well. She got to know about Agastya from him in 2010 and became involved. She would later join Agastya's board.

"I was always very impressed with RJ's skill in philanthropy," she says. "He had a similar approach as he did with markets. He had a gift for picking undervalued gems."

When Ramji first met Rakesh Jhunjhunwala, the investor was worth an estimated $500 million. By the time of Jhunjhunwala's all-too-early death in 2022, this figure had ballooned to nearly 12 times that amount. Jhunjhunwala's interest in – and later affection for

– Agastya was born from a tendency towards curiosity to which he attributed his own incredible successes. When speaking about his upbringing on various interviews, he described himself as a deeply curious child, a trait he credited to his father for always encouraging in him.[6]

"He valued integrity, and he had a liking for self-made people," says Vishal Gupta, Jhunjhunwala's nephew, who knew him better than most. "He didn't care much for familial wealth. He was proud of what Agastya had achieved. In 2010, on his fiftieth birthday, we made a video of his life. The only two organizations we featured were Agastya and St Jude.[7] He always said, 'If you intervene in a child's life, the ROI is much better.'"

Known mainly as a stock market virtuoso with an insatiable appetite for large numbers, Jhunjhunwala would often come across as exceedingly well read over a range of topics far outside the realm of finance. This breadth of knowledge allowed him to understand and appreciate what Agastya was trying to achieve, beyond the obvious goals of reach and scale.

As an investor with a lot of media exposure, Jhunjhunwala constantly championed Agastya's cause, bringing mention of the foundation's exemplary work into nearly every interview he gave. He would sometimes joke that he was becoming more famous for his contributions to Agastya than he was for his stock market successes.

"Agastya was everything for him," says Jhunjhunwala's wife, Rekha Jhunjhunwala. "It was very dear to his heart. He had a lot of respect for Ramji. Education was his first love. If a person was genuine, he would not think twice [about giving them support]."

Jhunjhunwala made his only trip to Agastya's campus shortly after making his first ten-year commitment.

Sadly, he never got to see the remarkable transformation that his contributions enabled. He was accompanied at that time by Bhaskar Bhat, the then managing director of Titan – India's largest manufacturer of branded jewellery and a favourite among Jhunjhunwala's diverse portfolio. Bhat confesses to having been blown away by his visit to the campus. More than that, both he and Jhunjhunwala were astounded by the scale at which the founders were imagining the development of their organization.

"I think the thing in Agastya was Ramji," Bhat says of Jhunjhunwala's decision to fund the foundation. "I think Jhunjhunwala was a great judge of good managers as well as good people. If the manager happened to be a good person, then he would strike up a relationship with them. With Ramji it was a combination of both. He would always talk about what great work Ramji was doing."

Amit Chandra, the chairperson of Bain Capital India, whose own efforts in charitable giving are themselves altering the very fabric of Indian philanthropy, was another close friend of Jhunjhunwala.

"I think inspirational people, like Ramji, would get a person like Rakesh – who essentially bet on people to create great outcomes – excited," Chandra reflects. "Rakesh was always a big believer in the power of curiosity. He himself was an incredibly curious person. I think he believed that what Agastya did was fairly unique and this whole concept of igniting curiosity in hundreds of thousands of children was an amazing opportunity. He also liked that it wasn't just conceptual, but that there was a well-defined framework to it with an emphasis on making sure that there was impact being measured. I think all of that appealed to Rakesh."

Ramji's reflection on Jhunjhunwala is particularly poignant. "He had this ability to see around the corners," he remarks, "During his visit to the campus, he had seen a boy, unkempt with snot running down his nose, but with a certain self-assuredness about him. RJ immediately remarked that he saw curiosity dancing in the child's eyes. This ability to meld mind and heart to assess impact and value was what set him apart. To top it all, there was honour in his word. He would sometimes appear to make a casual commitment; but a lot of thought would have gone into it. Once made, his commitments were gold; he always honoured them."

At board meetings – always held at his 15th-floor office in Nariman Point – Rakesh Jhunjhunwala was generally more concerned with how Agastya was evolving its methods than with how his money was being spent. He had a deep and profound trust in Ramji and the Agastya team and would never question the allocation of funds beyond an academic interest in costs and their impact.

His legendary temper was unusually subdued when dealing with Agastya and on the rare occasion that he did erupt in anger, it was on behalf of, rather than towards, Agastya. It peeved him when others didn't bestow on Agastya the same trust, benevolence, and generosity that he felt the foundation clearly deserved.

This trust was born both from his remarkable ability to evaluate a person's character and from the very visible impact Agastya was making with the use of his funds. In Jhunjhunwala's mind, Ramji was a vital conduit through which the investor's immense wealth could be put to the best possible philanthropic use. His interactions with Ramji over the years only reaffirmed that Ramji had both the integrity and the ability to deliver on their collective ambition for Agastya.

When Jhunjhunwala and Ramji appeared on stage together at an event at the Bombay Stock Exchange hosted by Vidya Shah's EdelGive Foundation, Ramji had praised the billionaire, saying his commitment to Agastya was "unprecedented." Jhunjhunwala had responded: "Agastya's achievement is unprecedented."

The last time the two men met was in July 2022, at the Breach Candy Hospital in Bombay. Jhunjhunwala's health had been steadily deteriorating for a few years, and Ramji had called on him at the hospital to pay his respects. Despite Jhunjhunwala's physical frailty at the time, his mental capacity remained undiminished. He was confident that he would emerge stronger than ever. He spoke optimistically about both India's and Agastya's future and urged Ramji to keep fighting the good fight.

His death, a few weeks after that meeting, sent shockwaves across the country. Jhunjhunwala's rise was a thing of inspiration for everyday Indian people. For any humble investor, he was a glowing example of the endless possibilities in wealth creation that India had to offer. Apart from his colossal fortune, the crown of his legacy sparkled with Agastya as one of its most prominent gems.

With Jhunjhunwala's passing, the reins of his estate passed to his wife, Rekha. A strong, committed and compassionate individual, Rekha Jhunjhunwala has shouldered the responsibility admirably. With Vishal Gupta – Jhunjhunwala's nephew – for support, she has worked tirelessly to ensure that her husband's legacy endures. In July 2023, this commitment was evident as the first payment after Jhunjhunwala's death was received by Agastya from the R. Jhunjhunwala Foundation.

Over the years, Rakesh Jhunjhunwala would often say that his two greatest investments were Titan –

the company that made him his early millions and in which his holdings eventually exceeded $1 billion – and Agastya. When asked what it was that he saw in the foundation, he often proclaimed, "I love the crusade, I love the crusader."[8]

1.   Sources cite this number as anywhere from 54% to 63% – mind-boggling figures themselves. However, Vishal Gupta – Jhunjhunwala's nephew and a financier in his own right – did a more in-depth analysis of the late billionaire's assets and confirms the figure to be just north of 67%. Shared in conversation with the author.

2.   Brother of Robert Oppenheimer, who led the Manhattan Project, which made the first atomic bomb.

3.   It would not always be easy. The very specific nature of Agastya's demands would often mean that it might take months to find a fabricator willing to take the job up, especially as it would be a one-off and have an unusual design that Agastya would rarely compromise on.

4.   Agastya's actual achievement over this period would be double the target, reaching 6.2 million children.

5.   Jhunjhunwala's ability to take these intense power naps was legendary. They were particularly effective in letting the presenter sink into a sense of complacency only to be suddenly put on the spot by Jhunjhunwala. From a seemingly blissful reverie, the billionaire would instantly reanimate, more alert than before, and ask a question whose pertinence belied the idea that its source had been asleep just a moment ago.

6.   A bust of Jhunjhunwala's father currently stands at the Jhunjhunwala Discovery Centre. Sadly, Jhunjhunwala passed away before it could be formally unveiled and inaugurated. A similar bust of Jhunjhunwala himself now stands proudly at the entrance to the Discovery Centre.

7.   A not-for-profit organization that provides free-of-charge shelter and holistic care to children who are undergoing cancer treatment.

8.   In 2023, Agastya recommended Jhunjhunwala for one of India's national awards. Jhunjhunwala was posthumously awarded the Padma Shri – India's fourth highest civilian honour.

CHAPTER 9

A PHYSICAL AND PHILOSOPHICAL EXPANSION

For any entity to survive and possibly thrive, the importance of ready, liquid cash cannot be overstated. Studies done across businesses will often highlight that enterprises usually shut down not because of a faulty model but because they simply cannot maintain the influx of capital needed to simultaneously finance their operations, manage their credit terms and fuel their growth. Even a company with high profitability and excellent net credit can struggle to stay afloat if the growth it is aiming for forces it into a negative cash flow spiral.

Agastya's status as a charitable venture meant that there was no revenue model – no profits to plough back or line of credit to run behind when payments fell due. Growth could only be driven by the infusion of regular, externally raised cash donations. Up until 2006, the erratic nature of the inflows forced the operations to run in an almost ad hoc, hand-to-mouth manner. If funding for a programme was pulled, the programme needed to be suspended. If the financing for a new building on campus was suddenly held off, the project was stalled indefinitely or until some new benefactor could be located. The founders themselves took no salaries. Any available funds were used purely for keeping the lights on, the engine running and the conviction alive that reaching one more child was worth the sacrifices being made.

Such constraints forced an extreme element of caution in Agastya's overall approach. This was especially frustrating considering the plans for growth were so markedly daring in contrast. With the advent of the R. Jhunjhunwala Foundation's involvement, things finally began to change. Brave decisions could now be taken without worrying about where the money would come from. Long-term commitments could be made even when funding into a particular programme or region had hitherto been unpredictable. Nowhere was this shift in attitude more apparent than in Agastya's expansion in North Karnataka.

By any standards, Agastya's pilot project in Koppal was an unmitigated triumph. Until the project was launched, Agastya had operated mostly around the campus. Programmes were closely monitored and even the founders could physically look in on things frequently to ensure that quality was being maintained.

However, the efforts of Suresh and Hamsa had illustrated two things: firstly, that a satellite operation – some nine hours away from the campus – could be just as effective, and secondly, that the stellar teaching talent, brought into Agastya by so many eminent academics, could be made to permeate down to the instructor level so that the 'wow factor' was not limited to a few individuals at the top.

All this brought about a change in perspective even for the core team. They now began to understand that the long-term purpose of the campus was to be a centre for ideation and experimentation, and to serve as a point of confluence where thought leaders could connect and synergize their efforts. Meanwhile, it would fall to the science centres and their mobile labs to penetrate rural India and take the various pedagogies developed on campus to the minds of young children and their teachers.

In 2006, the Karnataka government took notice of Agastya's work in Koppal. It had already pushed Agastya to engage with government schools close to Gudupalle. However, after seeing what impact Agastya was having at the other end of the state, their confidence was further boosted. This marked the beginning of the Sarva Shiksha Abhiyan (SSA) of Karnataka – Agastya's first private–public partnership.[1] It was, incidentally, the sort of model that Rakesh Jhunjhunwala had always recommended that Ramji use to expand Agastya's operations.

The SSA agreement called for the launch of 17 mobile science labs and 12 science centres in North Karnataka. The government would pay the operating costs of the programme over three years. Agastya would provide the capital to acquire vans, models and equipment. It was a significant outlay for Agastya and until just recently it would have been a bite too large to chew. However, with the new funding coming in, such bold and path-breaking opportunities could be grabbed with a lot more certainty.

It was also during this time, as Agastya was making its first attempts to scale its precariously developed ideals around teaching, that it appeared on the radar of the Deshpande Foundation.

The Deshpande Foundation – headed by Boston-based billionaire philanthropists Gururaj 'Desh' Deshpande and his wife, Jaishree Deshpande – was similarly involved in charitable activities in North Karnataka. The couple, originally from Hubli, the largest city in North Karnataka, were keen to focus their philanthropic endeavours around that region. It was a matter of some providence for Agastya that the nature of its goals for education and the geographies it was targeting saw a lot of overlap with what the Deshpande Foundation was looking for. After hearing of the Deshpande Foundation's enthusiasm for supporting Agastya, Ramji met with Desh and Jaishree. Busy schedules all around meant that they had only 20 minutes to discuss things. However, it was enough time for Desh and Jaishree to buy into Ramji's vision. Ramji recalls that, as they parted, he asked Desh, an alumnus of the Indian Institute of Technology in Chennai, whether he spoke Tamil, which was Ramji's mother tongue. Desh replied, tongue-in-cheek, "Yes, but only *rikshaw-wala* Tamil."[2]

For its part, the Deshpande Foundation was casting a far wider net in the area. Altogether, grants had been made to some 183 organizations, although Desh admits that only two of these took the opportunity to scale and become truly unique. One of these was Akshaya Patra, the iconic non-profit that has successfully managed to implement a gargantuan midday meal scheme for children across India. The other, of course, was Agastya.

Nish Acharya, a senior fellow of the Clinton Foundation who was CEO of the Deshpande Foundation at the time, recalls the decision to back Agastya.

"Desh said, 'Let's find organizations that can scale and that have leadership that want to scale,'" he recounts. "In Ramji we found a leader who could speak in conference rooms and speak in the villages. That is a rare quality."

Nish's excellent book *The India–US Partnership* is emphatic in its praise for Agastya, stating:

> Early on, [Agastya] developed a culture of experimentation and an internal innovation cycle. It is one of the first NGOs to truly utilize the traditional corporate innovation cycle to improve its programmes. Indian NGOs like the Agastya International Foundation ... are bringing the best corporate practices in management and innovation to the non-profit sector. ...
>
> The American non-profit sector can learn from and emulate Agastya's series of innovations and programme adjustments. Very few NGOs in the US innovate in a sustainable manner, and hardly any utilize innovation as a means to achieve scale as Agastya has done.[3]

It is a sentiment echoed by Desh Deshpande himself. Known for his passion for innovation, Desh is a life member of the MIT Corporation. His contributions and support led to MIT creating the Deshpande Centre for Technological Innovation.

"There are 3.5 million NGOs in India and the US combined and 99.9% are useless," he declares with finality. "They have no scale, no balance sheet. You're lucky if you can find 25 that are any good. Most have noble ambitions, but what they lack is execution." He adds that Agastya is among the mere handful of NGOs he considers worthwhile in the present environment.

Desh's views on the charitable space have been honed by years of experience. Having conquered the corporate domain, his mind is now focused on all aspects of sustainable, scalable social change. His foundation supports causes in the US, Canada and India. He draws interesting parallels between the profit and non-profit space and illustrates where the latter tends to fall short: "The for-profit space has execution excellence, and the non-profit has compassion. The reason why NGOs fail is that there is no feedback mechanism in the non-profit space. The people giving money are not the end customer, unlike in the for-profit space."

Deshpande believes that NGOs that adopt the best practices from the for-profit space are the only ones that equip themselves for long-term success. Back in 2006, he saw Agastya's attempts to weave a corporate ethos into its otherwise compassionate and altruistic cause as something worth investing in.

He is known to have often stated that "impact equals relevance plus innovation."[4] It is a phrase far more nuanced than it seems. Especially in the digital age, where there is an app for nearly every societal malady,

Desh feels that innovation is being over-engineered without a basic appreciation of the underlying problem that needs to be solved. He is a firm believer that unless you spend time understanding the relevance of the problem, any attempts to innovate a solution will eventually fall short. In this sense, he respected Agastya's approach, which consisted of working its way up from the grassroot level to gauge what problems plagued education, before trying to develop macro-level answers around how they could be alleviated.

When all was said and done, Agastya was now finally in a position where it had the ammunition it needed to march forward. It had two billionaires and a state government rooting for it, and money – for the time being at least – did not pose any limitations.

All that remained was to prove that what had started around the fringes of Gudupalle could be amplified across a region the size of a small country with no loss of impact. It was time, yet again, for the Agastya team to show its mettle.

Given his success in Koppal, Suresh was the obvious choice to head the North Karnataka expansion. His learnings from the pilot project, while not insignificant, would need to be built upon further in order for him to taste success once more. Along with Hamsa and Dilip Kumar, and with the blessings of his seniors, Suresh embarked once more on delivering for Agastya.

The challenges the team faced were many, but for each they devised an actionable, on-the-ground solution.

The recruitment of teachers was anything but straightforward. For one, Agastya's name did not yet carry the weight needed to entice new recruits. The ones who did join needed to conform to a whole new teaching style where, rather than traditional chalk-and-talk formats, they were interacting with different children each day and needed their approach to be immediately captivating to a child. For teachers who saw Agastya as merely a stopgap while they were waiting for a position to open up in a government school, adapting to a completely new teaching method didn't seem worth the effort.

The region also did not produce enough science graduates, so arts graduates were hired and trained in science. This proved to be an unexpected asset, since arts graduates seemed to be more effective in communicating with children. When even arts graduates were running low, Suresh and Dilip broadened their criteria to "anyone who was hungry, committed and willing to learn" (an oft repeated mantra at Agastya with regards to recruitment). This included hiring dropouts, leading Ramji to coin his BEE acronym (bachelor of energy and enthusiasm, as described in *Chapter 6*). The initiative to train dropouts became known as Operation Vijay, after the mobile lab driver who showed considerable aptitude as an instructor.

Overall, the establishment of a motivated front-line teaching staff required a fine balance. Filling the rosters could not be done at the expense of low-quality instructors. By instituting one-to-one mentoring, the team guaranteed that each member took on post-training responsibility for one new member.

Suresh also insisted on 'organizational flexibility.' Bucking the trend that teachers were only meant to teach, they trained all staff on administration, finance, and vehicle and premises maintenance. This not only allowed them to ensure operations remained smooth even if someone suddenly left but also helped the teachers to better understand how their role affected the larger mission.

Ramji often cites a story told about President John F. Kennedy during a visit to a NASA space centre in 1962. Seeing a janitor carrying a broom, JFK walked over to him, saying, "Hi, I'm Jack Kennedy. What are you doing?" The janitor responded, "Well, Mr President, I'm helping put a man on the moon."

It was this attitude that the Agastya team were looking to inculcate when it made the broader duties and the mission itself accessible to everyone involved. In this manner, teachers gained an appreciation of how vital the project's success was and took on whatever responsibilities were needed to allow for the smooth functioning of activities.

Like in Koppal, a lot of time needed to be spent in gaining vital community support. Agastya's was a radically different approach to education, meaning that school authorities and local government officials would need to be sold on the aims and objectives of the programme and see its value and benefits for children.

Finally, costs continued to be a constant battle. Despite the arrival of funding, Agastya was determined not to allow inefficiencies and complacency to set into the manner in which money was treated. Ultimately, the internally advertised tagline was that the more money that was saved, the more easily Agastya could make its way to the next school or region. This belief was reinforced by management and acted as a compass in guiding staff to be habitually careful with expenses.

Even for Agastya's founders, the North Karnataka project offered valuable insights. The idea that they could remotely review and evaluate projects was quickly quelled. It was immediately apparent that personal visits carried tremendous value. For one, the staff were motivated by management's efforts to travel so far to see their progress. Equally important, the visits provided a plethora of new or updated pedagogical learnings to the founders, meaning that decisions taken in Bangalore and on campus were done with a real-world perspective. This culture of always having a finger on the pulse of grassroot activities allowed Agastya to remain relevant even as it scaled further.

By 2007–8, the North Karnataka programme looked well on its way to stabilizing. Sensing that he needed to branch out once more, Bala Warrier left Agastya to join the Manipal Foundation as its CEO.

"I learned so much from Ramji and Mahavir about how to build from the ground up," Bala reminisces, before adding, "I owe it to them."

Fully aware of the massive void he would be leaving in his wake, Bala introduced the founders to Ajith Basu. A former architect and the founder of his own design firm, Ajith joined Agastya as chief of new programmes. He was keenly interested in the philosophy of education, and this attracted him to Agastya. An ideas man to the core, Ajith had worked with children through his design firm, which had reached about 60,000 children. However, the sheer ambition and pace of Agastya enticed him.

"I was intrigued by the scale," he confesses. "Very few NGOs talk about scale at this level. We have 300 million children in India and Agastya intended to reach everywhere!"

Ajith was quick to imbibe the Agastya way and soon became a vital member of the team.

"Education is in action at Agastya," he says. "Right in front of your eyes you can see the philosophy as it evolves. Even the senior team were exceptional learners, and the management was promoting this culture of learning. The culture is now in our DNA. We are like a bamboo plant. We grow fast and we multiply fast, and we are useful in so many ways."

By 2009, operations had scaled to the point where the foundation truly needed a formal COO to take charge and bring more order into the system. When the founders were concerned about how they might afford such a high-level resource, Desh Deshpande stepped in and offered to fund the first three years of the COO's salary. He requested Sushil Vachani to help Agastya shortlist a suitable candidate.

Sushil was a professor at Boston University and a board member of the Deshpande Foundation and would later serve as the director of the Indian Institute of Management, Bangalore. He had visited the Agastya campus in 2008 and been blown away by what he had witnessed. He also observed that the style of management at Agastya was very collegiate and collaborative. There was a lot of back-and-forth between senior management, and this allowed for quick, decisive action when big decisions need to be made.

"What also impressed me about Agastya was that they were able to get these enthusiastic reactions and the involvement of the kids," he says. "You rarely find educational systems where you get positive feedback from children. They had found these creative ways to use models to explain the scientific process."

Like Desh, Sushil felt that Agastya was at risk of imploding unless it brought in someone to steady the ship. A former consultant with Boston Consulting Group, he had a mastery of business and operational strategy. He understood how precariously placed Agastya was, considering the numbers now at stake.

"I get very restless about scale," he confesses. "One of the thoughts we had was around what was keeping Agastya from scaling. The feeling was that Ramji was too involved in operations. We urged him to hire a CEO or COO. I had thought that it would not happen because most founders are very attached to running things themselves. But Ramji said he'd be open to it. This surprised us and this is how we started looking out for someone to fill the role."

The man they recommended would go on to become the beating heart of Agastya.

In 2008, K. Thiagarajan – or Thiagu as he is always called – was serving as the head of the infrastructure firm Maytas in Hyderabad. In a somewhat oblique stroke of good fortune for Thiagu, back problems forced him to resign and move back to Bangalore. In 2009, Maytas' parent company – Satyam – rocked the Indian markets with a scandal that, at the time, was considered the largest in Indian corporate history. The scandal took Maytas down along with it.

A former classmate of Sushil Vachani at the Indian Institute of Management, Ahmedabad,[5] Thiagu was still reeling from the fallout at Satyam when Sushil approached him regarding Agastya. Although not directly impacted, he worried at the time that his association with Maytas might tarnish his otherwise spotless reputation.

"Satyam had just imploded and Thiagu had bailed out just before," Sushil recalls. "He felt hit by the scandal, but we trusted his integrity."

Thiagu's impressive background, global experience and seal of approval from Desh Deshpande and Sushil Vachani convinced Ramji that he might be well suited to the role of COO.

"I was impressed with Thiagu not only because of his record as a professional manager but because of what he said when I asked him what he was most proud of in his life," says Ramji of their first meeting.

Thiagu's answer: "My son, Arvind."[6]

His answer surprised and impressed Ramji for its frankness. Equally important, Thiagu was seeking a larger purpose in life. He believed that working with Agastya might provide him with that purpose.

Thiagu adapted quickly to the world of Agastya. An articulate former CEO who had managed a group of over 9,000 professionals, he brought to Agastya a capacity for strategic and innovative thinking. He was supportive of the founder's desire to scale new ideas. He communicated Agastya's vision effectively, both in public and to important donors and partners. Above all, he urged Agastya to be entrepreneurial and aim for the moon.

His views on organizational design echo the very manner in which Agastya had built itself up from the beginning.

"The most important thing in terms of the sustainability of an organization," he maintains, "is to keep the vision fixed even as we are pulled in different directions. Getting the right people is second. Money is only the third. If you have one and two, three will follow. I believe we have proved this time and time again."

True to his mandate, Thiagu, along with Ajith, began to infuse professionalism into Agastya's activities. Standard operating procedures, management information systems, formal training manuals and a host of other corporate processes were implemented over the next few years. A firm believer that Agastya could bring about a force multiplier effect through government schoolteachers, he encouraged the creation of a teacher training network that became the backbone of the teacher training programme on campus. Selva Sekhar, who Ramji describes as the "champion of the teacher training programme on campus," would ably spearhead these initiatives, his efforts eventually culminating in a Mobile Teaching Lab – another unique delivery mechanism that Agastya will no doubt use to great effect in the years to come.

"We run like a well-planned corporate," says Thiagu with a characteristic smile that underlines the joy he finds in working with Agastya. "We follow the three 'C's – curiosity, creativity and confidence – but we have added a fourth 'C' to it: caring." It is a matter of some significance that Thiagu declares that his years with Agastya are possibly the best of his career. In a heartfelt speech given at an Agastya event in 2023, Thiagu would outline the gratitude he felt for the opportunity that was Agastya. It was a humble tribute by someone whose legacy will be permanently entwined with that of Agastya.

Having put Agastya on the map in North Karnataka, Suresh and Hamsa prepared to return to Bangalore.

Nitin Desai, who joined Agastya from Rishi Prabhakar's ashram in early 2009, took over from Suresh as the Karnataka region head later that year. Exposed to a humanistic view of life at the ashram and to Hindu philosophy, Nitin possessed an enquiring, spiritual bent of mind.[7]

"I joined the ashram intending to be there until the end of my life," Nitin says of his journey before Agastya, "but my teacher at the ashram came and said, 'I want to train more Nitins. You need to go out and spread what you have learned.' I started meeting a lot of people in education.

Home schoolers, open schoolers. My wife and I thought of starting our own *gurukul*[8] in our village, but we realized that we would be reaching barely 50 children. We needed a movement that would reach a lot more children and that's how we heard about Agastya."

In time, Nitin would don many hats within the foundation, but in 2009, his first leadership role would be an extremely challenging one.

The team that Nitin inherited was fiercely loyal to Suresh. This, compounded by the fact that Nitin lacked experience in teaching, meant that acceptance was proving difficult. The staff resisted his leadership and even went as far as writing a six-page letter to senior management questioning Nitin's ability to effectively head them. Things escalated to the extent that some members refused to enter the science centre.

A gentle man, blessed with immense resolve and passion, Nitin had considered resigning. When he brought the possibility up with Ramji, he was instead advised "to be adjusting, resilient and persistent like water." The advice seemed to motivate Nitin to strive harder to win his team's respect. He began to spend time with individual team members, getting to know them and demonstrating a willingness to bend and adapt to their styles. It took many months, but – as is usually the case when pride and ego are supplanted with humility and perseverance – he eventually won them over. It is almost shocking to know that Nitin, who now commands such tremendous respect within Agastya, began his journey so very much on the back foot.

Nitin's responsibilities in North Karnataka included establishing a strong personal relationship with the Deshpande Foundation and with local government officials, both of whom had also held Suresh in high regard.

For their part, the Agastya seniors provided Nitin with all the support and guidance that they could muster from Bangalore. However, consistent with Agastya's 'sink-or-swim' philosophy, it was Nitin's organization to fashion and win over. Nitin showed patience, dexterity and maturity in dealing with the challenge of getting the organization that he had inherited from Suresh to back him. He emerged as a leader open to innovation and ready to expand Agastya's work further in North Karnataka.

Ramji recalls Desh Deshpande remarking to him at a science fair in Hubli that Agastya "had found a leader in Nitin." Nor was Nitin's success purely subjective. The five years that he headed the region in North Karnataka saw the operations spread over a total of 13 districts. Of these, Dharwad – where the Deshpande Foundation was funding the programmes – had complete coverage by Agastya across all the addressable population of schools in the area. In effect, the region became a testing ground both for Agastya's methods and to experiment and implement new concepts – something that Nitin would exploit to great effect in the coming years.

"I think what Ramji, Thiagu and Mahavir are showing us is how to be a true trustee of this philosophy and this movement," Nitin professes. "There is a strong sense of family and although there are disagreements, we are all ultimately pulling in the same direction. There is a beautiful balance of mind and heart. I feel we have a strong footing in the education space. What Agastya spoke of 20 years ago, today everybody is talking about."

———————

While North Karnataka was coming to terms with new leadership, the ground back at the Agastya campus had started to seem shakier.

When Agastya built its first hands-on centres on campus, it was faced with the need to find a suitable candidate to lead this new 'school of schools.' B. Subramanyam – or Subbu – had done an admirable job of shepherding the campus during its earliest, most formative phase. However, his departure had laid bare the not inconsiderable challenge of finding someone equally suited to the task. Not only could Agastya ill afford to pay the campus head a high salary, but also, the campus's location was hardly a draw for qualified educators. However august the campus might one day become, its initial avatar was merely that of a collection of small labs in a very remote, rural setting. What Agastya needed was a pioneering and adventurous spirit – someone keen to take on the challenge of building a new kind of institution.

Subbu was initially followed by a teacher and then a former headmistress of a school in North India. For a few years, there were genuine worries, as without a strong manager, the campus appeared to be floundering. Teamwork deteriorated, projects were being delayed, and tensions flared in the face of a void in able leadership. However, the campus finally found some stability in 2009 when Dr. Shibu Sankaran, a former veterinarian, took over as campus head.

Shibu had been working with the Raymond Group before joining Agastya. His intention was to move closer to Kerala, where his family had continued to stay. Although not an educator by background, he possessed a flexible attitude and the willingness to manage both the educational activities and the administration of the campus.

"I visited the campus with Ramji in 2009 and there were very few buildings," Shibu recalls. "The main centre, the dining hall and the biology lab. A few other partially built buildings. I saw a lot of opportunity to do things – it was an unknown area."

Shibu proved to be a committed and competent leader. He oversaw the building and commissioning of several new projects. He made visitors feel welcome and introduced hospitality into the campus aura. Visitors who stayed at the campus remarked on the friendliness, commitment and passion for service that Agastya's staff displayed.

Shibu successfully navigated the campus through a time of great uncertainty. It is without question that the various projects on campus that were executed and completed under his watch would have had a rough time of it without his steadfast guidance and supervision. With the expansion of the labs on campus, Agastya began encouraging children from surrounding government schools to visit. As activity grew, the campus began drawing visitors from beyond its local sphere and indeed beyond India.

"We had 200 to 300 people coming into campus for these programmes and I had to manage that," Shibu says. "Whenever Ramji used to come down to campus, he would ask me, 'What is new?' He was always looking for progress and wanted me to engage out of the box. I would rattle off things and he would remember them the next time we met, so I knew he was really paying attention."

Eventually, however, Shibu's separation from his family reached the point where it was taking a toll, so in 2015, after six years managing the campus, he returned to Kerala. His legacy was a campus so full of life and learning that Agastya was now spoilt for choice when looking for his replacement.

The benefits of scale for Agastya went beyond the numbers. True, having a larger reach made it immeasurably easier to gain an audience with new, prospective donors. However, the feedback from the field – a product of the impact assessment project that Hamsa launched in Koppal and then augmented in North Karnataka – was also allowing Agastya to rapidly fine-tune and even alter its approach based on actionable, real-world inputs from the end customers: the students and teachers.

The result was that Agastya began delving even deeper into the fundamentals of education. It used its findings to formulate more holistic perspectives on how its own efforts were influencing and even transforming the children it reached.

Along with the concept of rote learning, Indian education had somehow also developed an affinity for STEM subjects. It is a common jibe in India that all parents expect their sons to become engineers and their daughters to become doctors. This is reinforced by schools, which generally place more emphasis on math and science than on the arts.

In his book *Seven Kinds of Smart*, Thomas Armstrong points to as many different kinds of intelligence: logical, linguistic, kinaesthetic, spatial, musical, interpersonal and intrapersonal.[9] In effect, syllabuses focusing on STEM subjects mainly give importance to logic, with some credence being afforded to linguistics by way of language education. By ignoring the others, schools potentially discourage students whose strengths do not necessarily lie within the STEM bracket.

For students growing up in Indian schools, it is usually the children who excel in math and science who are considered 'brainy.' A child with exceptional spatial intelligence might, however, excel at art and design. Similarly, a child with kinaesthetic skills would stand out in sports or dance. These, however, are usually seen as a bonus, rather than as fundamental intelligence indicators. To complicate matters further, success in STEM subjects is easily measured by marks, while progress in more creative or subjective fields is harder to quantify.

While Agastya had started with a focus on STEM education – the foundation's teaching curriculum was largely aligned with the NCERT[10] – the importance of the arts and the appreciation of soft skills was forcing it to take another look at the broader purpose of its mission. With creativity as its guiding principle, Agastya was able to step back from seeing itself as purely science-centric and employ a wider evaluative lens to assess the children it reached. Taking into account that curiosity and creativity are hardly restricted to the STEM domain, Agastya began looking at how non-STEM subjects might be approached and better included in its curriculum.

It was also becoming evident that Agastya's intervention into India's system of education was more than purely academic. A strong trait of Ramji – abetted no doubt by a certainty that his cause was just – was his ability to call on anyone he felt might help him better understand education. He called these 'curiosity conversations' and never shied from boldly approaching anyone he felt he might be able to learn from.

Agastya's connection to Hayagreeva 'Huggy' Rao was made through one such throw of a stone. A professor of organizational behaviour and human resources at the Stanford Graduate School of Business, Huggy Rao is an outspoken and passionate advocate of design-based thinking. He has a genuinely warm and caring personality, is loath to mince words, and refers to Ramji as a "tempered revolutionary."

"I met him by chance," Huggy reminisces about their first interaction. "I had no idea what Agastya was, and I get an email out of the blue from Ramji saying he wants to come and meet me. He was like an activist. He wasn't a manager; he was driven by a cause, and he wanted to get s**t done. He spoke about his uncle [P. K. Iyengar] and he said, 'We're teaching science,' and I said, 'Are you sure? From what I can see you're teaching people love.'"

Huggy's observation was pertinent. In sparking curiosity, Agastya was certainly helping children and teachers better understand their subjects. However, it was also infusing confidence and changing the very way the students and teachers approached all problems – not just the ones they were expected to solve at school. More importantly, Agastya was altering the way it saw itself and allowing for ambition to kindle where earlier there may have been none.

Huggy's involvement would result in his team conducting a formal study at the Agastya campus sometime after his initial meeting with Ramji. The study measured the impact of design thinking on confidence and creativity.

"Great educators create the conditions for people to choose the more curious and confident versions of themselves," Huggy articulates. "I think this was what Ramji did for himself and his team. He chose to be a curious and generous version of himself. I think Thiagu and Mahavir did this as well."

The notion that learning, when experienced properly, leads to positive knock-on effects in personality is echoed by Ron Berger, the chief education officer at EL Education in the US. Like Agastya, EL Education works with public schools to encourage the concepts of action-based and project-based learning.

When you speak with Ron, you are instantly confronted by a profound humanity. Within his first few sentences, you get the impression that you are, at that moment, the most important person he wishes to interact with. It is a trait that no doubt helped him immensely in his 28 years as a public school teacher.

Ron's teaching style – which encourages children to "be kind, be specific and be helpful" – was honed further to help EL Education develop a curriculum that has shown impressive results across the 400-plus schools that have adopted its methods.[11] In addition, he has collaborated with the Harvard Graduate School of Education, where he has used his learnings to teach the course Models of Excellence.

Ron's views on the power of collaborative peer-to-peer learning are best showcased in an online video titled 'Austin's Butterfly.'[12] Here, he takes a group of young students through the various iterations that Austin – a six-year-old – created when asked to copy a picture of a butterfly. Encouraged by peers who constructively critiqued his work, Austin eventually created an illustration that defies belief that a first-grader could have produced it.

Ron's philosophy extends beyond the mere absorption of learning and into what that means for the child and the society they live in.

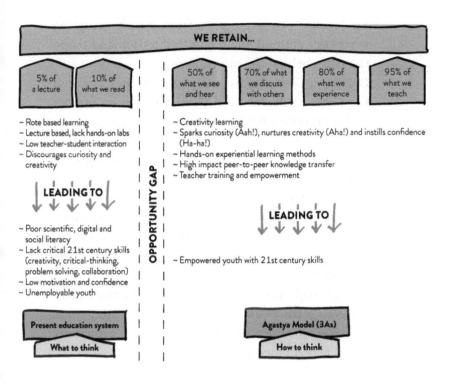

"We need to join character with learning if we want education to make a meaningful difference," he states. "What if the idea was not to get ahead, but to get everyone ahead?"

As Agastya came to better understand the children it was reaching, it further accepted that education was indeed a stepping stone to it having a much deeper impact. In fact, if this was done properly, Agastya could ensure that the children it reached would themselves go on to be torch-bearers to take the mission further.

Five behavioural shifts were eventually distilled that would define how Agastya looked at its impact going forward.

- *Yes to why* – children move from merely accepting what they are told and begin to question and probe the truth behind the information
- *Looking to observing* – children do not merely watch the experiment but push themselves to go further and appreciate what is really happening and how
- *Passive to exploring* – rather than simply be receptacles for information, children begin playing with the ideas and merging different concepts to gain a deeper understanding
- *Textbook to hands-on* – moving away from the pages, children start replicating experiments and confirming for themselves that what is written can indeed be brought to life
- *Fear to confidence* – in the final piece of the puzzle, children move from being afraid to becoming more assertive and surer of themselves, allowing curiosity to guide them forward

With hands-on learning as the vehicle, it would be these shifts that Agastya would ultimately back itself to deliver as it prepared to use its message and its model to influence a generation of children across the country.

1. The SSA is the Government of India's flagship programme for boosting the quality of primary schooling. It looks at opening new schools, improving infrastructure, and providing adequate support to teachers and students by way of materials, grants, and training programmes.

2. When Rakesh Jhunjhunwala announced his intention to back Agastya, Desh sent him a note congratulating him for his foresight in spotting the value of Agastya before others did.

3. Nish Acharya, *The India–US Partnership* (Oxford: Oxford University Press, 2016), p.105-107.

4. See, for example, David L. Chandler, "Bringing Innovation to the World" (MIT News), last modified 18 October 2010, https://news.mit.edu/2010/deshpande-1018.

5. Thiagu, Sushil and Desh were also contemporaries at the Indian Institute of Technology, although Desh and Thiagu were at the Madras (now Chennai) campus while Sushil was at Kanpur.

6. Arvind Thiagarajan – Thiagu's son – was a Gold Medallist in the Indian Institute of Technology (IIT) Joint Entrance Exam in 2001 and was awarded the President's Gold Medal for standing first in the entire BTech engineering class at IIT. He also has a PhD in Computer Science from MIT. Thiagu, however, rightly maintains that his pride extends well beyond his son's stellar academic and professional achievements.

7. A pleasant by-product of Nitin's association with the ashram was that he was able to lure away one of its cooks – Sharmaji – to come and manage the kitchen at the Agastya campus. It is worth noting that after a hard day on campus, the pure, unimaginably tasty food that Sharmaji's kitchen puts on offer is a reward beyond compare.

8. A type of education system followed in ancient India where the students and teachers live in close proximity and academics and daily life are experienced in tandem.

9. Based on Howard Gardner's theory on multiple intelligences, more recent editions of the book add 'naturalist' and 'existential' to the list. While not altogether considered a scientific approach, the idea that intelligence is a much broader term than we have traditionally accepted is certainly worth appreciating. See Thomas Armstrong, *7 Kinds of Smart* (New York: New American Library, 1999).

10. The National Council of Educational Research and Training, which advises the Indian government on policy matters pertaining to education.

11. In the school opened by EL Education, 98% of students graduate and go on to college.

12. "Austin's Butterfly: Building Excellence in Student Work" (EL Education), last modified 9 March 2023, https://vimeo.com/38247060.

CHAPTER 10

THE BEGINNINGS OF A MOVEMENT

An adage from ancient Greece draws a much-explored comparison between the fox and the hedgehog. Often attributed to the poet Archilochus, it states that "a fox knows many things, but a hedgehog knows one big thing."

In a nutshell, the parables created around this saying explore the idea that in trying to hunt the hedgehog, the fox may employ a variety of tactics. Ultimately, however, the fox fails because the hedgehog – although less wily and cunning than the fox – knows how to defend itself. The hedgehog excels at one big thing – its own defence – and this ensures that it consistently comes out on top.

The expression found its way into corporate lore in 2001, when Jim Collins used it in his much-lauded book *Good to Great*.[1] Collins drew a contrast between companies that keep trying new and different things (foxes) and those that survive and even thrive by being unbeatable at one big thing (hedgehogs). Collins's own reflection on this was that companies aiming to be great should evaluate their strengths and develop into hedgehogs. Think Google and the search engine, Microsoft and Office, or Apple and the iPhone. He used this concept to develop a framework for companies that would help them become hedgehogs within their own industries.

A more interesting take on the proverb, however, lies in understanding that an organization – or indeed an individual – may need to flit between these two extremes to achieve success.

According to Ramji, "Agastya knew one big thing, namely the value of curiosity and creativity and the methods to trigger them. It had never lost sight if this. But it also needed multiple pathways and angles to achieve its goals. The key was knowing when to be which."

Agastya's carefully constructed and meticulously honed philosophy on education had gone deeper than any other grassroot initiative had dared to. With this at its core, it allowed its eclectic team of academics, ex-corporates and an army of BEEs (bachelors of energy and enthusiasm; see *Chapter 6*) to use every trick in the book to facilitate its proliferation. It is in finding that balance that the foundation has flourished.

By 2008, Agastya's name had become somewhat synonymous with hands-on education. In February of that year, Sam Pitroda, the chair of the prime minister's National Knowledge Commission,[2] invited Ramji to join the commission's working group on attracting children to science and math.

Members of the commission visited an Agastya science fair and the campus. During this time, the members also inaugurated the Jhunjhunwala Discovery Centre, which was finally ready after two years in development.

Impressed with what they had witnessed, the commission asked the foundation to present a plan for expanding the Agastya model across India. The plan recommended a massive expansion of mobile science labs and science centres, student peer-to-peer teaching, and the creation of 20 campuses like the one at Gudupalle across the country. The investment in the programme would have equalled less than 3% of the education budget of the nation at the time, and some of it would be contributed by the private sector. The benefits would be massive. The Agastya management predicted that the programme would have a groundswell impact on innovation and that Indian education would be transformed within 15 years. The commission recommended a number of Agastya innovations, among them mobile labs and the Young Instructor Leader programme, to popularize science at the grassroots. Budget constraints, however, prevented the plan from becoming operational. In time, with the dissolution of the knowledge commission, this particular opportunity faded completely.

It was, however, encouraging to note that Agastya – which still operated within the confines of some key hubs in South India – was being recognized nationally. In addition, Ramji was now specifically being asked to come and give talks on education, and this was bringing in interest from corporates and high-net-worth individuals from across the world. It gave the team the impetus to start thinking about a pan-India presence.

From the very beginning, the founders were keen that Agastya should evolve from being a singular organization to becoming an educational movement that covered the country and left no child behind. To facilitate this, Ramji often declared that he had no qualms about other foundations using models developed by Agastya to further the cause of hands-on education in India. The process of planting seeds and observing how they grew was set into the Agastya culture from the start. In 2009, the team would glimpse a rather unexpected and fantastic result of this approach. Like so many things relating to Agastya, it was wholly organic and – once recognized – brilliantly adopted for mass dissemination.

It happened one evening, when Ramji took a guest from the Agastya campus to a village nearby where Agastya had taken to doing some community events at night.

The night visits were a necessity-based innovation that had originated with a meeting that Ramji had had with a government official of the Chittoor district in Andhra Pradesh. The official had asked Ramji to review an initiative that the government was undertaking in the villages. While interviewing a woman from one of the villages, Ramji noticed her young son clinging to her saree. Ramji asked the boy whether he had seen an Agastya mobile lab. The boy nodded and went on to describe a biology model he had seen. However, the mother seemed completely unaware of her own son's interactions with Agastya. The community night visits were suggested as a way to bridge this gap and create awareness among the parents.

It was an almost ethereal sight: a group of children staring enrapt at an instructor as the humble glow of a solar lamp illuminated him and the experiments that he was guiding them through. Like any such event should be, the noise quotient was high as peals of laughter and shrieks of excitement filled the warm evening air. At the insistence of the guest, he and Ramji climbed to the terrace of a nearby house to take pictures from a better vantage point. It was then that they spotted a girl, away from the rest of the crowd, surrounded by a few children. She appeared to be holding a model in her hand and explaining it to her younger brethren.

Intrigued, Ramji went up to her and asked why she was not with the rest of the group.

"I like to teach," she replied and then pointed to the mobile lab. "The things the Agastya teacher teaches – I like to continue teaching the children here."

She showed them a model of the food chain that she had borrowed from the mobile lab. She said that she had gone through Agastya's programmes when she was younger and now wanted to use what she knew to help other children. Leading them to her home, a modest room, she showed them a blackboard and a piece of chalk.

"I teach here every night," she said with a big smile.

"What's your name?" Ramji asked.

She replied, "Vasantha."

The sheer simplicity of the idea astounded the Agastya team. Operation Vasantha (OV), as the night-school concept would come to be known, was remarkably scalable and low cost, and could use the force multiplier effect to project Agastya's impact without adding more staff. In effect, it was a levelling-up of the peer-to-peer teaching structure that Agastya had pioneered years earlier, now being taken forward by the very students in whom Agastya had once nurtured curiosity.

The programme became extremely popular among the children, their parents and the schoolteachers. The parents were happy that the children were learning and not watching TV or creating mischief. The children said that they much preferred the hands-on classes to sitting at home and doing chores for their parents. The schoolteachers felt that the children came to class well prepared and with their homework completed. Everyone, it would appear, was winning.

The OV volunteers were typically young women aged between 18 and 25. Sometimes they were college students who had returned home (often because their family believed it was time to get them married!) and had time in the evening to engage with the children.

Agastya began to support the volunteers with a modest stipend and by supplying them with the models and even the training they needed to execute their tasks. Teaching and engaging with a class of some 30 children every night, the OV volunteers gained enormous knowledge, confidence, and communication and interpersonal skills. The community was happy that one of their own was teaching their children.

OV was a low-tech, high-impact grassroots operation that began to quickly spread across the Agastya network and beyond. It complemented and reinforced the mobile lab sessions.

But managing the growing army of volunteers was no mean feat.

In 2005, Jayamma P.S. was working near Gudupalle when she heard about Agastya and the work it was doing. Despite her misgivings about being unqualified to join what she considered an "international project," she really felt she needed to be a part of Agastya.

"I lived in a village at that time," she recollects. "I would leave at 5:30 am and reach Gudupalle[3] by 7 am. From there it was four kilometres to campus. When I first saw the campus, I really felt I wanted to work there. I used to also see the mobile labs going up and down and it sparked my interest. I was the first woman to work at the Agastya campus. Ramji called me and he even spoke with my husband, Raghava, to ask if it was safe. Raghava was worried, but I wanted to work here even if there were struggles."

Jayamma busied herself for a few years by working on campus in various capacities as required. An energetic personality blessed with unique compassion, her brand equity within Agastya would skyrocket with the emergence of OV. As it transpired, the OV volunteers were very receptive to her, and she was entrusted with the coordination of the programme. Under Jayamma's wing, OV would grow to cover 700 villages in India and monumentally boost Agastya's reach. Every evening, some 18,000 children would gather around an eager OV instructor and learn new things about science. OV was a shining example of the kind of movement that Agastya's momentum could create and remains one of the most successful initiatives that the foundation has launched.

Within Agastya, Jayamma is referred to as the 'Mother of OV.' To the young volunteers she shepherds, she is simply 'Agastya Madam.'

The OV origin story is in and of itself a heart-warming example of Agastya's ability to spot potential in the quietest corners and infuse purpose into that potential to drive change. With Agastya now approaching its tenth year, such anecdotes were becoming more frequent, although no less touching and worthy of reflection. Agastya's methods did not promise any overnight change in exam marks or economic conditions. In terms of impact, it would still be a few years before any formal metrics were tracked to quantify the Agastya effect across the organization. But a decade of sparking curiosity was slowly starting to stoke flames that were difficult to ignore. In these flames, Agastya saw the beginnings of an inferno that could one day lift a nation of underprivileged children to soar well above their circumstances.

On a hot summer day, two young village girls – Rani and Roja – were seeking refuge from a pitiless sun. They settled under the welcome shade of a peepul tree and, as friends are wont to do, commenced chatting about whatever it was that held their fancy that morning.

As they continued chatting, their curious minds led them down a path of inquiry that had game-changing consequences.

They started with a question: "Why do we feel cool sitting under the shade of a tree?"

This led to a follow-up question: "Is there a difference in the cooling properties of different leaves?"

Rani and Roja's investigation at Agastya into the cooling properties of leaves would win them the Special Award at the IRIS National Prize. It was noteworthy, considering that IRIS (the Initiative for Research and Innovation in STEM) invited nearly a thousand students from across the country to compete. This meant that the girls were up against children from private schools, who had the resources and the time to create far more elaborate studies and experiments.

IRIS was started in 1999 as a collaboration between Intel, the Confederation of Indian Industry, and the Department of Science and Technology.[4] Sharon Kumar, who joined IRIS in 2010, has a special fondness for the children that come from Agastya.

"We target students from grades five to twelve," she describes. "IRIS reaches out to students pan-India and Agastya has been facilitating these workshops. It gives us a great deal of pleasure and hope when we see how Agastya impacts the perspective of the students. It's so much in sync with what is required. We have always had students from Agastya coming into IRIS. We look out for them. Somehow or other they always make it into the top hundred. Their research and projects are always focused on problems that they have experienced. It's so different from the projects that the more privileged kids come with."

Following in Rani[5] and Roja's footsteps, Agastya children would win at IRIS five years in a row. In 2011, 10% of the IRIS finalists were Agastya children. The projects always had the same vein of science infused with reality. The children had a perspective that more well-off students may not ever have had access to. Some youngsters worked on correcting urban problems such as traffic or pollution.

Agastya's projects were always aimed at minimizing the hardships that many of these children and their families faced day to day. In 2010, two girls – Bhargavi and Jyotsna

– studied the medicinal value of plants and identified certain plant species that, if planted alongside crops, would not allow weeds to propagate and steal nutrition from the soil. Another project, a device invented by a boy who did not want his grandmother to have to bend while working the fields, looked at improving the ease with which seeds could be planted. One girl presented her innovation for a pair of gel-padded gloves, meant to ease the pain of callouses that formed on her father's hands while he worked cutting stones at the quarry.

Gavin Dykes, programme director of the Education World Forum, recalls his first interaction with Agastya students when visiting in 2012: "In my first conversation with them, I thought I'd talk about the London Olympics, but there were a lot of mystified faces. When I asked how many knew about the Olympics, only one hand went up. The girl who answered gave me a textbook definition. When it was their turn to ask me questions, their first question to me was, 'What crops do you grow?' For me this was a great lesson that if you are a teacher, don't presume your picture of the world is their picture."

These examples were certainly heart-wrenchingly touching but were also profoundly indicative of the effect that Agastya could have. As hard as some of their lives were, these children were not looking for handouts. They had been introduced to the tools they needed to influence change in their own communities, and with Agastya's help, they intended to use these tools to the fullest.

The IRIS prize winners from Agastya were not children who had just had a passing experience with Agastya's teaching techniques. They were a part of Agastya's Young Instructor Leader (YIL) programme, which had its beginnings on that fateful morning in 2000 when

– grappling with a crippling staff shortage – the founders had accepted the help of a few enterprising girls and trained them to be instructors (see *Chapter 5*). Witnessing the earliest benefits of peer-to-peer learning, Agastya had expanded on the idea to identify students with exceptional aptitude and attitude and help them harness this potential further.

The YIL programme was begun in a rather unconventional way. Kimberly Karlshoej, the heiress of a Danish family with businesses in shipping, had heard of Agastya and wished to see the Agastya campus. While on the drive down from Bangalore, Ramji described the YIL programme to her. Struck by the power and simplicity of the idea, she offered her foundation's support even before they reached the campus.

Over time, the YIL programme would grow to involve nearly 30,000 children. Most of these YILs were aged between 11 and 15. They would benefit from additional sessions with Agastya instructors and get special assistance on projects, such as those intended for IRIS. For a while, a few YILs were even housed on campus and had access to the labs and teachers there. Older YILs would sometimes find themselves moving into OV roles, giving Agastya another example of how its multiplier effect could create self-propagating ripples across the organization and more broadly across the landscape of education itself.

From 2010 to 2014, Agastya would try to hone the YILs further by introducing them to a Gifted Children programme. At the behest of the government, Agastya was asked to identify potential diamonds in the rough from among the children with whom it interacted.

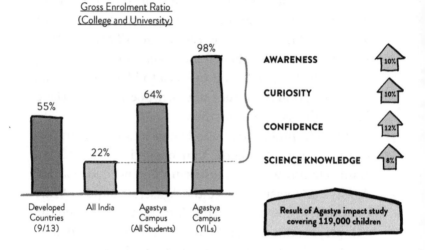

THE AGASTYA IMPACT

"The government wanted us to initiate a programme and Thiagu asked me whether I was up to it," says Ganu Subramanian, who spearheaded the project. A former senior executive at Hewlett-Packard who had been a year senior to Thiagu at the Indian Institute of Technology, Ganu's passion for education is evident in the way he speaks about Agastya's impact on the children he was working with.

"The YIL was much more a social leadership programme. The Gifted Children programme was not a nurturing programme, it was an identification programme. The idea we proposed was to give us 50 gifted children that we would work with on weekends, and each year we would take another 40 students, and then we would work with them up to college. The goal was that all would opt for higher education and that a significant portion would get into institutions of some repute."

"A child does not grow up in a knowledge vacuum," Ganu observes. "A child develops a lot of envelopes – intellectual, emotional etc. – you cannot teach them only one thing and not hope to influence the others. One of the major things that Agastya does is to provide a 'nurture gap,' which the child does not get at school or even at home. This is why we see so many success stories coming out of Agastya."

However, within a few years, budget constraints would force the programme to shut down. The Gifted Children programme would cease and only the YIL would continue.

A study done a few years later would highlight an incredible statistic. The YIL programme appeared to be impacting the gross enrolment ratio into higher education for the children who passed through it. The national ratio for India as a whole was 22%. For developing countries, it was 37%. For developed countries, the number rose to 55%.

The number for Agastya YILs was an astounding 98%. Marks or no marks, there was something life-changing happening and Agastya was unmistakably at the centre of it.

IMPACT STORY – SANDHYA

Sandhya was in the 4th or 5th grade when she first saw the Agastya campus in Gudupalle. Visiting with her cousin as part of a summer camp, her first impression was that it might be a park. Sandhya was mesmerised by all the art and the plants that surrounded her. She recalls participating in a soil experiment, which gave her valuable, practical insights. The very experience of being on campus struck a chord with Sandhya. She was determined to be a part of the foundation in some way and wanted to benefit as much as she could from the abundant learning and the unique experiences that Agastya's teaching provided.

In the 7th grade, Sandhya sat one of Agastya's trademark tests and was selected as a Young Instructor Leader. Agastya's YIL programme was especially effective in spotting young talent and Sandhya's inclusion into this elite cadre was to prove to be life changing.

Brought up in a family of four, Sandhya's mother is a tailor. Her now late father was a farmer. Her parents did not know much about Agastya but supported her through her journey once they learned how it might benefit their daughter. Through Agastya, Sandhya was able to secure a scholarship from the Puranam Family to further her education. This came at a time when her family's financial situation was dire, and she was on the verge of having to drop out of school.

Sandhya quickly found that Agastya was a place that encourages all talents. As a keen reader and a lover of music, Sandhya was allowed to hone her skills. She believes that Agastya's methods allowed her to develop an analytical mindset enabling her to better deal with problems and handle personal issues.

As an introvert, Sandhya had never been comfortable speaking to people. She is grateful to Agastya for providing her with a platform and the opportunity to build her self-confidence, courage and public speaking skills. Some years later, as an anchor at a YIL Alumni Meet, Sandhya addressed an audience of around 3000 children.

During her time as an Agastya YIL, she participated in several projects. One of these was Operation Vasantha.

Coming from a remote village, Sandhya had witnessed multiple problems with the state of education in her hometown. The number of school dropouts was staggeringly high due to the inability of parents to pay the school fees. A narrow minded and ignorant view towards the importance of education – especially for girls – saw children being pushed into farming, or marriage, at a young age. Sandhya was inspired to bring about a change. She joined Operation Vasantha and helped with night schooling for school dropouts in her village. She conducted various science experiments with them and encouraged them to spark their creativity. Deeming it as a wonderful experience, she observed that her students' minds shone in that environment of learning.

Her students praised Agastya's practical, hands-on science learning, stating that "Two visits from Agastya are equivalent to a month of school."

Sandhya was also able to make a difference by involving herself in various other Agastya programs such as science fairs and awareness sessions on child marriage. She also participated in Swachh Bharat (Clean India) initiatives in railway stations near Kuppam.

When asked about her passions, Sandhya says that she wishes to become an Office in the Indian Administrative Service (IAS), fulfil her father's dream and her own responsibility to serve society, and work towards having a positive impact on the education of girls. She dreams that no girl should suffer due to illiteracy or be a burden to their families, but should rather become strong, independent individuals. After she becomes an IAS Officer, she wants to protect the young girls in her village from child marriage and provide them with support through Agastya.

She also wants to look after her mother and see her smile as her mother has sacrificed a lot for Sandhya.

Sandhya is 22 years old now and has graduated from college. She is presently pursuing her Master of Computer Applications (MCA) whilst working at a call centre to support herself financially.

As a former YIL, she advises every student at Agastya to be as curious as possible, learn everything, and most importantly, use the platform given to them very judiciously and properly because "If learning starts from childhood, life will be beautiful."

IMPACT STORY – PAVAN

Pavan Kumar, a young man associated with Agastya, offers an interesting piece of advice to those he meets: "By sharing your knowledge, your influence will be improved and your values increased."

Pavan grew up in a small village in Chittoor District, about 20 km from Agastya's Campus. He absolutely loved his time at Agastya. Emphasising the strong support he received from his family, he says that he and his friends felt that going to the Agastya campus was like a grand festival for them; the new classes and experiences were something out of the ordinary.

Pavan, who humbly describes himself as an enthusiastic, hyperactive, but average student, was selected as a Young Instructor Leader when he was in the 7th grade. He claims that at the time he did not know much, but that the emphasis on creativity and curiosity set sparks flying in his mind.

Pavan recalls the influence Agastya had on his education and on him as an individual. He appreciated the abundant nature on campus, the friendly faculty, and the hands-on learning experiences that Agastya provided. In addition, he believes he gained important life skills such as leadership, teaching skills, and the ability to stay calm and regulate his emotions, which he attained by meditating for 5 minutes each time before entering the YIL lab.

The son of a cattle farmer, Pavan has had a connection to grasslands since he was a very young boy. He understood the difficulties of the profession and identified the danger of farmers having to water their crops at odd hours of the night due to the presence of snakes.

In the 8th grade, with the help of his YIL team, Pavan created an automated irrigation system. Using sensors that connected

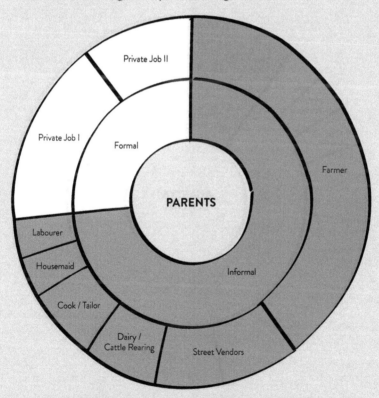

INTER-GENERATIONAL PROFESSION CHANGE BETWEEN AGASTYA ALUMNI AND THEIR PARENTS

a phone to motors, Pavan's system would help farmers irrigate their crops easily and from the safety of their homes.

The invention won him 2nd place at a state-level competition, which he describes as an extremely memorable achievement.

In addition to this, Pavan also identified the issue of multiple accidents taking place on the road in front of his school because of no sign board. Calling it the best initiative of the YIL team, he organized a donation drive in his village to install a speed breaker on the road to ensure greater safety and reduce accidents. Pavan also participated in awareness campaigns in factories, offices and trains regarding cleanliness and the reduction of waste.

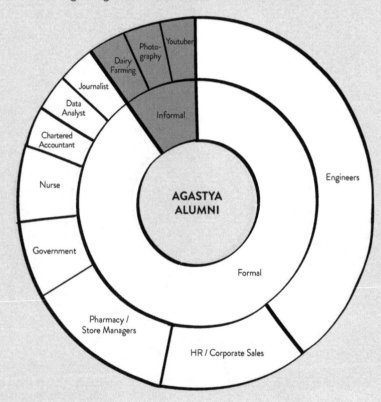

INTER-GENERATIONAL PROFESSION CHANGE BETWEEN AGASTYA ALUMNI AND THEIR PARENTS

Pavan recently graduated from college with a degree in computer science. Wanting to share the knowledge he gained at Agastya, Pavan's career morphed into one involving social media. He has one YouTube channel about science facts and experiments and another channel about wealth creation. Pavan speaks about how one must be a job creator rather than a job seeker. He amassed almost 250,000 subscribers within 3 months of starting his channel. His love for wealth creation is so deep that he has founded a start-up to further his influence and spread knowledge about this field on a much larger scale. His initiatives include teaching around 5000 students online and conducting 2000 plus seminars offline as well as planning free courses in self-development, money management and marketing.

Determined to help reduce the increasing unemployment around him, Pavan also looks to assist people to leverage social media to monetize their knowhow. For instance, he taught a farmer how to make informative videos about the process of watering plants and managing fields, helping him earn some extra income.

Pavan hopes that once he establishes his start-up, he can give back to Agastya and its students. He credits Agastya for helping him improve his speaking and marketing skills and mentions that the foundation is quite underrated despite its huge impact.

When asked about his hopes for the future, Pavan responds by saying that he wishes to see Indian knowledge develop companies in India rather than abroad and hopes that future generations would develop life skills rather than merely chasing a degree.

His final message to all Agastya students was to explore and learn everything, share that knowledge with others and utilize all of their resources prudently; and last but not least, seize every opportunity that comes their way!

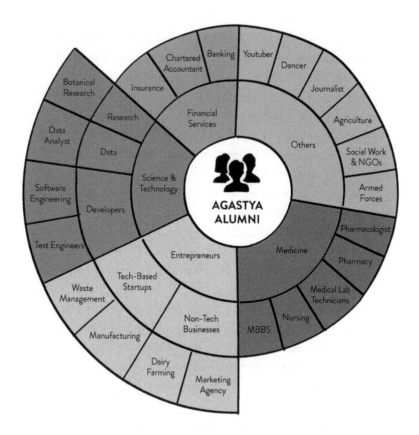

PROFESSIONAL ROLES OF AGASTYA ALUMNI

The YIL programme was far from being the only scalable offshoot of the early science fairs. Having captured the fancy of so many children, teachers and parents, the science fairs themselves would frequently be used as a medium to reach out to communities and market Agastya's techniques. It was an infallible way to win over sceptics. Those who attended usually went back to their respective towns or villages asking their local schools why Agastya's mobile labs could not be persuaded to make trips to their neck of the woods.

From the humbler fairs of the early 2000s, which each drew in only a few hundred children, Agastya had started to envision bolder and larger exhibitions. In 2008, Agastya launched its first mega-science fair at the Indira Gandhi Glass House in Hubli, Karnataka. The fair attracted nearly 10,000 children, teachers and community members. Several mobile science labs parked around the main hall showcased different theme-based learning modules. Visiting scientists and educators conducted Q&A sessions with children. The Hubli mega-science fair created an appreciable buzz; attracted the local community and the media; and trained hundreds of children to teach science to their peers.

Two years later, at the Bangalore Army School grounds, an even bigger spectacle would follow. Some 40,000 children would attend a science fair over six days. Logistically, it was a monumental undertaking, as Agastya buses flitted across the city picking up and dropping off schoolchildren at pre-designated locations.[6] Two years later, a fair in Bihar would similarly host 14,000 children.

Mega-science fairs became a centrepiece of Agastya's strategy to popularize science. In time, the fairs included interactive art workshops, ecology and even yoga. The intensity of the work involved stretched Agastya's resources and capacity, almost to breaking point. Hundreds of YILs had to be trained in advance and scores of Agastya teachers and facilitators had to be transported to the location from different regions across the country. The challenges to which the Agastya team were exposed as a result of the mega-fairs went far beyond the realm of education. Apart from logistics, the organizers needed to be mindful about crowd control, food distribution, meeting and greeting important visitors, managing the venue itself (including the erection of tents), and working tactfully with local government schools, officials and VIPs.

The staff learned in equal measure from their successes and their failures. Mistakes were always treated as opportunities to learn and advance rather than as excuses to reprimand. By bringing people together from across the country and focusing them on a critical project mission, the mega-science fairs helped to break barriers, promote communication, build cohesion, and foster a spirit of teamwork, camaraderie and celebration across Agastya.

A by-product of the mega-science fair was Jignyasa – a model-making competition for children launched in Hubli under Nitin Desai's watch. Supported by the Deshpande Foundation, Jignyasa – which translates, quite fittingly, to 'curiosity' – became a tremendous success. Starting with only 12 districts, Jignyasa quickly grew to cover the state before going national. By 2018, the competition would be attracting close to 15,000 children from across 11 states. Over 1,400 projects would be submitted, with about 100 children being selected as finalists. Again, the task of sifting through, understanding, evaluating, and judging these submissions was nothing short of herculean. By now, however, the Agastya team was regularly eating large numbers for breakfast.

In 2017, Ramji would be approached by a young man on a busy road in Bangalore.

"Are you with the Agastya Foundation?" the boy asked. Ramji replied that he was.

"I am an orphan," the young man said and continued, "I participated in Agastya's Jignyasa model-making competition in Hubli from the seventh grade onwards."

Ramji was delighted and asked him what he was now doing.

"I am an orphan, sir," he repeated before adding, "but thanks to my exposure to Agastya's Jignyasa fair, I am now studying for a degree at the M. S. Ramaiah Institute of Technology in Bangalore."

It was one of those poignant moments that stunned Ramji. As he watched the boy walk away with confidence, he was overcome with a sense of renewed purpose.

Jignyasa, in turn, paved the way for an innovation fair called Anveshana – which translates, equally fittingly, to 'innovation.' Supported by the IT giant Synopsys, the idea for Anveshana came from N. Ayachit of the B. V. B. Engineering College in Hubli. It was managed by Ganu Subramanian.

The idea was to pair two high school children with two students from an engineering college. Over a six-month period, the team would ideate and develop an innovation of their choice under the guidance of an Agastya facilitator.

Forty teams from a pool of over 100 project submissions would be invited to the final round of the competition in Bangalore, where they would compete for a prize. Anveshana winners would then be invited to a follow-up session at the Agastya campus. Besides promoting a spirit of innovation, Anveshana offered a unique opportunity for schoolchildren to connect with college students through a common project. This engagement with college students not only allowed for osmosis of ideas but also raised the aspiration quotient for the underprivileged children. Collaborating and innovating with older children also gave them an opportunity to acquire vital skills around communication and teamwork. The college students, in turn, were learning how to simplify ideas and concepts and transmit these effectively to younger children.

Erin Guzman, who leads corporate social responsibility at Synopsys in Mountain View, California, explains why the company decided to collaborate with Agastya on Anveshana.

"One thing that is very fascinating is the innovation and the drive," she says. "Agastya is demystifying science in the villages. Even if you can get only a few girls whose families have changed their minds, it's such an impact and is so holistic. In Bangalore there was a science fair. Then there were some discussions with Agastya on how we scale that in a much bigger way. We spoke about how to get older students involved. This was the genesis for Anveshana."

In 2021, Anveshana reached its ten-year anniversary. During this time, it had expanded from Bangalore across ten states, covering 200 schools and over 100 engineering colleges.

On a blindingly bright day in the summer of 2012, the mood on the Agastya campus was considerably more electric than usual. The preceding five years had seen new buildings brought to life, including the Jhunjhunwala Discovery Centre, a planetarium, and a host of other labs and accommodation. With this infrastructure, the campus was able to welcome around 500 children from surrounding schools each day. Hence, it was not unusual to see and hear groups of children animatedly chatting and running around, clearly enthused by their day on campus.

But this particular day was different. All in all, a few thousand children and scores of their teachers flocked to the Agastya campus eager to catch a glimpse of the iconic man whose visit had been announced a few weeks ago.

Ramji's first meeting with Dr. A. P. J. Abdul Kalam happened in 2003, when Dr. Kalam was still president of India. The introduction had been made via scientists who had worked with Kalam in the past and were now friends of Agastya. These included Dr. R. Krishnan and

K. Ramchand, who had heard Ramji speak at a seminar at the National Institute of Advanced Studies in 2001 and had subsequently invited him over for dinner. The connection was further strengthened by Dr. Aatre, who had succeeded Dr. Kalam as the head of the Defence Research and Development Organisation.

"My first meeting with Dr. Kalam took place at his office at Rashtrapati Bhavan, the presidential palace in Delhi," Ramji recalls. "Dr. Kalam questioned me about my plans. Why had I returned to India? What did I hope to achieve? He was keen to know about the mobile science lab that we had launched less than six months ago in Gudupalle. What science experiments did the lab carry? How many children could it reach? Who was the teacher, how was he trained and by whom? For an iconic president, Dr Kalam had a friendly and easy manner. As he listened closely to my answers, he would count the worry beads in his hand. He leaned forward at one point and said that the problem with most leaders in India was that they were interested only in working from a comfortable office in the city. 'Very few people want to go out to the field. If you want to make a difference, go to rural India.' I asked Dr. Kalam what he felt the country needed most. 'Three things,' he said. 'Curiosity, skills and confidence.' As I bade him goodbye, Dr. Kalam wished me success and said he would like to visit Agastya someday."

Given Kalam's hectic schedule, Agastya would not have a chance to showcase its work to the president for another three years. On a visit to Bangalore in 2006, Kalam asked to see the Agastya mobile science lab. He spent time reviewing the experiments and talking to the children who had gathered. He even posed for a photo in front of the mobile lab. To the unruly throng of reporters that was throwing a volley of questions at him on India's social challenges, he said, "Why don't you write about Agastya's positive work?"

As he got into his car to leave, he turned to Ramji and said, "I will help you if you decide to expand your mobile labs into India's backward areas in the north." Kalam believed that most organizations were satisfied to work in and around urban areas, where connectivity was good, and staff were easier to hire. However, in many of India's poorest states, there were areas that remained completely ignored. He wanted Agastya to reach into these parts, believing that children there would truly benefit from exposure to Agastya's methods.

True enough, a few years later as Ramji was boarding a flight, he received a call from Kalam. Kalam had been awarded the S. R. Jindal Prize for exemplary service to humankind. Ramji congratulated Kalam on his winning the prize. Kalam laughed and replied that he wasn't calling to be congratulated but rather to deliver some good news.

The prize carried a cash reward of 1 crore rupees ($150,000) and Kalam had decided to split this between four NGOs. He intended to give one of these portions to Agastya to buy two mobile science labs to serve the poorest children in the remotest areas of Bihar.

In 2012, Kalam's long-awaited trip to the Agastya campus was finally planned. Ramji remembers being called to meet him at the Raj Bhavan[7] in Bangalore, at midnight, the night before Kalam was set to visit the Agastya campus.

"At 80, looking remarkably fresh at the late hour, he listened to my update on the Bihar mobile lab programme, enquired about the following day's schedule and expressed his eagerness to help Agastya in any way he could," Ramji recalls.

Kalam's visit to the campus was truly a sight to behold. As he marched through the campus, the army of children followed him like a million flecks of iron stringing behind a powerful magnet. The noise level was incredible, and the thundering of young, eager feet churned the land's light, chalky earth into an enormous pale cloud of fine dust. When Kalam took to the podium to give his speech, the rousing crowd cheered him like he was a rock star.

His talk and stimulating presence at the Agastya campus left a lasting impact on many underprivileged children. The same day, he would inaugurate Agastya's newest building: VisionWorks, the model-making workshop that Agastya had envisioned nearly a decade ago when building its discovery centre.[8]

It was on Kalam's insistence that Agastya launched a mega-science fair in Darbhanga, Bihar, later that year. A deeply compassionate man, Kalam felt genuine concern that certain poorer pockets of India – Bihar in particular – were being left behind by the progress that was washing over the rest of the country.

Kota Harinarayana, who had worked with Kalam and later managed the latter's Viksit Bharat Foundation, recalls the passion that Kalam felt for the state of Bihar.

"We wanted to improve the education levels in Bihar," he explains. "One of the major vehicles for Dr. Kalam was science education through the mobile science labs. Agastya trained the people there and implemented the programme. Dr. Kalam felt that Agastya was one place where the students were experimenting with their hands; that there was so much energy in the work Agastya was doing. Dr. Kalam was very deeply appreciative of Agastya. He used to hear about Agastya from me and Dr. Krishnan. He knew all the work that they were doing, and he was keenly aware of the positive impact of the mobile labs in Bihar."

Kalam's connection with children was indeed remarkable. One Diwali, Ramji remembers visiting Kalam's Rajaji Marg home office in Delhi with his 17-year-old daughter, Jeena. Visibly elated by Jeena's presence, Kalam asked her, "What is your passion?"

"Painting," she replied. (Jeena would go on to earn a degree in fine arts from the prestigious Parsons School of Design in New York).

"How wonderful," he beamed and followed up with his next question, "What is the first thought that comes into your mind when you paint?"

She thought for a moment and said, "Colour."

"Aha!" he said with delight, as if she had solved a puzzle.

Much later, as they rose to leave, Kalam asked an assistant to fetch a book from his library. He walked Ramji and Jeena out into the cool night. Under the lights outside, he softly read out words of wisdom from his book of poems to Jeena like a grandfather reading to his favourite granddaughter, and asked her to repeat the words after him.

He pointed to the dark silhouette of a large tree in his garden. "That tree is called Arjuna," he explained. "It is 500 years old."

Ramji could not help but be struck by this remarkable man who, against all odds, had risen to the highest office of the land. For a few precious minutes this famous scientist – the son of a poor boatman – had made a young girl feel as if she was the most special person on earth.

As Kalam and Ramji made their way through the mist on a cold winter's day in distant Darbhanga to inaugurate the Agastya mega-science fair in Bihar, Ramji asked him to reveal the secret of his almost limitless energy.

Without the slimmest shade of pretence, Kalam replied, "When you give selflessly, you gain energy."

Dr. Kalam's involvement with Agastya was yet another endorsement that launched the foundation's image and reputation onto the national stage. His belief that Agastya's approach could bring about a mass transformation was a validation that infused new energy into the foundation and allowed it to push forward with even more gusto and aplomb.

1. Jim C. Collins, *Good to Great* (London: Random House, 2001).

2. The National Knowledge Commission was an Indian think-tank created to advise the Prime Minister's Office on matters of policy related to education, research institutes and reforms needed to boost India's standing in the knowledge economy.

3. The nearest bus stand to the Agastya campus.

4. It began as the Intel Science Talent and Discovery Fair and took its current form in 2006. Presently it is funded by the Broadcom Foundation, the EXSTEMPLAR Education Linkers Foundation, and the Department of Science and Technology.

5. Rani would go on to earn her PhD and is now an Assistant Professor of Plant Pathology at the Dr. YSR Horticulture University in Andhra Pradesh.

6. Sadly, traffic woes in larger cities have prevented fairs of this size from happening since 2010. Smaller towns simply do not have the volume – even if their roads are immeasurably quieter!

7. The governor's house.

8. Funding for VisionWorks was supported by Axis Bank.

CHAPTER 11

THE FOUNDATIONS OF SCALE

If you were to be so brazen as to ask Ramji Raghavan to empty his pockets, a curious object would invariably emerge. At first glance, it appears completely unremarkable: a small, coloured wooden ball, hollowed out on one side, with a short peg sticking out of the scooped-out portion. Anyone having made a road trip across South India might have seen similarly painted wooden toys sold in roadside shops.

The tippe top, however, deceives you with its simplicity.

Without too much coaxing, you could convince Ramji to demonstrate how the top works. Holding the short peg, the top is spun by hand, much like snapping one's fingers. For a few seconds, the top spins on its spherical surface with the peg upright. Then, the peg appears to lean sideways and, in an instant, the top flips upside-down and starts spinning on the peg. The astute onlooker might also notice that the top changes the direction in which it rotates.

A photo taken at the Institute of Physics at Lund, Sweden, in 1954 shows Wolfgang Pauli and Niels Bohr half-crouched comically over a spinning tippe top, smiling like schoolchildren marvelling at a fascinating new toy. Indeed, as humble as the design is, the tippe top's behaviour requires a fairly advanced knowledge of friction, angular momentum and torque to be sufficiently understood or explained.

For Ramji, however, the top seemed the perfect talisman to complement his phrase encompassing the soul of Agastya: 'Aah! Aha! Ha-ha!'

Much like reading, writing and arithmetic were once known as the three 'Rs of learning, Aah! Aha! and Ha-ha! were coined by Agastya as the three 'As of curiosity. Nowhere is the revelation behind this rationale more evident than when you initially witness the tippe top in action.

When the unassuming little toy starts spinning, there is not much to surprise the observer. Then, when it flips over, it delivers a sense of sheer astonishment. This feeling of watching something behave contrary to expectation is the 'Aah!' It is the same wonder that a child feels when seeing their first rainbow or when they first graze their hand against a touch-me-not plant and witness its leaves spontaneously fold in response.[1] It is not uncommon to hear a whoop of amazement from someone watching the top when it flips before them.

Having seen something that warrants explanation, the observer – should they be so inclined – seeks out the truth, the science behind the occurrence. Finding this answer is the 'Aha!' – the child who allows their curiosity to evolve into understanding now has the tools to use this knowledge as they see fit.

'Ha-ha!' is the final step of the journey. It signifies the joy that can be derived from the know-how acquired from this expedition of inquisitiveness. The same principles that govern the motion of the tippe top can be used to explain a host of other phenomena in physics, or even to create alternate versions of the top itself.

Agastya's mission to spark curiosity is as much about igniting the flame of inquiry as it is about leading the mind of the child to a place of understanding. The phrase 'Aah! Aha! Ha-ha!' would be carved into the mindset of every Agastya employee, because it represents the ultimate goal of the foundation and underlines joy as its main destination.

Apart from the science it encapsulates, the tippe top is also an excellent icebreaker.

In his first meeting with Deepak Parekh, the chair of the Housing Development Finance Corporation (HDFC) and one of the most respected names in Indian business,

Ramji spoke extensively on Agastya's mission, vision and future goals. For most of the 20-odd minutes of the meeting, Parekh barely spoke. Ramji sensed that he was not making much headway.

As the meeting concluded, Ramji pulled out a tippe top from his coat pocket and spun it on the table. True to its reputation, the colourful top tipped over and spun on its stem. Parekh smiled and told Ramji that it reminded him of his childhood when he used to play with tops. The meeting ended on that note. A few weeks later, Neil Joshi of the H. T. Parekh Foundation called to say that the foundation had approved a grant to fund Agastya's new biodiscovery centre. Neil added that Parekh had mentioned to his team, "Agastya has ambitious plans. We should help them." This was just the kind of enlightened social vision that Agastya needed in its corporate donors. The H. T. Parekh Foundation became one of Agastya's largest and most consistent long-term partners.

The spinning top was not the only Aah!-inducing apparatus in Agastya's repertoire.

In 2011–12, the foundation, with the help of M. Shivkumar and Dr. V. K. Aatre, made a presentation to S. V. Ranganath, the chief secretary of Karnataka. With the continued success of the Sarva Shiksha Abhiyan (SSA) programme in North Karnataka (see *Chapter 9*), Agastya was looking for ways to drive its mission further.

While visiting the campus, Ranganath was fascinated by a wooden model that visually explained the Pythagorean theorem ($a^2 + b^2 = c^2$). Overall, he was sold on the idea that Agastya was delivering something that needed mass dissemination.

"I was impressed by what I saw," says Ranganath. "The current situation will not help to improve the education system in India. I felt what they were doing in Kuppam needed to be taken forward. Unless you have mastered the foundational learning skills, you cannot master the higher level. The rule in education is that 85% of children should have an 85% level of competence in 85% of the competencies. In India we have 20% of children who are very bright, another 60% are average and will fall by the wayside unless tapped, while the remainder may not be strong students and will need a different kind of intervention."

Ranganath also believed that Agastya's approach had important advantages that made it easy to integrate into the government education system. Agastya's content was aligned with the school curriculum, its creative pedagogy helped teachers and students to effectively complement their syllabus with hands-on learning, and its methods were scalable at a low cost. These features meant that the existing school system could absorb a new way of learning without going through any major systemic adjustments. Ranganath, an avid chess player, used the following analogy to outline the importance of Agastya's efforts: "Manuel Aaron never became a chess grandmaster," he explained, "but he created the foundation, the Tal Chess Club in Chennai, which produced a world chess champion, Viswanathan Anand. We must build the foundation now to transform tomorrow's education."

This viewpoint aligned well with Ramji's idea that you can either sing and dance or you can create an environment that encourages others to sing and dance. Agastya was creating such environments for children in virtually every field of knowledge.

With Ranganath's backing, Agastya was eventually given approval to launch five large core science activity centres (CSACs) in North Karnataka. Unlike the smaller science centres, the CSACs were more like mini campuses, located on plots of about two acres in area and able to house significantly more models than the erstwhile centres.

Ramji would often ask visitors how much they might pay for the wooden model that had so captured Ranganath's fancy. Figures offered would not go far beyond a few hundred rupees. He would then reply that this inexpensive but very educational model had been powerful enough to convince the chief secretary of Karnataka to authorize a multi-crore (i.e. hundreds of thousands of dollars) project.

By the end of 2012, Agastya was preparing to embark on its next chapter.

Balasundaram had passed away in 2009; K. V. Raghavan in 2010; P. K. Iyengar followed in 2011. The three wise men were no more, but they had left an indelible mark on the foundation.

"My father and I were very different," says Ramji, reflecting on his father's inestimable impact on Ramji's own ability to stay the course. "Through uncertain and troubling times, he remained calm and collected. He had scaled great heights in the corporate world, which I had wanted to emulate. We would talk about Agastya every day. Not once, through those excruciating years of toil and hardship, did he express the faintest disappointment or suggest that I might have made a mistake in quitting my banking career."

Shortly after Kalam's visit to see the Agastya Mobile Lab in 2006, while enjoying a drink with Ramji in the veranda of his home in Bangalore, the elder Raghavan momentarily gave voice to his inner thoughts.

"My father said that he had wondered all along how I, with little experience of working in India, would handle the challenge of navigating through India's demanding and oftentimes frustrating socio-economic environment. He concluded with a compliment: despite significant odds, Agastya had created something that had attracted the interest and attention of the president of India, an achievement that deserved a celebratory drink." Ever his father's son, Ramji remarks, "Growing up, my father was my hero, who became my adviser. His compliment meant a lot to me."

There was virtually no aspect of Agastya's work or culture that the three elder co-founders had not played a part in shaping. They departed knowing that their vision for Agastya had been sculpted into reality and with a certainty that the hunger for reach that they instilled in the founders would be realized in the coming years.

However, they had also foreseen that as Agastya scaled further and prepared to go nationwide, the issue of growing pains would become very real and start to chip away at the foundation if not addressed properly.

Even with close to 70% of the activity focused on Karnataka, operational standards were proving difficult to regularize. It was now occurring to the core team that in order to shift gears, the systems that had held things in place thus far would need to be upgraded and perhaps even reimagined. The more remote Agastya's locations were becoming, the higher the risks of miscommunication, mistranslation or a complete lapse in quality that would not become apparent to the teams in Bangalore or on campus until it was too late. As had been the case from the very beginning, Agastya could not risk any loss of face, lest it permanently damage the reputation it had so painstakingly cultivated.

Sai Chandrasekhar joined Agastya in 2012 to bolster the management and to complement Thiagu's efforts to streamline operations. Having earlier been a vice president with Hewlett-Packard, Sai had decided to quit working and commit himself to a social cause. An alumnus of the Indian Institute of Management (IIM), Calcutta, Sai had been invited to an IIM Ahmedabad event showcasing various NGOs. Agastya was among these but, surprisingly, did not impress Sai whatsoever.

"Somehow, I thought this seems to be too rudimentary for me," he recalls in his frank, unvarnished manner that is both known and loved across the organization. "But I was looking at it from my perspective and not that of a child in a government school. Only after joining did this perception really change."

Eventually, after a few meetings with Thiagu, Sai decided to join Agastya. Despite the fact that there was no defined role on offer, Thiagu was certain that someone of Sai's intellect and drive would bring about a positive change in the way Agastya worked. It proved to be an excellent move. Sai quickly adapted to and then thrived in the role, allowing Thiagu to step back from day-to-day management and focus more on Agastya's strategy and long-term goals. Within a few years, Sai would function as Agastya's de facto COO.

Sai's management style was all about giving honest, real-time feedback at the point of delivery. Almost immediately after joining, he was travelling for half the month, personally visiting the myriad schools and science centres in Agastya's network in order to stay as close to the action as possible.

It was often gruelling work. On a cab ride from Varanasi to Azamgarh, Sai realized a few kilometres into the journey that the air conditioning had ceased functioning.

For the remainder of the two-and-a-half-hour journey, he travelled with the windows down as heat, dust, and fumes enveloped him. Arriving at his destination covered in dust and sweat, he proceeded to audit a class, as a very confused instructor tried his best to conduct proceedings as though nothing was askew.

"It was a disaster of a class," Sai chuckles, "The poor instructor was distracted and to make matters worse, the children just weren't grasping the concepts. After an hour-long class on magnetism, they were still saying 'like poles attract.' The instructor was beside himself. Eventually, I had a short discussion with him and left. I travelled all the way back to Varanasi to catch a train to Patna. The train was delayed, so I had to wait on the platform for hours, still looking very dishevelled. I finally reached Patna only at 3 am!"

"In one case," Sai explains of his classroom observations, "children were spending 15 to 20 minutes doing an activity that would help them to experience a concept. However, the discussion that followed this activity was very short. The ratio of time spent on discussion to time spent on the activity was enhanced to ensure a greater internalization and retention of the concept. Elsewhere, in some schools where the strength was on the higher side, we had seven or eight children in a group. The material available in the mobile science lab was increased to enable more groups to be formed, with each group having a maximum of five children so that there was better participation."

These first-hand insights into Agastya's end-customer interactions allowed Sai to make on-the-ground changes that would consistently have an impact at the organizational level.

"For me, if you ask, 'What is Agastya?,' what happens within the four walls of the classroom is Agastya," he explains. "Everything else is incidental. I would spend whole days sitting in the classroom. Instructors would get nervous initially, but subsequently they would come and ask, 'Why didn't you come to my class?' At the end of the lesson, I would not leave without giving some feed-back, usually in a friendly manner. The discussion with the instructor at the end of the session is, for me, a very important thing because that's what moves the needle."

Sai's example forced the area leads to be more rigorous about spending time observing classes and ensuring that the instructors knew where they might be falling short.

The following year, Hariharan Ganesan was also roped in. A neighbour of Sai's, Hari had worked in the IT industry as an independent consultant for seven years before joining Agastya. Like Sai, Hari joined without a clear idea of where he might focus his talents.

"I was working with start-ups and early-stage organizations that had to struggle for new customers. In Agastya, the difference was that it was for social good," Hari says. Like Sai, Hari carries with him a keenly honed sense of purpose and subscribes to an infrangible moral code.

Eventually, Hari decided to involve himself in corporatizing Agastya's fundraising operations. While Ramji had shouldered the bulk of this activity thus far, changes to India's corporate climate necessitated a team to manage the outreach to potential donors. The Corporate Social Responsibility (CSR) Bill, which came into effect in 2013, specified that companies making over 5 crore rupees ($625,000) in annual net profits would need to give a minimum of 2% to charitable causes. Hari would set about creating a system to tap into the immense wealth that corporate India suddenly had on offer.

The addition of capable new members did not immediately alleviate Agastya's risk of growth instability. In fact, Ramji faced some pushback from within the organization during this time. Concerned about the possible dip in quality and standards, the larger team argued for the pace to be dialled back. Hari cautioned Ramji that there was too much ambiguity in the message being projected across the organization and that if the goal was to scale despite the risk, this needed to be made clear to all stakeholders. For both Ramji and Thiagu, this boiled down to whether they had faith in Sai and his team's ability to make this happen. They believed that Sai could deliver, and were willing to bet it all that he would.

"My strategy was for Agastya to occupy 'opportunity spaces' – including in the most remote areas – wherever and as fast as possible," Ramji explains, "besides reaching underserved areas, this would build Agastya's reputation as an organization that was prepared to scale with speed and go where no one else was ready to go. So, I pushed the gas pedal hard, and the team responded brilliantly."

The logic for massive acceleration was twofold. First, there was the time value of education. Agastya had to expand rapidly to permanently stem lost learning opportunities by reaching millions of children who were desperately in need of an Agastya-type creative learning intervention. Further, Ramji was confident that the stress and tension created by this acceleration would dramatically raise Agastya's game by forcing it to rapidly build systems to address the risks of massive expansion.

The issue, as had been apparent right from the beginning, was in maintaining a uniform quality of instructors across the organization. The models themselves left little room for doubt or misunderstanding.

However, communicating the science behind the models and doing this in the right way were what needed to be standardized.

In North Karnataka, this was mitigated by the presence of Suresh and later by Nitin, both of whom personally made sure that quality levels did not dip. In other areas, Sai's regular visits placed some onus on the local teams to hold themselves to the high standards that Agastya had instilled in them during training. However, for Agastya to scale uninhibited, it could not depend on individual efforts. The system itself would need to be so well defined, so unapologetically thorough, that even an instructor left to their own devices for months on end would have no doubt regarding the right way to be doing things.

In 2012, Revathi Narayanan visited the Agastya campus, wholly convinced that it was nothing more than a recreational trip. Her husband, K. G. Narayanan, had formerly been the director of the government's Aeronautical Development Establishment and was a close friend of R. Krishnan. He had been associated with Agastya from as early as 2001 and had even served as a judge at the Anveshana fairs. He was visiting the campus for a meeting, and Revathi had accompanied him intending only to take in the natural beauty of the burgeoning campus and to finish reading a book she had brought along with her.

The meeting that K. G. Narayanan was attending was with Baluragi. A retired physics professor, Baluragi had become associated with Agastya in 2003. A man with a reputation for seemingly limitless energy, Professor Baluragi would travel some 400 kilometers from his hometown in Dharwad to reach the Agastya campus. From the foundation's earliest days, he had been training its teachers and instructors. His impact was almost immediate. His ability to communicate with the new teachers at their level without compromising on content or discipline resonated with Agastya's culture. Besides his animating lectures, Baluragi would go on to produce dozens of science models and experiments at Agastya's VisionWorks, where he also trained a young man named Manjunath Prakash.

Manjunath had joined Agastya in 2003, only a few months after the first mobile lab was launched. He had an MSc in microbiology and was a vital cog in the engine that was Agastya. His involvement extended into nearly every critical project. From starting as an instructor in the first mobile labs, he contributed significantly to the early initiative at Koppal and designed the kits that were sent to Operation Vasantha volunteers across India. Manju, as he is called, possessed a gift for teaching that Ramji describes as "magic," making concepts come alive in a way that other instructors would often try to emulate.

Revathi and Manju connected instantly. When Manju complained that a few instructors who were meant to attend Baluragi's training sessions that day had failed to show up after the first session, Revathi agreed to go and seek them out. Finding the trainees walking about a little aimlessly after having gotten rather lost, Revathi decided to accompany them to their class and observe how things were being done at Agastya.

"Sometimes it is like serendipity," she laughs, showcasing the enviable joy of someone that truly loves what they do. "I had retired from formal work. I have a PhD from the Indian Institute of Science, but I never wanted to work in a lab. I moved into the social sector and was working with women and girls from marginalized communities."

After seeing the session in action, Revathi was intrigued.

"I could not resist, so I asked Krishnan if we could do things a little differently. We decided to put people in groups and encourage participatory training. Somehow this clicked, and at the end of the day my head was full of ideas."

During further discussions with the team, Revathi and Manju highlighted three specific areas that needed to be addressed. The first was an absence of a planned training schedule. Instructors were arriving at random and expecting to be trained. The second was that there were no handbooks or manuals for the instructors to take back and use as a reference. The third concern was that there was effectively a cap on the quality of trainer that Agastya could get, given that salaries were a constraint. Without addressing issues one and two, Agastya was certain to very quickly be sucked into a vicious cycle of instructor quality that it would be difficult to ever escape.

Revathi shared her ideas with Ramji, which she assumed he would reflect on and potentially incorporate as he saw fit. She had every intention of returning to her book as soon as the conversation ended. Instead, she was presented with the counter-suggestion that she herself spearhead the initiative and bring some method to all the madness.

The resulting work would, in many ways, form the backbone of the foundation and be the very platform on which it was able to scale so effectively. Revathi began working with Baluragi and Manju to develop a new system for the teacher training programmes. To get into the mind of an instructor, they brought in Syed Mohammed Peershavali – known to all by his nickname, Sony.

A local from Kuppam town, Sony had joined Agastya in 2009. He had worn multiple hats in Agastya, working as an instructor before joining Baluragi in the teacher training team, and then assisting Manju at VisionWorks. "Sony brought a completely different kind of leadership," Revathi declares. "He is quiet and unassuming, but able to work with everyone across the board. He truly is Agastya's 'Mr. Reliable.'" Sony brought an invaluable on-the-ground perspective to the team's work. One of the things he emphasized right at the beginning was that training must start in the field.

"The reason teachers are first sent into the field is because we want to know whether they are capable of the job or not," Sony stresses. "Else we would be wasting our time. We have seen people get training and then leave [when they realize how difficult field work is]."

The team decided to adopt a three-pronged approach. The first prong was to develop a training and implementation plan that would incorporate the entirety of Agastya's network. The second was to create a framework for the standardization and decentralization of quality. The third was to focus Agastya's force multiplier inwards to create a home-grown army of instructor master trainers (IMTs). An IMT would be an instructor who had been upskilled to impart further training to other instructors. It was a tactic that took a leaf right out of Agastya's peer-to-peer learning approach and generated an appreciable buzz within the instructor groups across the foundation.

The possibility of becoming an IMT carried significant aspirational value to Agastya's teaching staff. However, gaining membership of this exclusive cadre was anything but easy. Given that demand from within the ranks was extremely robust, the instructors were put through a demanding selection process involving written exams in the sciences and in logical thinking. In its first iteration,

120 applied, 81 took the exam and 35 passed it. These 35 would go through a lengthy interview process where they would be evaluated on everything from their knowledge on basic science to their familiarity with the models and the ease with which they could explain a new concept to a child. When it was over, 14 instructors formed the first generation of IMTs. This number would expand to only about 45 by 2021, illustrating the exclusivity that Agastya maintained in its IMT programmes.

The purpose of the IMTs would be to audit classes and provide real-time feedback, much like Sai had been doing, but with the increased frequency and reach that additional resources could provide. In addition, video feedback was used as a powerful tool, as the instructor could see for themselves where they may be going right or wrong. However, the IMTs needed guidelines against which to evaluate the sessions they audited. This was where the framework came in.

Revathi describes the initial discussions around instructor training, which involved a large number of meetings with region heads, midlevel managers and field teams from July to October 2012. She recalls Thiagu's talisman of 'educate, educate, enforce' as being a driving mantra behind getting the buy-in of instructors and really pushing the idea of training as a core requirement across the instructor cadre.

"We started by asking: What does a really good class look like? How long should it be? What are all the things that need to be in it without losing the rigour of the content? We had the curriculum; we had the activities; we had the models. Now the thing was defining the structure. The term 'Super Start' became important."

The fact was that most schools would only offer 120 minutes to Agastya. In these two hours, the instructor needed to maximize impact and engagement. The word most commonly used by children any time they were amazed or excited was 'super.' The Agastya team decided that they needed to start by defining what a 'super class' would look like and see how closely and how consistently they could get their instructors to hit this mark.

The super class contained many elements, all of which were dynamic and would continue to evolve as the team's understanding did. It broke the two-hour time slot into smaller portions and defined a 'super start' and a 'super finish' as bookends. A super start could not be more than ten minutes long, including questions. A super finish could not be more than 15 minutes long and should include a recap. There were specific times allocated for activities and observations and for inquiry-based learning, and buffer time for any supplementary work involved.

To drive the training and quality assurance (TQA) further, Agastya assigned Shrishail Dhanawade to spearhead implementation.

"The main issue was that we work with different languages," he describes. "There were a lot of errors happening when content was being translated from one language to the other. We needed to find a better way to ensure that quality was preserved as content changed."

In order to refine the evaluation process, the Science Learning Observation Schedule (SLOS) was launched.

"We made five buckets: content, pedagogy, child-friendly learning, safety and caring," Shrishail explains. "Each bucket had some seven to eight parameters. It took us 30 to 35 iterations to come to a first-draft SLOS. Then the big task was implementing it. We went around India and observed the engagement of instructors and their performance against the SLOS. Then we would go back after a month or a month and a half and see what improvements there were."

Using the SLOS parameters, the TQA extensively charts how the approach of the instructor must be evaluated. Ratings are given on approachability; relatability of content; the use of simple, child-friendly language; the volume, tone and modulation of the instructor's voice; efforts to include all children; and the use of quantifiable measurements to avoid confusion. Instructors are also gauged on whether they treat the children with empathy and whether they encourage an atmosphere of harmony and respect between the children. Most important – especially for an organization dealing with children – is the rule that instructors will not touch any child unless the child is in some imminent danger or is ill.[2]

"In the early days there was a lot of resistance from older instructors around the extra rigour we were bringing into the whole process," says Shrishail. "But we brought them into the programme and had them do the observations themselves and then use the SLOS to evaluate their own sessions."

Agastya's TQA handbook is fascinating as it shows the extent to which the foundation has gone in defining what a productive teaching session must entail. Early observations of classes threw up a number of areas for improvement. Instructors were spending far too much time introducing Agastya, activities were not always properly linked to concepts, some classes lacked excitement, and girls were often ignored by the instructors and stayed quieter than the boys.

With the TQA and training schedules in place, and IMTs to conduct quality assessments and disseminate feedback, Agastya had finally introduced a corporate-like system to govern instructor management. Over the next three years, the approach was piloted, fine-tuned and rolled out. Eventually, it was formally combined with instructor appraisals so that awareness of and adherence to quality metrics were not merely 'good-to-haves' but essential parts of an instructor's move up the ladder. Agastya would also launch an app to manage its vast instructor network. The app stores data on which schools were visited on which dates, which subjects and topics were covered, and the number of children in each session. The data collected would provide invaluable feedback on reach and coverage and allow for under-serviced areas to be easily mapped.

In many ways, this is similar to the manner in which large corporations gear up for proliferation. The fast-food industry, for example, very efficiently implemented similar frameworks to allow for uniformity across a network of franchises spanning the entire globe. Agastya was doing something similar for education. A fundamental difference, however, was that in the hunger for reach, Agastya was somehow managing to keep its core philosophies extremely well preserved.

Ramji's own perspective on the structure of Agastya's teacher training programme goes beyond the metrics and implementation alone. He describes a philosophy that he believes to be at the core of Agastya's success in developing an army of hungry, motivated instructors.

The single most important thing that Agastya did, according to Ramji, was to create a bond between the instructor in the field and their immediate senior. This view was reinforced by an interesting interaction he once had with a general in the Indian Army.

Ramji was posed a question as to whom the soldier was fighting for when in the thick of battle. Ramji suggested that the soldier, being a patriot, would clearly be fighting for his country. The general, a veteran of the Kargil War, smiled and shook his head, saying this was a romantic thought: when staring down at death, patriotism was not a soldier's most immediate concern.

Ramji then offered that perhaps the soldier was fighting for his friends and family at home.

The general relented slightly, accepting that it was certainly possible that loved ones were on the soldier's mind and that the thought of getting home in one piece might motivate them to fight harder.

At the battle of Gallipoli, Kemal Atatürk is said to have stood sick with a high fever on the battlefield and roared to his soldiers, "Men, I am not ordering you to attack. I am ordering you to die. In the time it takes us to die, other troops and commanders can come and take our places." The sight of their commanding officer pressing them forward – even to certain death – drove the men into a frenzy that eventually won the battle.

Thus, the general concluded, the person that soldiers really fight for is their immediate commanding officer. In the thick of battle, there is no directive soldiers will not follow if they trust the person giving those orders.

This is not a phenomenon restricted to the armed forces. In the corporate world, often, an employee will strive to succeed not for their CEO but for their immediate manager. It is often said that employees don't leave companies, they leave bosses. Conversely, when good managers move on from a company, they usually take a few loyalists with them – those who believe that their careers will be better served under a leader that they trust.

Agastya's ability to instil in its front-line staff a profound feeling of commitment and loyalty to the cause may have benefitted from those staff members' belief in the foundation and indeed its founders. However, Ramji maintains that it was the IMTs and regional leaders who drove this loyalty to create a cadre of self-catalysing change agents on whose efforts Agastya's true impact was ultimately delivered. These agents, in turn, created bonds with the students, thus ensuring that the enthusiasm for learning and innovation remained undiluted across the spectrum of Agastya's delivery mechanisms.

The structure of the TQA along with this trust would ensure that the spirit of Agastya would remain undiminished no matter how far removed from the core Agastya team a location was.

In 2014, the teacher training programme would receive validation of the highest degree. Through Desh Deshpande, Agastya would connect with Sudha Murthy and Narayana Murthy of the Infosys Foundation. Both legends in their own right, they would see Agastya's efforts in teacher training as something worth supporting.

"The biggest bottleneck for developing countries aiming to scale up the process of quality education is the availability of good teachers," says Narayana Murthy, one of India's most respected captains of industry. "The only way you can scale up is by scaling up the training of teachers. I think the beauty of Agastya has been to leverage the power of experimentation to communicate scientific ideas. I can't think of anything better than that. It creates the foundation to enhance the curiosity of children. The result of all that comes when they complete their education, but the initiative has to start today, right at the primary school level."

Being familiar with the challenges of financially sustaining an NGO, Sudha Murty was the first donor to offer Agastya endowment money through the Infosys Foundation. The money continues to be used to fund the education of close to 5,000 teachers from Odisha and Maharashtra each year. The Infosys Science Foundation also supported Agastya to train teachers from Karnataka. Besides the money, the Infosys foundations' engagement with Agastya added significant credibility to Agastya's work with other private and public donors.

The endowment allowed Agastya enough funding to bring teachers to its campus for extended training courses. These could sometimes span three weeks during the school holidays. The range of hands-on labs and materials available on campus provided a rare opportunity for teachers to acquire new skills and knowledge that they could then take back to their schools. The interactive training programmes emphasized learning content through teaching-learning methods. Equally important, the campus instilled in the teachers an appreciation for the environment and the joys of caring for it. So highly prized would a visit to campus become that, going forward, teachers who had had the good fortune of visiting it would refer to themselves as 'Kuppam Returned.'

"I'm leaving this place with a heavy heart but feel happy that I got such a once-in-a-lifetime experience," one government schoolteacher's testimony says of their time on campus. Another says: "We did the activities by 'learning by doing methods,' which enhanced the utility of this training programme. Most of the training I attended elsewhere was only lecture-based, chalk and talk. This training was unique."

While teacher training flourished on campus, the team in North Karnataka was continuing to innovate new methods to improve teacher quality.

Babitha Rajashekhar, who joined in 2015 and rose to become a regional manager, was put in charge of the Acharya Initiative, which looked at teacher training in the districts of North Karnataka. Ramji credits her for taking a leaf out of K. V. Raghavan's earliest suggestions to emulate a teaching hospital model (*see Chapter 3*). Babitha began engaging B.Ed college students and involving them in hands-on training workshops. The YuvAcharya (Yuv = Young, Acharya = teacher) programme, as it was coined, was a tremendous success.

However as always, Agastya ensured that it was the end customer – the child – who provided the ultimate appraisal.

"I asked a group of students, on a sunny afternoon in a government school in North Bangalore, why they came to Agastya," describes Ramji. "'Because,' they said, 'Agastya's science models and experiments are better and more fun to learn with than our textbooks.' 'Okay,' I replied, 'I will give your school a set of models. Will you still come to Agastya?' After the students exchanged a few whispers, a girl said, 'We will, because Agastya's teachers have been trained to make the models come alive in the classroom.' 'Alright, we will train your teachers,' I countered. 'Will you still come?' The girl spoke again after consulting her friends. 'Yes, we will still come to Agastya.' Intrigued, I asked her why. 'Because the Agastya teacher treats us like a friend,' she replied."

Although Agastya had always maintained the importance of teacher training, the TQA illustrated how seriously the foundation was looking at this aspect of education.

In 2016, Agastya would host the Maverick Teachers Global Summit at its campus. Some 70 teachers from around the world would congregate at the campus to share thoughts and methods with one another. Gavin Dykes, programme director of the Education World Forum, was the compere at the summit. He had connected with Agastya when he heard Ramji giving a speech in Delhi a few years prior.

"In one of the initial discussions, an Indian teacher stood up and asked why we were using English as the language of communication," he recalls. "It was an interesting point; it helped to challenge the mindset. I think India is at a very interesting point. I've been coming to India for close to 20 years and I've worked with schools up and down the country. There was a lot of old-fashioned thinking. It was stuck. The distance that India has travelled in this time is remarkable. The education plans that were put in place have been excellent. It's interesting to think what the ambition for Agastya should be. Measuring it in numbers is maybe not the best way. Measuring it as a movement is probably a better way to look at it."

1.   The Mimosa Pudica, whose leaves fold in when touched.

2.   Initial findings saw that while instructors were fine to engage physically with boys – which might include a tussling of the hair or a pat on the back – they could not act in a similar manner with girls. The solution, of course, was to encourage equality by ceasing all physical contact whatsoever. It may seem an obvious measure to most, but in a culture where gender equality is rarely addressed – especially in rural areas – it was an important distinction that needed to be hard-coded into the TQA.

CHAPTER 12

EVOLVING FOR TRUST

In a country like India, trust is, somewhat understandably, at a premium. Many different arguments exist for why this might be. You could blame centuries of oppression as having imparted a status quo of constant suspicion among people. Or, you could point to a rigid social system that has promoted hierarchies and thereby hard-coded a me-first attitude in individuals. Post-independence, the chasm between the haves and have-nots only widened, further reinforcing people's instinct for self-preservation. Meanwhile, an arduously slow judicial system eroded any belief that conflicts could be quickly resolved and that the genuinely afflicted might see justice in their lifetimes. Whatever the reasons might be, India's move from a low-trust to a high-trust society is likely to take decades more.

This lack of trust generally requires everyone to keep their cards close to their chest and remain, by default, sceptical of the intentions of others.

Breathing life into a charitable organization within this system is therefore an undeniably difficult task. For one, the stereotypically murky perception of an NGO as being some kind of front for a nefarious undertaking needs to be overcome. It doesn't help that even genuinely altruistic, well-meaning organizations often fall short of maintaining proper standards of accountability.

As someone who has engaged in philanthropy for over three decades, Narayana Murthy laments the fact that much of the Indian non-profit space has still not reached the levels of transparency needed to inspire confidence in donors: "One of the good things about the corporate world – particularly the listed corporations – is that we have a mechanism that forces transparency in terms of performance," He explains. "There is a very simple and straightforward number that tells us whether a corporation is doing well or not and that is EPS [earnings per share]. Everybody understands it. But in the case of the non-profit world, somehow in India we have still not come to a mechanism whereby we can say 'this NGO is doing well' or 'this NGO is not doing well.' So many NGOs that I have contributed to, they don't send me any information on what objectives they have taken up, how much money has been used for each of those, what is the overhead, what is the next year's target, what new things they want to take up. That is simply not there in the mindset of the non-profit."

By instilling an airtight corporate culture from day one, Agastya was certainly able to break free from this perception. Considering the founding team members had all been exposed to a variety of organizational structures, the requisite that no number could be left unexplained was an obvious one from the beginning. Consequently, Agastya usually found donors pleasantly surprised when metrics – such as cost per interaction, operational expenses, and capital outlays – were readily and regularly submitted. Agastya's ten-year plans, which were updated each year and presented at board meetings, provided a forward-thinking roadmap. All this allowed for resource planning and quantifiable feedback that matched anything seen in the corporate sphere.

Internally, these numbers are just as important to the core team, as they allow them to compare the costs across programmes, assess project effectiveness and create more robust projections. Board meetings are usually intense, spanning many hours. They focus both on the subjective aims of Agastya and on specific metrics that tell a deeper story about where the foundation is headed financially.

Amit Chandra, who along with his wife Archana and close friend Anuj Bhagwati co-founded the A. T. E. Chandra Foundation, has spent more than his fair share of time thinking about the hurdles of professional reporting in the non-profit space. As the chairperson of Bain Capital's India office, Chandra is a bit of an anomaly within the business world.

Considering Chandra is known for his intention to give away a significant majority of his income to social causes, you could comfortably see him as deeply charitable. While he does admit that many NGOs do fall short of providing the right feedback to their donors, he believes that this can be alleviated if the organizations are provided with the right guidance.

"Social challenges are far more intimidating than corporate challenges," he postulates. "These are challenges that have been shaped by societal issues over decades or even centuries. In my mind the ecosystem has simply not been developed to support solutioning, and adequate investments have simply not been made in organizations to go out and solve these problems. If you want to see high-quality measurement and impact, the question to ask is: are you actually willing to fund that? It takes a high-quality team if you want comparable results to what you get in a corporate audit function. What kind of resources does a CFO have in an NGO? I think these comparisons are therefore unfair. If you see the Agastya journey, many of these reporting mechanisms were evident in the early stages and some were capabilities that Ramji built over time. I think that's what endeared Agastya to many people in its impressive roster of backers."

Indeed, the challenges for managing a social organization like Agastya go well beyond the numbers alone. The scale, while impressive, often masks the complexity of managing the sheer diversity of stakeholders including children, parents, teachers, headmasters, educators, government officials, politicians and social investors. This, combined with an unpredictable cash flow makes managing Agastya in many ways far more challenging and complex than running a corporation. It requires no small measure of mental agility and adaptability. Ramji, Mahavir, Thiagu, Sai and Hari had to learn to blend their corporate skills with the new social-entrepreneurial skills needed to succeed in the social world. In the excellent book *Uncommon Sense, Common Nonsense,* Jules Goddard and Tony Eccles say, "Success flows to those firms that authentically operate an idiosyncratic, self-discovered and coherent belief system."[1]

By Ramji's own admission, Agastya's aim was to shape exactly this kind of success. The belief system was that for an NGO to mature into an institution and then into a movement that would stand the test of time, it needed to break free of small-business mentalities and practices that may have served it well at the start. At the same time, much of the flavour that drives innovation can easily be sucked away by over-reporting, corporate hierarchies, and ivory tower management. An equilibrium exists between these two extremes and Agastya appeared to have found a way to position itself at exactly the right spot so that both donors and stakeholders were effectively managed. Ramji highlights the key elements for this as being a scaling mindset, a collegiate style of management, rapid decision making, a bias for action, an obsessive focus on quality and innovation, and a spirit of caring and trust.

While trust among its benefactors was built via professionalism and stringent adherence to financial best practices, trust within Agastya's own organization needed to be a far more nuanced affair.

Speak with any Agastya employee and the words 'trust' and 'freedom' pop up with heart-warming consistency.

The founders always understood that these elements were fundamental in nurturing a team of self-starters and kindling a sense of ownership of Agastya's successes and failures. Further, any joy around learning that Agastya hoped to inculcate in children would ultimately be an outright reflection of what the staff and teachers themselves felt.

A fragment of this ethos was apparent right from the time a new employee walked in for an interview. In a number of cases, there was no role on offer. High-level appointees – including Ajith Basu, Nitin Desai, Hariharan Ganesan and Sai Chandrasekhar – recall being told that there was nothing specific that they could be hired for, but that they should join nonetheless. The founders and Thiagu believed that proactive, hungry individuals would invariably discover what was missing from the existing structure and set about making it right. Time and again, they were proven right.

Building the organization around the strengths of the individual as opposed to the other way around would bring an extreme resilience to Agastya. Unusual backgrounds encourage diversity, which in turn instils plasticity and leads to what Ramji refers to as 'adaptive intelligence.'

However, to push this belief into reality, a lot of freedom needed to be allowed for. Ramji was notorious for encouraging free-thinking, expansive ideas that might or might not work. This was a mindset that was complemented by Thiagu, while Mahavir – ever the pragmatist – kept a firm eye on the finances so that runaway experiments did not prove unmanageably expensive. As the primary operating heads Sai and Hari were the bridges – unafraid to challenge the founders and Thiagu with alternative ideas and, at the same time, open to radically new possibilities. This balance allowed new thoughts and methods to flourish from all corners of the foundation at a tempered pace. Most importantly, failure was rarely reprimanded but rather treated as a teachable experience that could perhaps do without repetition.

"Every year I would try four or five new things and it was always well received by the management," says Dilip Kumar, who after starting out assisting Suresh in North Karnataka was made a regional manager. "There is a freedom for us to experiment and interact with people. I can directly call Ramji and Thiagu and Mahavir. The comfort level in Agastya is because higher-ups come and speak with all the staff."

"Ramji is a heart person," professes Nitin. "He doesn't do it knowingly, but he connects with people. The trust and the space I got were amazing. The backing for anything new that had to be done was given with so much confidence."

The importance of communication and respect for employees had been made clear to Ramji in his days at Citibank. He recalled a junior colleague sounding elated because Citibank's chair, the legendary Walter Wriston, had called on him for some advice on a specialized area that the colleague had recently been working on. The short call had provided the colleague with a morale boost that appeared to last for years.

That the mission must be familiar to all was another deeply ingrained idea. "When I was working for Citibank, Antonia Shusta, our division executive remarked that she would know we were on the right track if the office janitor could explain our mission," Ramji says. "This stuck with me. I worked hard to ensure that Agastya's mission was clear, inspiring and, most importantly, easily understood by everyone from the cleaner to the bus driver."

Regular and intensive calls between senior management and staff showcase the authenticity of this belief.

In these calls, the core team would reach out to staff, instructors, front-line workers and even the janitorial staff on campus to guarantee that the vision was communicated and that no one was omitted from the Agastya journey. Ramji makes frequent and usually unannounced calls to Agastya's mobile lab drivers and instructors. Besides testing their understanding of Agastya's mission, he spends time asking about their family, and encourages them to ask him questions and suggest ideas. After one such call Ramji learned from an instructor's colleague that an instructor who had decided to leave Agastya was so moved to tears by an unexpected call from Ramji that he decided not to leave.

The benefit of inquiry-based brainstorming was hard-coded into all modes of communication within the organization. The management believed that open-minded curiosity was as vital to their own interactions with staff as it was to the children that Agastya was reaching. The curiosity conversations that Ramji looked for with external thought leaders (see *Chapter 9*) were equally important between key personnel within Agastya. They ensured that ideas were disseminated internally with the same fervour as they were in the field. Sai began exploring the technique of question storming, which he began to encourage among Agastya's managers and instructors. The group starts with a statement or topic that it wants to pursue and discusses it threadbare through questions only (no answers!). Such counter-intuitive thinking techniques are important to get employees to learn to deeply question; to see that the superior or best answer often lies in the quality of questions that one learns to pose. This is an approach that runs counter to existing answer-based methods of analysis.

Agastya's innovative engine – including the framing of its unique mission of Aah! Aha! and Ha-ha! – has in no small measure benefitted from such question-oriented approaches.

Board meetings and management calls promoted candour and encouraged contradiction from all corners, no matter the seniority of the person voicing the opinion. Some of these calls show that despite Ramji's growing aura as a leading voice and thought leader in the global education space, staff were never reticent in pointing out improvement areas even for him.

"People are afraid to sit near him because he will assign them new projects," laments one employee in an excerpt from a staff call in 2021. Another says, "Ramji needs to restart asking 'What's new?' again! Ramji used to do this all the time in the past, so we were on our guard and always ready with an answer – it helped fuel innovation."

Some of the comments can even seem somewhat harsh, if you ignore the fact that they were spoken by staunch Agastya loyalists. One person says, "Ramji needs to make people feel free to come and talk to him about their problems and not react immediately." Another muses, "Staff wonder if Ramji's visions are practical and achievable – he needs to simplify and demonstrate 'actionable items.'" A third opines that "Sai is very focused on data and numbers – he intimidates the centre in-charge." However, others felt his candid feedback methods had helped them to grow immeasurably. Some said Agastya was losing its core identity by "corporatizing," while some others felt it needed to look more like a corporate. A manager likened Agastya to be playing a long-haul cricket test match, but with a frenzied T20 approach!

The senior team believes that it is exactly this ability to extract honesty that ultimately preserves trust and drives success. "The secret to an organization's culture and, therefore, its success or failure, can be inferred from the content and nature of interactions among its people," Ramji says. "Very few management books give you an insider's view and insight into these conversations."

The management's ability to hear these critiques and act dispassionately to make amends was also picked up by the staff. The same staff calls also threw up opinions such as "Management expresses gratitude to all employees – it has trust and faith in employees"; "There is equal treatment of everyone, freedom and responsibility. Management treats people with humanity – it takes ideas from anyone"; and "Management made us feel that we – each and every employee responsible – owned Agastya."

Fostering freedom – of both action and speech – went hand in hand with encouraging respect. Like in the case of Jayamma, who believed she was unqualified to work at Agastya and yet went on to expand the Operation Vasantha project exponentially (see *Chapter 10*), the seniors at Agastya were always concerned that women employees should feel safe within whichever role they chose to pursue.

Sridevi M., who joined Agastya in 2013, reflects on this: "Even though I was the first woman mobile lab instructor, I never felt any difference within the organization. Even though I had to travel a lot, I love to travel, so it was good."

In the earliest days, when the labs were still simple and few, Chayya Devi – who presently manages the Innovation Hub and VisionWorks on campus – remembers doing some chemistry experiments out of the biology lab: "Ramji was showing visitors around and he asked me what I would like. I said I would like a chemistry lab and three years later the lab was ready. The fact that management takes us so seriously and values us makes a lot of difference."[2]

Ramji would maintain that in this particular case, a chemistry lab was already on the cards. However, the incident highlights that management was thinking and moving in the same direction as the team thought necessary. This alignment in ideals and agenda only ever manifests in organizations where stakeholders actively listen to one another, no matter how candid, provocative or even toxic these discussions might sometimes be. It is little surprise that Agastya has been certified as a Great Place to Work® since 2019.

———————————

The most valuable by-product of the freedom that Agastya infused into its people was innovation. Most importantly, offering employees the chance to try, fail and try again without penalty brought about a self-sustaining culture of inquiry and problem-solving that began to pull the foundation forward in ways that surpassed even the founders' outlandish ambitions.

Vinay Dabholkar, who has co-authored the book "8 Steps To Innovation: Going From Jugaad To Excellence" and works in the field of creativity and design thinking, recalls his initial encounter with Agastya. He describes the foundation as a genuine 'sandbox.'

"I didn't have too much exposure to experiments in the educational field," says Dabholkar, who since 2011 has also been a visiting faculty at the Indian Institute of Management in Bangalore. One of the things we were writing about is called a 'sandbox,' where you take an idea and run with it, setting a few constraints without necessarily knowing the outcome. I had not seen too many sandboxes, even in corporate settings. Agastya had constraints about education, but they had also taken a position on creativity, and they also had constraints on cost and the fact that the experiments needed to be low cost and easy to move."

As with the children that Agastya was reaching, anecdotal episodes around the staff members' own remarkable exploits were cropping up with regularity. This underlined the drive and can-do spirit that were becoming habitual across the organization.

When Agastya was looking to expand into the state of Maharashtra, it was able to get the Indian conglomerate Larsen & Toubro (L&T) to sign off on a single mobile science lab. The catch was that L&T gave the foundation only ten days to execute the project. K. R. Ranganathan, who joined Agastya in 2012, was entrusted to deliver the project within the stipulated timeline.

"L&T wanted to have a mobile van in Ahmednagar in Maharashtra," he recounts of the incident that made him the gold standard for meeting deadlines within Agastya. "We had to procure a vehicle, get it registered and send it back to Bangalore for retrofitting. I was sitting with the fabricator for three days to get the work done. Both welding and fitting work needed to be done. There were a lot of mosquitoes! After retrofitting, the van had to be sent to the campus to load with the models. We took two Hindi-speaking instructors from campus and drove non-stop overnight to Ahmednagar. The L&T team was very impressed and then the mobile science lab programme took off in Maharashtra."

A. M. Naik, the legendary chair Emeritus of L&T, India's largest infrastructure company, was very taken by Ramji when they first met. He was especially appreciative of the fact that Ramji had chosen to give up a life in England to come and make a difference in India. A staunch patriot and a titan of industry, Naik now spends a significant portion of his time on philanthropy. "My grandfather spent a lot of time in tribal villages, working for their betterment," Naik recollects of his inspiration to actively involve himself in charity. "From when I was ten years' old, I would accompany him to the Adivasi colonies. He would go and sit in the veranda of one of the houses and children would surround him. He would distribute peppermints to all the children. It was his selflessness that motivates me even today."

"Two things always bothered me about education in rural India," Naik articulates. "There is no equipment in the schools, and where were they going to get good teachers from? When Ramji explained the van to me, I said I would buy it and if it was any good, I would get L&T to buy it for every location. I felt it was good, so we now have 11 or 12 mobile labs." (An amusing story often told in Agastya was of an early visit to a school, where the principal declared that they had no need for Agastya's models, as the school had already installed models of their own. When the Agastya team asked whether they could see the models, the principal proudly showed them a glass cabinet within which the somewhat expensive models had been perfectly preserved behind lock and key, with no child or teacher ever having the opportunity to interact with them.)

Agastya's ability to innovate and wring results from limited inputs was already evident from the Koppal and North Karnataka experiences. However, they were determined to hardwire this into the organization so that every employee would function and approach tasks with the mindset of a social entrepreneur.

The period between 2012 and 2018 saw a slew of breakthroughs in Agastya's dissemination methods. Key among these was an award-winning delivery system borne out of a cultural problem identified when the mobile science labs were first launched. The unspoken class divide between a driver and an instructor was proving frustrating, as combining the roles would significantly reduce Agastya's labour costs for running a single mobile lab. Compounding this was that schools would not afford a driver the same respect as they would a 'proper' teacher. In other words, neither upskilling a driver nor convincing a teacher to shoulder the driver's role seemed like viable options given the current mindsets in place.

Around the same time, Agastya independently piloted a programme called the Lab-in-a-Box, or LiB. It consisted of ten boxes with miniaturized models, each box addressing a set of different science concepts. A box would be given to a school and periodically rotated among them. It was a way to lower the cost per interaction and allow even the smallest of schools – where mobile science labs would not necessarily have the critical mass needed for a visit – access to Agastya's models.

The solution to the instructor–driver problem was a masterpiece of lateral thinking that Thiagu is credited with having struck upon. The LoB – or Lab-on-a-Bike – was launched in 2012 by mounting the LiBs onto the sides of a motorbike and letting a single instructor ride across the countryside to conduct sessions at different schools. The perception of riding a bike was not the same as that of driving a van. Instead, it made the instructor seem 'cool' and added a sense of panache to the way they entered the school compound. The LoB completely negated the stigma that otherwise prevented the roles of driver and instructor from being combined.

The LoB became an instant hit. Among its advantages was the fact that the cost per interaction was far lower compared with that of the mobile science labs. Further, the LoB could pierce much further into rural areas than the mobile science labs could, often traversing unpaved narrow routes to reach the smallest of schools in the remotest of locations. While Agastya's fleet of mobile labs continued to roam denser regions, expansion into the further reaches of India would be done using the cheaper, more agile LoBs.

In 2014 Agastya decided to compete in the Google Global Impact Challenge. The proposal submitted was the TechLaBike, a name coined by Thiagu. The TechLaBike combined the LoB's activity-based learning with digital literacy by adding a laptop and targeting both students and teachers.

At 4 am while on a fund-raising trip to Boston, Ramji was sound asleep when the ringing of his phone awoke him. At the other end, barely able to contain her excitement, was Janani Subramanian, the TechLaBike product manager. Excitedly, she informed Ramji, "We have won the Google award!"

Apart from the LoB, the LiB and the TechLaBike, Agastya would launch a range of other initiatives, each with differing levels of success and sustainability. Chief among these were the Lab-on-a-Tab, a digital lab loaded on tablets and distributed to schools, and the Maja Box, a small collection of experiments in a compact case that primary school kids could take home to play with.

Overall, this was a time of immense abundance, successfully melding both heart and originality of thought. It was as though in spreading creativity across the country, Agastya had itself become irrevocably drenched in its own philosophy. The resulting slew of innovations was an almost predictable outcome of the culture and sense of purpose that the foundation had managed to instil.

Dirk Smit, vice president and chief scientist at Shell, had partnered with Agastya to launch a LoB programme on the outskirts of Bangalore. He was fascinated by what he saw in Agastya: "One thing that I like is that in order to foster creativity, people need to work in teams; they need diversity of thought. That is something that Agastya has built in. The other thing is that it needs to be fun. The whole stifling culture of rote learning is not helping. Creativity is very important in any science. The more you get, the more you see the right people coming out of education systems. Also, the courage to propose something different is something that children need to be encouraged to have. This is what Agastya is doing – pushing for the 'Aha!' moment."

The foundation's success in infusing curiosity into its every fibre was also observed by Soumitra Bhattacharya, who at the time was president of the Bosch Group in India. Bosch's innovations, he had told Ramji, sprang from its excellent process management systems. He remarked that Agastya's strength was its unique hands-on learning culture and its emphasis on curiosity.

"We decided there was a benefit in working together," says Ramji. Bosch, a major corporate and social responsibility partner of Agastya, would train Agastya's staff on process management and Agastya would help Bosch to spark curiosity among its staff.

By 2014, the pieces were all in place. With the TQA (training and quality assurance) handbook (see *Chapter 11*) as its backbone, a young and motivated cadre of staff free from legacy thinking, and an enviable range of dissemination methods and channels, Agastya was ready to launch itself on a national scale.

Shiv Kumar Chaudhary was entrusted with the regions of Delhi, Haryana, Madhya Pradesh, Rajasthan, Uttarakhand and Uttar Pradesh. The beginnings were relatively humble, with about four or five science centres and around 15 mobile science labs to start with.

"It was a very challenging situation," says Chaudhary of the initial years. He had a background in quality control and wanted to bring these elements into Agastya. "Things were not very organized, and there was also some amount of groupism. We had to bring people together and make them understand that we were working for a cause using the money given to us by others."

Like in North Karnataka, Agastya needed to use a variety of methods to win over local authorities and convince schools of its value. The difference here, of course, was that unlike in North Karnataka, Agastya was entering a new space without the government's express involvement or support.

When the foundation received funding for a mobile lab from Blue Dart, it was told that the lab needed to be run only in Delhi. However, operating in Delhi required special permissions and Agastya had little or no influence with the local governments in the north.

"I started exploring how we could get past this," Chaudhary describes. "A couple of my cousins were teaching in government schools, and they said to forget it as I would not even be allowed inside the Deputy Director of Education office. I went anyway, thinking, 'What is the worst that can happen?' I met the head of the office, and she was very happy to see the Agastya card. She was an ex-science teacher and was so delighted. In front of me she called her boss and asked him to speak with me. I met her boss the next day and she too was delighted. She asked me to submit a file for approval, which I submitted the next day. We didn't hear back for a month. Eventually, Ramji approached Akshaya Patra to ask if they could provide a connection. Some time later, I got a call and was asked to come immediately to Delhi.

We had received permission. Eventually we had more than 22 projects in Delhi."

The tendency to push forward with impunity, knowing that a worthy cause deserved nothing less, appeared to have rubbed off from the founders and onto Agastya's many employees and volunteers. Within two years, the North India operations would expand to the extent that they needed to be split into North One and North Two.

Mukesh Kumar, a graduate of Azim Premji University, would join Agastya in 2016 and be given North Two to manage. A native of Patna, in Bihar, Mukesh was especially passionate about extending Agastya's involvement to the east of India. As new operations flourished in Bihar and Jharkhand, Mukesh would guide their implementation.

As demanding as the expansion in North India was, Agastya strode forth with confidence, no longer the fledgling charitable venture it had once been. The foundation now had a brand, an enviable track record, robust systems and even a heap of guerrilla-style best practices gleaned from its early triumphs in the south. These best practices would continue to be vital, as even a professional organization like Agastya was not immune to the mercurial nature of local educational and government bodies. Every rollout required its own tailored approach. Having implemented programmes in multiple areas, the Agastya teams had become adept at concocting the exact formula that would work in any given setting. As a result, the rollout in the north was far more surgical than the one in the south had been, its build-up measurably more structured.

While on a visit to Jodhpur, Ramji recollects a rather interesting series of events that culminated in Agastya launching its operations in the fabled city:

On the road from the airport to my hotel, I asked the driver if there was a government school on the way that I might see. Ten minutes later he pulled over near a handsome building made of Jodhpur stone.

The principal was taken aback by my uninvited presence, but warmed after hearing about Agastya's work and suggested that I should meet the children. Most of them, he said, were children of labourers, stonecutters and security guards. I was introduced to a boy, Himanshu, 13 years old and the son of a labourer, who the principal proudly announced as 'the smartest kid in the class.' Never one to be impressed by the traditional definition of a 'smart kid,' I asked Himanshu, 'Where do you see science?' 'Science is here,' he said, pointing to a creaking ceiling fan, 'and here,' pointing to a small piece of chalk, and 'here,' pointing to his body. He turned his head towards the trees and plants outside in the yard and beyond and said, 'There is science there.' Startled by his insightful response, I asked him what he wanted to be. 'An army officer,' he replied. 'Great. I am sure you will become a general,' I said to spontaneous giggles and laughter.

I told the children about a study in the US that had measured the performance of children who had learned to play a musical instrument. The students in the study had been divided into three groups: the A group aspired to be musicians, the B group said they would play a instrument through secondary school and the C group said they would play it through primary school. Neither innate talent nor hours of practice seemed to explain the marked difference in performance between the children in the A group (who performed the best) and those in the B and C groups. 'What was the missing factor?' I asked the class. Silence. And then,

Himanshu spoke. 'It's inner confidence.' 'Aah!' I exclaimed, 'Almost right. It was confidence that came from an ignited personal vision leading to a long-term commitment to be a musician.'

Quite a remarkable boy, Himanshu, I thought to myself – a perfect candidate for Agastya's Young Instructor Leader programme. If only Agastya had a programme in Jodhpur, hundreds of kids like Himanshu might find expression for their precocity.

Ten months later, on a refreshingly cool morning in December 2017, His Highness the Maharaja of Jodhpur Gaj Singh – affectionately called Baapji – inaugurated Agastya's mobile science lab at the Government Girls School in BJS Colony, Jodhpur. The children and staff were visibly excited to have their esteemed Baapji visit their school. Under a white pandal[3] in the schoolyard, Baapji looked curiously at the dynamic and colourful hands-on models and experiments on display. Young girls freely asked him questions before they confidently explained the science behind the experiments.

In my speech to the children, teachers and government officials who had gathered, I recalled my inspirational meeting with Himanshu and Mr Vyas, his principal. I said that Himanshu had truly fired up Agastya to come to Jodhpur. Sporting a tuft on a full head of coal-black hair, Himanshu – a special guest and the only boy present at the BJS School – walked up to the dais and shyly acknowledged the cheers of the girls and teachers. As he graciously welcomed Agastya to his city, Baapji lauded Himanshu and remarked that there were assuredly many more Himanshus in Jodhpur. The newspapers mentioned Himanshu's catalytic role in bringing the mobile science lab to Jodhpur – a mobile science lab that would reach 3,500 children every year. I met Himanshu a few months ago in Jodhpur and offered to support him with an Agastya YIL scholarship. His goal is to complete his university degree and join the civil services.

If there was a concern at this point, it was only this: how large could Agastya grow before the personal touch that made it so successful would succumb to its size?

In his pathbreaking book *The Tipping Point*, Malcolm Gladwell refers to Dunbar's number.[4] Often rounded to 150, the number describes the point beyond which a social structure begins to fall apart. Within this number, teams or societies have personal connects that allow for quicker decision-making, fewer misunderstandings and a transactive – or joint – memory. As the number increases, the group begins to fray, factions are formed, and the camaraderie and interpersonal connections that aided cohesion slowly evaporate. It is a phenomenon often observed in large corporations that seemingly lose their initial spark once they grow beyond a point.

By 2016, Agastya was at a stage where such issues should have been regularly cropping up. With over 600 staff and 300 OV teachers spread across the country, all signs suggested that Dunbar's number had long been surpassed. More challenging was that managing Agastya required significant fluidity. The daily movement in remote areas of a large proportion of its staff, called for more management bandwidth than, say, handling 10 or 20 times the number of employees concentrated in urban centres.

Yet, cases to support the idea that Agastya was buckling under its own weight were few and far between. Agastya's management were well aware of the perils of oversized teams. Sai, in particular, had been actively breaking groups to conform to Dunbar's number.

Tadashi Tokieda makes a remarkable observation on Agastya's ability to adroitly balance its growth. A mathematics professor at Stanford University, Tadashi is an interesting man, to put it most mildly. He started out as a child prodigy artist whose paintings were exhibited in a major gallery in Tokyo when he was only five years old. Later, he moved to France on his own at age 14 and began a journey as a philologist.[5] Moving from languages to science, he studied biology and physics. Then, after coming across a maths problem that flummoxed him, he took it upon himself to master the subject. He was told that in order to fully comprehend the maths problem that he was unable to solve, he would need to refer to a textbook that contained a specific proof. The complication was that the textbook was in Russian. So, Tadashi learned Russian. This remarkable and rather roundabout journey resulted in him settling on mathematics as his subject of choice. Here too, however, he had a thirst for the unconventional, and this saw him start collecting and then creating toys to explain various phenomena in math and physics. Tadashi's toys, as they are called, are fascinating items whose behaviour – much like the tippe top – forces the observer's curiosity to be instantly sparked. Tadashi's videos on YouTube mathematically explore a range of everyday concepts and have garnered millions of views.

"My job is to supply a sustainable level of 'Aah,'" jokes Tadashi. "The best scientists in history were precisely that because they looked for surprises."

Tadashi had connected with Ramji via a meeting arranged by John Coates at the University of Cambridge. Tadashi had spent a significant amount of time studying and appreciating Agastya's models – whose purpose very much mirrored the toys he invented. A polymath, deeply invested in understanding different methods of education, his perspective on Agastya's growth is fascinating. He first draws out the contrast between the macro and the micro in any large-scale undertaking by recalling his experience as a volunteer in South Africa at the peak of the AIDS epidemic.

"I was helping in running a nursery school for HIV-positive babies," he says. "At that time, some statistics were saying that 25% of women were HIV positive. Many were saying that they were past the point of no return. I am a mathematician, and I am very sensitive to statistics. In a way the government has to stick to the statistics, but it is tough to ignore the individual issues."

Tadashi observed that while at the macro level, the government was forced to steer itself using statistics, at the micro level, each case was heart-breaking, even if statistically it might be considered insignificant. Hence, successes at the macro level, which may be assessed by looking at the overall percentages, may still see many failures at the micro level.

The disconnection between micro and macro can also be seen in education.

"It is possible to argue that what a state or educational establishment can do is to play the statistical game and ensure everyone learns the basics of arithmetic and geometry. I call this 'crossing the desert.' But the oasis you may encounter is in no one's control. It's pure chance."

Tadashi believes that Agastya is somehow bridging this gap between the micro and macro and operating in a sort of hybrid zone – or, as he has coined it, a 'mezzo zone.' By creating pockets of ownership across the country and by imbibing the regional heads with the freedom to use Agastya's framework and to execute as they see fit, Agastya has been able to scale across India while still ensuring that each child and teacher receives the same enlightened experience as those who visited its campus. Meanwhile, events, such as the science fairs, have brought people in from across the country and reignited friendships and familiarity. Ramji compares these fairs to the great hunts organized by Genghis Khan. Large expansive congregations of key members who are aligned to a common – even arduously challenging – cause tend to catalyse camaraderie, which lingers long after the event itself concludes.

Finally, the TQA has allowed for Agastya's message – which, far from being mired in stasis, has instead ever evolved and updated itself – to be regularly communicated across the instructor network.

"How do you operate between micro and macro?" Tadashi asks rhetorically. "It is not always possible. But there is something like mezzo. Agastya is managing to expand in a macro way, but within the micro level. This is mezzo."

1. An extension to the chemistry lab was later funded by Thiagu's family and formally launched in early 2023.

2. Jules Goddard and Tony Eccles, *Uncommon Sense, Common Nonsense* (London: Profile Books, 2013), p. 55.

3. A temporary covering/structure to shield from the sun.

4. Malcolm Gladwell, *The Tipping Point* (London: Abacus, 2001).

5. Someone who studies ancient languages. It is said that Tadashi speaks seven languages, but he will say that this is untrue – not because he cannot speak these languages, but because he believes that you cannot truly claim to know a language unless you have lived and loved in that language.

CHAPTER 13

THE NUMBERS GAME

When the developed and developing economies are compared, the capacity and indeed the impetus for charitable giving display a deep contrast. In the US, for example, the per capita contributions to charities are in the range of $1,500, or roughly 2% of GDP. In India, the figure is a forgivably more sedate 0.5% of GDP. However, the purpose of charitable giving is also vastly different. Indian households give roughly two thirds of their donations to religion, while in the developed world the distribution is spread more evenly.

The idea that religion should command the lion's share of charity in India is not particularly astonishing. Faith plays a major role in the lives of many Indians, and for most it is a haven of last resort. Even for the wealthy, however, religion offers a return on investment – in the form of acquired blessings and good karma – that other causes cannot claim to be able to deliver.

Agastya confronted this reality early in its journey. As already described, donations towards education lagged because poverty, nutrition and healthcare represented 'here and now' urgencies that education could never compete with. But, in addition to this, any marginal propensity to donate was usually dominated by contributions to any of India's myriad temples and spiritual institutions.

In 2013, the landscape of charity in India was seismically altered. As mentioned in *Chapter 11*, the Corporate Social Responsibility (CSR) Bill, which came into effect that year, specified that companies with over 5 crore rupees ($625,000) in net profits would need to spend 2% of their average net profits made during the preceding three years on CSR initiatives. The Bill turned what had hitherto been an admittedly ad hoc approach by corporates to charity into an obligatory exercise.

Harsh Mariwala, whose Marico Innovation Foundation does exemplary work in the fields of both innovation and mental health,[1] reflects on the Bill's introduction and on the impact that it had on corporates such as Marico: "For an organization like us, we were already doing a substantial part of CSR. I know corporates that were resistant, but I personally think it was a good thing, that corporates should add value to society. A lot of how they execute will depend on their own convictions."

Hariharan Ganesan had joined Agastya that same year (see *Chapter 11*) and saw the CSR Bill as a tremendous opportunity to create a framework around fundraising.

"When CSR happened, it accelerated the model for Agastya," he says. "There were organizations that had been involved in charity for a very long time, but a lot of them were doing it within their own foundations and they wanted total control over the work and reach. A lot of multi-national corporations had also been doing charity but were very focused on their own areas. The CSR law changed the scenario and made it mandatory and forced many organizations to look beyond their own space and seek out foundations like Agastya."

Hari's belief was hardly misplaced. The Bill not only pushed companies to start streamlining their charitable efforts but also proposed that anyone donating more than 1 crore rupees ($125,000) needed to get a third-party impact assessment done of the organization that they intended to support.

As Warren Buffett is widely reputed to say, "You only find out who is swimming naked when the tide goes out."

The murky, unstructured NGO space in India, which had steadily been becoming synonymous with underhand dealings, was forced to confront this new normal. Many name-only charities found that accessing this potentially vast reservoir of corporate wealth would require a track record in reporting standards that they simply did not possess.

Agastya, on the other hand, welcomed this new era. Years of effort in professionalizing and creating accountability across its operations meant that it was among a handful of NGOs that would willingly and confidently submit to an objective third-party evaluation. This gave it a unique advantage, as companies suddenly compelled to line up their charitable contributions discovered that foundations such as Agastya had the transparency needed to make their task of shortlisting viable candidates monumentally less arduous.

Paula Golden, the president and director of the Broadcom Foundation, seconds this opinion.

"I was asked by the company to advise them on how to deploy funds in India," she says. "This was when the CSR Bill came out and we were told we had to give 2% of profits for CSR. Hari invited me to have dinner with Ramji. At the time, I remember being struck by the fact that there was a glow to this guy. I had the impression that there was something a little bit on the magical side with him. There is a difference between those who talk and those who speak; he was speaking. He had a very clear idea about the infrastructure he wanted to create. He also didn't have what we call 'founder syndrome.'[2] When I went to the campus in 2015 or 2016, I had a very decent idea of the range of economic constraints on poorer students. The campus was visually and emotionally grounded on the fundamentals. We decided to leverage what resources we had to help the campus. We started supporting mobile labs and providing Raspberry

Pi technology. Agastya became the vessel for what we wanted to do in software and coding."

By 2018, nearly 60% of Agastya's donations were coming from corporate donors such as Fidelity, Honeywell, Infosys, L&T and Synopsys. This showed, unequivocally, that the numbers Agastya was putting out were solid and could withstand the highest degrees of scrutiny. Concerningly, however, retail funding (the smaller-denomination contributions made by individuals) hovered at only around 6%. This incongruity was only partly by design. Like Ramji, Hari came with an enterprise outlook and mindset, meaning that he believed the route to funding was via high-net-worth individuals or corporates rather than retail sources. However, it was equally true that early attempts to attract retail funding had proven largely unsuccessful.

C. K. Rao, who spearheaded the retail efforts until 2014, recalls the difficulties Agastya faced.

"Retail fundraising was a new concept for Agastya," he says. "Some 53% of [donations to charity] come from retail. You have to struggle a lot, but it can come. For Akshaya Patra, half their funding comes from retail. For Agastya it is a little difficult. We used to set up kiosks in cafeterias of software companies and would ask for money. After three days of standing there, we would raise very little. We would set up at the beginning of the month hoping to get employees to donate just after salary day. But sympathy would be more for food, less for education. We sent out many mailers, but not one person sent any money. We tried to get it going, but after a few years we shifted to corporate and CSR."

Agastya's inability to build a strong retail base could also be attributed to the larger ticket sizes of its programmes. Retail donors are usually converted by crafting a cause–effect narrative between the patron and their underprivileged counterpart. Telling a donor that their contribution could help one child eat for one week, for example, has a powerful emotional pull on the strings of even relatively modest purses. For Agastya, where the cost of one mobile van or even the low-cost Lab-in-a-Box is comparatively much higher, creating this connection with retail donors was not always easy.

Raising money via the retail route is significant for any non-profit. For one, retail funds are highly fungible – something that, as we have already seen, could be extremely helpful in allowing Agastya to smooth its expenses across operations. However, having a strong retail donor base also acts as a very effective tool for viral marketing. A humbling testament to Agastya's lack of success in creating a robust retail channel is the fact that despite decades of pathbreaking work across a mass audience, it remains one of India's best-kept secrets.

Another issue Agastya faced was with regard to corporate donors themselves.

As Einstein famously said, "Sometimes what counts can't be measured and what is measured doesn't count." Agastya had imbibed this viewpoint and placed it at its very core. It remained convinced that sparking curiosity was never about marks or pushing more knowledge into the minds of children. Certain individuals, like Rakesh Jhunjhunwala, held this same belief with unwavering conviction.

"He had a model of the campus in his office," recalls Pankaj Talwar (who, as related in *Chapter 8*, introduced Ramji to Jhunjhunwala). "Every time anyone would meet him and would ask what the model in his office was, he would say, 'This is revolutionizing education.' He would talk it up like a company he had invested in."

However, Jhunjhunwala was unique in being able to envision the long-term impact of the kind of intervention that Agastya was providing. Not all those who were involved in disbursing CSR funds remained similarly convinced, and fewer still were not answerable to a board that demanded quantifiable metrics against any money given to social causes.

In what Hari calls the 'three-year itch,' corporates would often begin to waver in their support after a few years, as Agastya was not always able to show rigid impact analyses for its programmes. This was equal parts due to the highly subjective nature of the programmes and because Agastya did not necessarily see output measurement as a priority.

Rakhi Advani Gautham joined Agastya in 2014 and has been instrumental in bringing in nearly 30 donors to the cause. Ramji describes her as a powerhouse, who has opened multiple doors for Agastya. Rakhi has a knack for converting even the thinnest of connections into engaged benefactors. Along with Hari, she has been a key lifeline through which Agastya has been able to tap into the corporate space and access the funds to fuel its growth.

"We have been good at raising funds from corporate donors, so that was our comfort zone," she explains. "But for companies that evaluate the optimization of the programme, the formal impact is very important to ensure the money is being properly spent. There are also those that want the assessments done. They want us to be able to take the attendance of each child." Paul Glick, executive director of the Rural India Supporting Trust, recalls his early experience with Agastya: "When we first started working with Agastya, one of the things we really wanted them to showcase was what monitoring and evaluation processes and policies they would be able to put in place. We did have reporting from Agastya on the impact of their programme, but maybe not as structured as we might have liked. But Agastya did have some internal data on the impact they were having."

The reporting that Glick refers to was based on the studies done by Hamsa on the project she started back in Koppal and continued to spearhead over the years (see *Chapter 7*).

"We were compiling data on whether the children liked science," says Hamsa, whose impact metrics were based on post-session interviews with students and teachers. For the most part, these focused on whether the classes were enjoyable and whether the students felt that they had learned anything.[3] "We also had a control school where we asked the same questions," she adds. "We also developed a self-assessment for the kids. But when it comes to convincing donors, the way donors look at things is very different."

Nor were the donors wrong in expecting numbers. With most other NGOs – be they in nutrition, health-care or even education – reach and effectiveness could be easily measured. and this could give a ready indication of success or failure. It was another matter that many non-profit organizations had not built systems to capture these numbers. However, corporates were more likely to align with these models, given that the data was there to be collected when needed. It was difficult to align CSR funds with Agastya's approach, especially when other more black-and-white options were available and could be seen as an easier sell to top management.

Agastya initially expanded on Hamsa's work by involving a third-party organization called the Best Practices Foundation.

"They would go sit in a classroom, give some tasks to the children and observe how they were doing," describes Sai Chandrasekhar. "They would question them and based on the answers, they would do an assessment and give us a report. The good thing is that it was being done by a third party. The bad thing was that it was expensive, and it simply was not scalable."

With pressure mounting from corporates, larger charitable foundations and even internally from staff who wanted more concrete data to help them understand their own progress, Agastya needed to find a way to improve impact assessments across its programmes.

As the former managing director of Titan, Bhaskar Bhat had experience with CSR, and this had brought him close to the funding and evaluation of several non-profit ventures. While his views are forgiving of the challenges that NGOs face in projecting impact, he nonetheless believes that there is no way around it.

"NGOs don't have to be governed in the way corporates are governed because with corporates, the relationship is financial in nature," he explains. "With NGOs the stakeholders are primarily the beneficiaries, and what is in the interest of that beneficiary needs to be at the centre of the governance mechanism. Corporates must accept that we have no capability to deliver that kind of impact. So, to sit on a high horse and say 'I'm giving you the money [so I require reports on results]' is so unfair. In fact, I would turn around and say, 'All you can do is give the money.' So, how can we make this relationship equal? Rather than make it emotional, we say we want impact and put processes in place, so the results are stakeholder based."

The complication, as Bhat describes, is that while all corporates necessarily use the same metrics, calculated in much the same way, NGOs need to tailor their metrics to their specific areas of operation and impact.

How do you measure curiosity, or innovativeness, or creativity and confidence? It was an alien concept in many ways, especially when anecdotal evidence was so abundant and could easily be referenced instead. Stories like those of Rani and Roja and of Vasantha (see *Chapter 10*) should have been enough to convince any thinking person that the Agastya effect, while intangible, was certainly not ambiguous.

Nonetheless, Agastya knew that banking on uplifting stories and the personal beliefs of a few benefactors was not a strategy that would hold them in good stead in a post-CSR Bill world. Internally, they had created an air-tight organization where every penny spent was accounted for and every activity was meticulously documented. However, end-customer impact was still largely subjective and could be seen as open to interpretation. If corporates needed to be convinced, the foundation would need to find a way to project its impact via graphs, charts and management-friendly spreadsheets. The challenge was in creating assessments that would capture the subjective impact of Agastya without reapplying the very same exam-centric pressures on the system that the foundation had categorically distanced itself from.

In 2016, Huggy Rao and Phanish Puranam – professors at Stanford University and INSEAD, Singapore, respectively – came to Agastya's campus to conduct studies on whether design thinking impacts creativity. Both men had interacted with Ramji on Agastya's efforts and were curious to know to what extent Agastya was influencing the creativity of the children it worked with.

"Ramji was enamoured by design thinking," says Puranam. "Science education was one way [design thinking was in evidence at Agastya], but it could have been anything. Ultimately, they were trying to instil confidence."

It was this confidence that the two men had come down to measure. In a paper published in 2022, they describe in detail the Guilford Intelligence Task, which was conducted on campus across a set of about 200 students.[4]

According to Puranam: "We ran the Guilford test. The surprising effect is that it increases confidence quite a lot. The main point here is that there are not many NGOs or even established companies conducting this kind of test and applying the results to their own work."

"The test showed that design thinking worked," says Huggy. "It clearly increased confidence in girls in the eighth grade. We took all the people who came into Agastya and randomly assigned tutors to guide them with design thinking. We also had a control group, of course. Then we asked them to do a simple task involving circles [the Guilford Intelligence Task]. We also asked them how confident they were about solving social problems. There was a definite improvement in the number of ideas and the categories of ideas."

The success of the confidence test bolstered the possibility of a more broad-based measure. In 2016, Agastya approached the Indian Institute of Management, Bangalore (IIM-B), to formally create a methodology to test the outcomes of its various programmes. The intention was to apply this across a significant sample of children that the foundation worked with on an ongoing basis. Professor Dinesh Kumar, whose work focuses on decision sciences and information systems, agreed to offer his time, pro bono. He roped in Shailaja Grover, whose first step was to research whether there existed any comparable methodologies to measure creativity and curiosity that they might access as a starting point. When none were found, it was decided that they would build a new model from the ground up. The features that Agastya specified were that the model had to be affordable, scalable and easy to administer even without skilled staff.

The IIM-B model – the costs for which were funded by Amit Chandra – incorporated the use of a 20-question multiple choice questionnaire, where each choice was marked on a Likert scale[5] for curiosity, confidence, awareness and creativity.

"We faced some challenges," explains Sai. "From a design perspective, there were a couple of things. Because each choice was marked on more than one parameter, each attribute was feeding into the other. So, someone whose answer suggested they were curious may have been getting docked points for confidence. So, we modified the questions to ensure that each question represented only one attribute. We also found that creativity cannot be measured in this fashion, so it was ultimately dropped."

The methodology went through multiple iterations before being piloted in a few select schools. In addition to the three remaining parameters – awareness, curiosity and confidence – Agastya also added science knowledge, at the behest of certain key donors. Along with the questions, which would constantly be updated and refined to improve the confidence level in the scores, the model also made recommendations on the acceptable sample size for testing, given the number of children that a certain programme was reaching in each area.

The process devised required the children to be given the questionnaire at the beginning of the year.

Then, after eight subsequent sessions with Agastya, the questionnaire was given again. In this manner, Agastya would get an indication as to the cumulative effect of its intervention.

The initial rounds were done by getting children to fill out their answers on a sheet of paper. The task of collecting and collating the data was time-consuming and subject to significant human error. It also led to an interesting problem that went right back to the very heart of the issue that Agastya was trying to solve. The purpose of the questions was to test whether Agastya was having any measurable impact. However, in a manner that showcased the quintessence of Indian education, students saw it instead as an exam that needed to be aced. Rather than provide honest answers, many took to copying from stronger students. The result was that sometimes papers would be submitted with 20 identical answers, and these needed to be discarded, lest they pollute the rest of the data being collected.

To address both these problems, Agastya adopted the PiCard system. Students were each given a placard with QR codes on the corners. Each corner corresponded with the letters A, B, C and D. Children would be asked a question verbally and would need to immediately hold the placard up with the corner representing their answer on top. The instructor would take a photo of the whole class, and this would be processed by the PiCard software to draw out the answers and effectively package the data into analysable reports.[6]

In 2019, Agastya ran its assessment model across 22 states and 2,300 schools. Over 100,000 students who had interacted with Agastya were assessed. The results were further divided across five main programmes – mobile science labs, science centres,

Labs-on-a-Bike, i-Mobile Labs[7] and the Young Instructor Leader (YIL) programme.

As expected, the numbers showed an improvement
of anywhere from 8% to 12% across all parameters.
This implied that a child who regularly interacted with
Agastya over the grades of five to nine could potentially be 50 to 70% ahead on the selected parameters as
compared with a child who had no access to Agastya.
The biggest improvements came from the YIL programmes, reinforcing the belief that the more exposure
a child got to Agastya, the bigger the improvement
would be.

The results served a purpose much like the Boston
Consulting Group report had done in Agastya's earliest days (see *Chapter 6*). It was an objective validation
based on a methodology developed by a very reputable
body. It immensely helped the foundation to quantify
the significance of its work and to provide annual metrics to its donors. (Shrihari Sridhar of the University of
Texas A&M is working on a model that would use AI
techniques to measure Agastya's impact.)

Using the study as a foundation, Agastya soon began
conducting micro-assessments within classrooms.
Students were given placards to hold up when asked
multiple choice questions. The same questions would
be asked at the start of the class and at its conclusion.
The placards could be scanned using an app available
to the instructor. In this manner, the relative improvement in science knowledge could be ascertained for
each session.

However, even with such metrics in place, Agastya
still believes that the true value of its influence is far
more nuanced and intentionally impalpable.

Ganu Subramanian, who headed the Gifted Children

programme between 2010 and 2014 and has a deep connection with the YILs, has this to say about impact: "We need to understand that we are working for a philosophical organization. Nothing we do is ever going to be easy to measure. There is enough evidence around that says that children coming from the same family or background do not turn out the same [when one is exposed to Agastya and the other is not]."

Ganu's observation is remarkably illustrated by the story of Shravani.

A 16-year-old girl from a village near Kuppam, Shravani came from a poor family. Financial constraints had forced her parents into the decision to sell their only cow. The sale would fetch them about 30,000 rupees, equivalent to five months of Shravani's father's income. Inspired by a sudden insight that a sacrifice today might lead to greater benefits in the future, Shravani convinced her father not to sell the cow. Instead, she persuaded her mother to find a job, as a coolie, to supplement the family income. Soon afterwards the cow gave birth to three calves. In time, the calves began to yield milk, which was sold to earn 24,000 rupees a month, or four times what Shravani's father earned as a government land inspector. The family now had enough money to send Shravani to a private engineering college.

Addressing a gathering of staff in Agastya's campus auditorium, Shravani said confidently: "If you change, your family will change. If your family changes, the neighbourhood and village will change. This will change the district, the state and eventually the country." No one who heard Shravani speak that day could leave without being hugely impressed. When asked what causes poverty, she replied with conviction, "Poverty is not real – it is a state of mind."

Shravani attributes her confidence and deep thinking to the holistic experience she had on campus training as a YIL. By allowing children not only to learn but also to understand the power of applying what they have learned, Agastya had fostered a unique blend of intellectual, creative and social awareness. This gave a girl like Shravani the ability to analyse her circumstances and trade-offs, the confidence to address them, and the know-how to craft the levers needed to pry herself free from them.

1. Using the five behavioural shifts (see *Chapter 9*) and the eight indicators (Persistence, Active Participation, Generation of Ideas, Development of Ideas, Linking Ideas, Attentive, Self-Regulative, Teamwork and Leadership) Hamsa developed a behavioural matrix, into which she fed data from hundreds of case stories that Agastya had compiled. The results showed a marked move from passive to active learning, and a continual trend of fear evolving into confidence. Encouragingly, other outcomes – such as changes in personal behaviour and changes in learning approaches – were also observed, validating Agastya's impact in terms of the positive knock-on effects on personality and identity.

2. *The Seven Sutras of Innovation* (2020) was released by the Marico Innovation Foundation and authored by Nikhil Inamdar. It featured Agastya as one of eight best-in-class organizations from India that have successfully made innovation the core of their enterprise.

3. The tendency of founders to be guarded about their creations and less open to new ideas, people or methods. Ramji and Mahavir had both always shown that the cause was more important than they were. This was showcased when the appointment of a COO was earlier suggested, and they embraced the idea.

4. Hayagreeva Rao, Phanish Puranam and Jasjit Singh, "Does Design Thinking Training Increase Creativity? Results from a Field Experiment with Middle-School Students," *Innovation: Organization & Management* 24, no. 10 (2022): 315–332.

5. A Likert scale is a psychometric scale commonly involved in research that employs questionnaires.

6. The company that launched PiCard sadly shut down. Agastya has presently moved to a 'clicker' system but is actively looking for a substitute for the PiCard system to implement.

7. Mobile Science Labs that had an added focus on IT-related learning.

CHAPTER 14

BEYOND SCIENCE

The Agastya campus at Gudupalle has had many stewards since the earliest days, from when the founders themselves worked the land, to when Subbu oversaw the commissioning of the first buildings, to when Dr. Shibu guided the campus through the rapid expansion between 2010 and 2015. Dr. Shibu handed the reins over to Nitin Desai, who after having stabilized the North Karnataka region was asked to manage the campus. In 2018, Nitin would be asked to spearhead Agastya's expansion in Maharashtra, leaving the campus in need of a new custodian.

A graduate of the Indian Institute of Technology Kanpur, Padmanabhan Kumar had worked as a vice president at both Deutsche Bank and JP Morgan before quitting to become a social entrepreneur. Kumar and his wife Shubalakshmi had forayed into education by building a K-12 school in Tamil Nadu. The project somehow didn't take off, and around the time Kumar met Ramji at a conference in Madurai in 2018, he had all but decided to close the school. Keen to stay connected with education, he asked Ramji whether there was anything he could do for Agastya.

Unsurprisingly, there was no clear role on offer in Agastya at the time. However, after a few meetings with Thiagu and Sai, Kumar was offered the role of campus head.

"I believed that Kumar possessed a good blend of idealism and management skill, so he would make a difference at Agastya," says Ramji of Kumar's appointment. Kumar himself was ambivalent until he visited the campus and saw for himself how artfully it had been developed.

"I spent some time on campus and Lokanatham [see *Chapter 6*] took me on the eco walk," he explains. "At the end of the eco walk, I knew that this was the role for me.

The only issue would be that I would be away from my family. We spoke a lot about it and finally my son said, 'I know from the look in your eyes that you will love it. You must take it.' Once he said that, there was no looking back."

Managing the 172-acre campus is no mean feat. All in all, nearly 30 vibrant buildings pepper the once barren landscape. Nor are these structures bunched close together. Agastya intentionally spaced them out, making the campus difficult to traverse without some kind of vehicle. The arrangement speaks to Agastya's foresight and planning. From the beginning, there was a belief that there would inevitably need to be ample room for more labs and buildings. The added philosophy that walking brings you closer to nature combined with the practicality and health benefits of a brisk stroll make a day on campus an exhilarating, if sometimes physically intensive, experience.

Starting with the Oberoi Centre and then the Jhun-jhunwala Discovery Centre, Agastya made it a point to constantly one-up itself with each new building. It helped, of course, that Sharukh Mistry and his team – comprising young and fiercely driven architects – ardently believed that this was exactly what the campus deserved. However, as a practically unspoken homage to Agastya's own 'sandbox' way of functioning, the architects set themselves up with certain constraints.

"We decided to stay local and use the materials that local people themselves would use," says Sunanda, an architect on Sharukh's team. "Even for the Oberoi Centre, which was more sedate, we used local stones and tried to innovate. We try and tread lightly on the land. There are minimal walls. We want the land to catch up with the construction over time."

"The idea of allowing the breeze to move through the buildings has been contentious," adds Sandeep, another architect, "but we wanted children to feel the openness."

"The concern is that once you expose them, they value their learnings and take pride from where they come from," Sharukh concludes. "The future of Agastya is in creating a system that inspires children to learn from the architecture and take that with them wherever they go."

Nowhere is this passion for inspiring children better illustrated than with the story of Agastya's Maritime Centre.

A curious man himself, Mahavir remembers being thrilled at the prospect of visiting a ship-breaking yard in Bhavnagar, Gujarat. "A ship had just come to be broken," he recalls. "The ship is dragged onto the beach, and they just start breaking it apart. There is only a rope ladder to go up to the ship's deck."

Well in his fifties by this time, Mahavir struggles with extreme stiffness in one leg, which he injured in an accident when he was younger. Regardless, he decided to climb the rope ladder to the equivalent height of ten storeys. As he stood on the bridge and waited for them to begin stripping the ship apart from the inside, Mahavir was possessed by a wild idea. He called Ramji and asked him what he thought about a Maritime Centre on campus. Mahavir believed that if he – a grown man – could feel such a sense of wonder while standing on the bridge of a ship, it stood to reason that a child would too.

On matters such as this, the founders were known to be very decisive. A quick back-of-the-envelope calculation told them that all the equipment on the bridge – which was to be sold by weight – plus transport to the campus would cost about 8 lakh rupees ($10,000). Both men agreed that it was worth it.

"They were about to start breaking and I told them to stop [while I spoke with Ramji]," Mahavir recalls. "I took a piece of paper and drew the layout of the captain's deck. I asked them to slowly break it down into parts and send it to campus. I marked each and every part on the paper. I then went across to the shops [near the ship-breaking yard] and bought some other items to add to what I already had. I spent an extra week there to get the job done. On campus, we altered a room so that the Maritime Centre could face the lake. Then, based on my drawing, the windows and doors were made to replicate the bridge."

The Maritime Centre was built as an appendage to the Jhunjhunwala Discovery Centre and positioned to overlook the Mustrahalli Lake. Inside, children would marvel at the controls, the layout and the maritime paraphernalia. A fully functional foghorn placed above the centre needed to be disconnected when, after it became an understandable source of extreme amusement for many a child, there were complaints from the surrounding towns about the noise. However, a smaller, hand-controlled foghorn was a replacement source of unbridled delight to every group of children that passed through the centre.

Equally astounding was the story of Agastya's astronomy centre and planetarium.

After receiving three tabletop models of the solar system, the Agastya team began to explore the possibility of building an astronomy exhibit that would hang from a ceiling. M. A. Ramaswamy showed Ramji the diagram of a model for an overhead solar system that he had developed as a hobby in the 1980s.

This became a project of some excitement and complexity. Mahavir suggested that the planets could run on monorails. After several brainstorming discussions with M. Shivkumar, the group decided to build a large solar system model that would have a diameter of 11 metres, making it possibly the largest suspended solar system model in the world. Initially intended to be housed within the Jhunjhunwala Discovery Centre, the proposed model was now so large that the team decided to build a separate dome-shaped astronomy centre to house it. The process took approximately 18 months to complete. Supported by the India Value Fund Association and investor Hemant Kanakia, the Guru Gruha Astronomy Centre was formally inaugurated by Dr. Abdul Kalam when he visited the campus in 2012.

Inside the astronomy centre, visitors could look up to see the planets moving in their orbits. An operator on the ground could adjust the controls to manipulate the movement of a particular planet to teach its characteristics. After interactively observing the suspended planets in motion, children could walk to a level above the exhibit to a planetarium to watch films on space. On the ground beneath the suspended system were displayed a series of tabletop astronomy models that students could manipulate with their hands to learn about celestial bodies and their effects, including eclipses, retrograde motion, how seasons change and the phases of the moon.

Many of the other buildings on campus draw inspiration from nature. The fascinating, grass-topped Innovation Hub was built to resemble a lizard. The bio-discovery centre was designed in the form of a butterfly emerging out of a cocoon. The Sensorium pays tribute to the humble termite. Finally, the main auditorium – for which Sharukh Mistry won the JK Architect of the Year Award in 2015 – was built to resemble the dung beetle. With each building, a story was also born and from these stories, Agastya – and indeed Sharukh – hoped to inspire the children who visited the campus each day.

In 2017, mathematician Sujatha Ramdorai and her husband, Srinivasan Ramadorai, offered to donate Agastya money to create a maths park. Created in collaboration with the Gyanome Foundation and Imaginary, the Ramanujan Math Park, as it is called, is located on a hillside overlooking the Jhunjhunwala Discovery Centre[1]. Along with it, an indoor maths lab was funded by the SBI Mutual Fund. Along the sides of the maths lab, and to the delight of anyone who spots it, is a seemingly never-ending line of apparently random numbers. Following these numbers to their source shows that the sequence starts with 3.14 – the value of pi. Designed by polymath V.S.S. Sastry, the Ramanujan Math Park occupies an important place on the Agastya campus – a fitting, if small, tribute to a great genius[2]. A bust of the great mathematician sits at the entrance to the park. It is one of a set of busts commissioned by Agastya, with the others being installed at the campuses of The Indian Institute of Science, The Indian Institute of Technology (Chennai), MIT, and Cambridge. In 2020, a study by the Museum of Mathematics, New York and Imaginary, Germany ranked Agastya's Ramanujam Math Park as among the top 15 math museums in the world.[3]

On the highest point of the estate sits the library that Ramji envisioned when he first saw the land and imagined its potential.[4] The terrace of the library offers a stunning 360-degree view from which all three states – Andhra Pradesh, Karnataka and Tamil Nadu – can be seen from a single point.

While the unique buildings could be considered the physical embodiment of Agastya's achievement, the soul of the campus is only truly awoken when children enter its gates. Early each morning, empty Agastya buses leave the campus, only to bring back nearly 600 children from surrounding schools. For these children, time at Agastya is a thrilling departure from an otherwise dreary school day. Many are aware of the propitious nature of their proximity to Agastya. It lends them the ability to hone their understanding of key concepts and gives them access to teaching resources that even students in private schools do not always have. It is therefore no wonder that the Camps on Campus programme – where Agastya allows groups of students from private schools to spend a few days at its campus – has proven so successful.

"I don't know whether there is any parallel for a campus dedicated to science learning anywhere in the world," says Anil Kakodkar, former head of the Atomic Energy Commission of India. He initially connected with Ramji through P. K. Iyengar. A titan in the scientific community, Kakodkar credits Agastya for creating 'wow' effects that expose children to scientific phenomena through hands-on experiences.

The children are taught, fed and can even be housed on campus, if needed. Residences with the capacity to hold nearly 300 students have been built. The insides of these residences are neat, tidy and intentionally minimalist, which bodes well considering children who visit rarely wish to remain indoors. However, the structures of the residences themselves are made with the characteristic flourish that Sharukh's team infuses into all Agastya buildings.

When Agastya began welcoming more teachers to campus for training, it found itself at a loss for space. Mahesh Naithani – a philanthropist and entrepreneur who over 30 years has made a habit of building and selling successful companies within the healthcare space

– offered to partly fund a new structure to house teachers. Naithani House, as it is called, is positioned along the highest contours of the Agastya campus with a breath-taking view of the valley and the lake below. The common areas are designed with informal seating, niches and nooks (of various sizes) that open out into the terrain. The wide-aspect view enhances your experience of the weather and changing skies, rooting you more deeply in nature. Is it any wonder that teachers clamour to come to the Agastya campus?

"The biggest thing for me was visiting the campus," describes M. R. Rangaswami, the San Francisco-based philanthropist and Indiaspora founder. Rangaswami has an unparalleled flair for networking that he is using as a force for good in spreading Agastya's word to the very successful Indian diaspora in the US. "Before that, I had seen a lot of information, but it wasn't doing much for me. Going there and seeing 100,000 trees was what hit me. Them taking a wasteland and turning it into an oasis is what hit me. For me that is a key thing, because it made me think: if they can do this, they can do anything."

Many have echoed this take on the impact that witnessing Agastya's campus has had on them versus merely hearing or reading about it. Visually, it bombards you with the sheer scale, size and audacity of what the foundation has been able to create.

However, risks remain in the form of the dry, sometimes threatening climate.

"In June of 2019, I was preparing to close the campus because there was no rain," Kumar recalls. "The borewells had dried up and we wanted to rebore, but the summer heat was so bad that we were unable to get any labour. By the end of June, the rains thankfully came in and the water problem was pushed forward."

To an appreciable extent, Agastya's rainwater-harvesting techniques have allowed the campus to experience longer rainless spells without courting catastrophe. However, artificial measures can only do so much in an area that is officially recognized for its low average rainfall. For now, however, the campus is experiencing a deservedly green renaissance, reaping the rewards of two decades of earnest ecological manoeuvres that have been blessed by the rains in recent years. Bursting with a thousand different colours, the campus is truly a spectacle of creativity come alive. Its morning air is drenched with dew and the very earth sings through its incredible buildings – buildings that are as alive as the ever-increasing fauna that finds welcome refuge in the campus's emerald thickets, growing bolder with each passing season.

As Peter Patch, a friend of Ramji's, once described, "It is a magic door coming into the campus. You enter a different world, a different reality."

Breathing life into the campus also pushed Agastya to understand that science could never be appreciated – or indeed harnessed – in isolation. The foundation's trysts with ecology, art and architecture all incorporate the scientific method in no small way. The resulting beauty of the campus – both natural and artificial – inspired Agastya's foray into art, theatre, music and design. During an event on campus, Aatre was once asked how Agastya compared with other institutes that he had been associated with. An alumnus of the prestigious Indian Institute of Science (IISc), Aatre had replied with characteristic flair: "When I walk into the IISc campus, I think 'science.' When I walk into the Agastya campus, I think 'innovation.'"

Around 2007, Vasant Nayak was visiting Hubli and happened to come upon one of Agastya's spectacular science fairs. Nayak was a professor of photography at the University of Maryland at the time, and ran the Murthy-Nayak Foundation along with his wife, Sheela Murthy.

"We had come as a group with the United Way [a nonprofit that assists other charities in fundraising] to set up the Indian chapters in Hubli and Delhi. The people involved in United Way took us to see the fair," he describes of the first time he learned about Agastya. "They had the science fair in Hubli. It blew our minds. Ramji was there personally. I pursued Ramji to the airport and that's where we met. We were thrilled to meet the guy who started the whole thing. I remember catching his interest by saying we would make a film for him [on Agastya]."

Never one to turn down a freebie that furthered Agastya's cause, Ramji invited Nayak to see the Agastya campus, where he was amply provided with the necessary inspiration for a film titled *The Spirit of Agastya*. The experience has stayed with Nayak, who recalls the challenges faced in getting aerial shots before drones became more commonplace: "We took a helium balloon – eight feet wide – and procured helium from a nearby town. A guy landed up at 2:30 am with helium and that's how the first aerial shots of the campus were taken."

Nayak and Murthy – like so many wayfarers willingly enticed and joyously ensnared by the heady purity of Agastya's mission – became deeply involved with the foundation from then on. Although based in Baltimore, they would visit frequently enough to have a meaningful impact, conducting media workshops on campus and adding to Agastya's library of media content. Along with the film, they also launched Agastya's first media lab. The lab may have been ahead of its time, considering Agastya was still only getting the hang of disseminating basic science learning. However, Nayak convinced Ramji that it would be significant in time to come.

"Going from science focus to the media lab, the main question was why these children had no access to any concepts of design," says Nayak. "The thing about Ramji is that if he sees something that somebody says is relevant and he trusts that person, then it's a done deal. He didn't see why it was relevant [to have a media lab] at the time, but he trusted that I knew what I was talking about and went with it."

In order to ensure that his work was carried forward even when he was away in the US, Nayak began working with a young, hungry graduate named Subramanya Shastry. This second Subbu had recently completed his engineering degree and, not wanting to code for a living, was looking for something more creative. As usual, his meetings with Agastya told him that there was nothing specific that the foundation could use him for, but he was asked to join all the same and placed under the capable wing of Nayak.

"I was asked to speak with Vasant [after I joined]," Subbu says. He told me "Agastya is doing some phenomenal work that no one knows about. The job is to get the word out about Agastya."

Under Nayak's guidance, Subbu would bring Agastya into the realm of social media and work to improve the foundation's online presence. Together, and with the help of Nayak's colleague Shay Taylor, the team would release a book in 2014 titled *The Wisdom of Agastya*. The book was issued on Agastya's 15th anniversary and recorded the contributions of the founder trustees and many others. Interviews with the three wise men had been conducted some years earlier and were featured prominently in the book.

A short while later, another book, *Rise of the Fireflies*, featured the case stories of 50 of Agastya's precious YILs. In each of these stories, the key behavioural shift that the child experienced was highlighted.

Both Nayak's and Subbu's passion for Agastya is infectious. How else might you superimpose arts on a foundation so doggedly determined to further STEM education?

"Any time I tell people about what Agastya did or started with, they are always amazed," Nayak laughs. He even went as far as to try and set up an Agastya mobile lab in the US. However, the nature of the experiments and models demanded that the van and instructor both be fully insured. This pushed the costing well above any available budget and the project was dropped.

Sheetal Kataria, Mahavir's daughter, had always been actively involved with Agastya from the very beginning. Her design company – Creative Workshop Inc. – was responsible for much of Agastya's distinctive, playful artwork that made the mobile vans so easily recognizable. As Agastya embraced arts more eagerly, Sheetal and her team would make frequent trips to the campus, spending innumerable hours conducting workshops and outreach programmes for staff and students alike.

Despite being known for her contributions to Agastya's arts initiatives, Sheetal prefers not to use the word 'art.'

"I am very against the word," she says, stating that it limits the vision of what art is to only drawings and paintings, "Our work has always been about 'creativity.' The way I see it: observation plus creativity equals art. Observation and creativity start from within, and both can be triggered by the right instructor."

"We faced two major challenges," Sheetal describes of the initial launch of the programmes on campus, "First, we did not get instructors. Everyone wanted to get into either science or maths. They did not see any future in arts. Eventually, we handpicked school dropouts and spent 8-9 months training them."

"The second challenge was materials. Not only were paint brushes, crayons, and paints expensive, but children and instructors would refuse to do anything without them. We had to redefine what it meant to create art. We used stones, sticks, and even cow dung! The students were slowly taught to understand that art was much more than just drawing and painting."

Delving deeper into arts and media meant that it was becoming essential to formally inculcate these learnings into the foundation's framework. Luckily, support came from the same man who had bought into Ramji's mission at the very beginning. In a meeting in Alok Oberoi's office in London, Ramji and Oberoi charted plans to further Agastya's effort in this space.

In 2018, the Sarga Samvad programme was launched in partnership with the Oberoi Family Foundation. Sarga Samvad – which is Sanskrit for 'creative dialogue' – attracted scores of artists and educators to the Agastya campus. The stimulating workshops held with these innovative thinkers and doers led to many new ideas, works of art and learning methods. They also led to a burst of activity around dance recitals, drama and musical performances. The insides of Agastya's dung-beetle auditorium were suddenly teeming with activity. Its stage was rarely empty, and the tranquillity surrounding it was often gilded with hoots and peals of excitement and laughter from within.

Sarga Samvad transformed Agastya's image from being purely STEM-centric to having a more holistic approach to education.

Paul Collard, the chief executive of CCE (Creativity, Culture and Education), which helps the UK government to deliver creativity programmes, spent three weeks on Agastya's campus as part of Sarga Samvad. He describes Agastya's extensive and intensive focus on creativity as unmatched.

"The fundamental problem with education systems around the world is they find it takes such a long time to change anything," he observes. "Agastya, by working as an NGO outside that system, is able to convert ideas and new approaches within weeks into something that is happening in a classroom somewhere. I think there is a lot to learn from the dynamism of Agastya. It is an amazing place for fantastically creative conversations."

In addition to attracting thought leaders to the campus, Sarga Samvad reached out to eminent personalities across the world to garner their thoughts via online interviews in a programme called Inspirational Indians. Academics such as Anil Kakodkar, Sujatha Ramdorai and Manu Prakash of Stanford have been featured, as have distinguished philanthropists such as Ram Shriram, Kris Gopalakrishnan and M. R. Rangaswami.

According to billionaire, philanthropist, and Alphabet board member, Ram Shriram, "Agastya is making a difference to young, aspirational Indians by sparking their curiosity. It changes the way they think from rote education to one based on innovation."

The flavour lent to Agastya by its embrace and encouragement of the arts cannot be overstated. By bringing different pieces of the education puzzle into a single campus, it created a self-sustaining synergy of creative ideas and shared learnings – a veritable melting pot of knowledge, innovation, questions, curiosity, discussion and debate. It opened a nearly endless well from which children could unabashedly draw out the best versions of themselves. Free from the limitations of only maths and science, children could explore nearly any avenue that called for creativity and curiosity and know that the end result would be fruitful, valued and accepted.

It also showed that even after nearly 20 years, Agastya was far from done evolving. If anything, it had merely reached the end of its rather illustrious beginning.

1. Sujatha Ramdorai and Tadashi Tokieda featured the Ramanujan Math Park in the 2018 International Conference of Mathematicians on two separate occasions.

2. In 1989, a decade before Agastya was even born, Ramji was fortunate enough to visit Ramanujan's wife in Madras (now Chennai). The old lady spoke fondly of her husband's all consuming love for mathematics but lamented in Tamil: "No one remembers my husband." The experience left an indelible mark on Ramji and became a strong motivation for having an homage to the great mathematician on campus.

3. https://yourstory.com/2020/11/agastya-ramji-raghavan-blended-learning-pandemic

4. The library was funded by Kimberly Karshoej's TK Foundation.

CHAPTER 15

NEW AMBITIONS BORN FROM CRISIS

An analysis of the Earth's ice ages throws up an interesting theory that organizations can perhaps take insight from.[1] For an ice age to have formed, the theory suggests, it was less about how harsh the winters were and more to do with how mild the summers were. In other words, to build an ice age, some ice needs to survive at the end of each summer. In the case of the earth, numerous mild summers allowed each winter to build on existing layers of ice, eventually spinning into a self-sustaining cycle that left the planet permanently altered multiple times, many millions of years ago.

The parallel that we might draw with an organization is this: survival is less about how well the organization does in the good times and far more about how much resilience the organization shows during the bad times. A rising tide, it is often said, lifts all boats. However, it is only the ships that survive the storm that rule the tides of tomorrow.

For its part, Agastya had weathered all kinds of hardships as it tried relentlessly to scale up, each time coming away with yet another 'layer' to build upon. However, few would test both the foundation's character and its grit like the pandemic of 2020.

If you were to describe a perfect storm for an organization whose very existence relied on face-to-face interactions, peer-to-peer learning and hands-on models, you could simply refer to the arrival of COVID-19. In early March 2020, over a fortnight before a national lockdown was imposed, the Agastya seniors convened to make a decision on whether to suspend operations, considering the unabated advancement of the pandemic.

Ramji remembers running what he called the 'Daughter Test': "If I would not feel comfortable sending my own daughter to the schools as an instructor,"

Ramji said, "then we should not feel comfortable carrying on in this environment."

The decision was ultimately a simple one: Agastya would need to cease all activities immediately. The mobile labs and bikes would remain parked at the science centres and the campus would close its doors until the situation improved. Staff on campus were sent home, barring those who lived on campus and would need to oversee day-to-day functions there.

Agastya's survival through the pandemic was yet another case study in the foundation's steadfast resilience. There were many hard knocks, obviously. Salaries across all levels were cut by 15%, while senior management took a 30% cut. Here the trade-off was between laying off staff while keeping salaries as they were or reducing salaries so that everyone shared the burden. Resoundingly, the Agastya staff and workers opted for the latter. Managers later told Ramji that one of the chief reasons for the Agastya staff's energetic response during the COVID crisis was because they felt that the organization had always cared for them. They highlighted the difficult decision taken by Agastya management to suspend operations even before the government had mandated a lockdown as a key factor in raising their morale, energy and commitment during an extremely trying period. The move was yet another illustration of Agastya's habit of putting its people first.

However, with caution creeping in across economies and with Agastya having no programmes to run, corporate money began to be withdrawn. Over the next year, Agastya would lose close to 45% of its funding.

Still, the foundation had monies to fall back on. A legacy of frugality instilled by Mahavir at the very beginning meant that there were savings that could be dipped into.

More importantly, high-net-worth benefactors such as Rakesh Jhunjhunwala and Ram Shriram assured Ramji that their contributions would continue, giving Agastya enough breathing room to stay in hibernation until the pandemic subsided.

With survival guaranteed – at least in the short term – Agastya prepared to enter an indefinite period of stasis. However, the admittedly inevitable thing about building an institution of self-starting innovators is that its members don't necessarily like the thought of staying still.

Within only a week of lockdown having been imposed, some of the staff in Agastya's North Karnataka region had started to get restless. Sensing the beginnings of what would eventually be recognized as a national-level problem, they realized that unlike most children in private schools, government schoolchildren would not have access to any online teaching resources.

A misconception that would exist among the elite during the pandemic was that mobile phone penetration in India was sufficient for even less privileged children to get access to an old phone and attend online classes. In truth, most rural families survive with a single phone, with the breadwinner often needing the device to carry out their daily work. This left the children at home with no access to education of any form.

Nimesh Patel and Geeta Patil were both Agastya instructor master trainers (IMTs) who had risen through the ranks to manage their respective regions in Gujarat and Karnataka. Unwilling to accept the hand dealt by the pandemic, they began discussing whether there was a way to get information out to their students at home without flouting the COVID safety restrictions.

"During lockdown, we got permission to continue operating a centre," says Geeta. "We did online sessions for grade ten students. We were recording videos and sending them to the local TV channels. It cost us 4,000 rupees (US$50) per month, but we reached 55,000 children. Today we are designing our own newspaper. We will publish 1,000 copies and distribute them to the schools."

"As the lockdown extended, the classes started moving to WhatsApp then Google Meet or Zoom," Nimesh adds, noting that groups of children were somehow managing to rustle up a single phone between them to be able to stay online. A member of Nimesh's team sent a WhatsApp message with some origami instructions and the response was amazing. "We were learning how to do sessions online and fine-tuning the process as we went."

The online learning model that emerged from this initiative was called EPL – or Explore, Play, Learn. Through EPL, Agastya showed children how they could use commonly available materials at home to build home labs and models. Seeing its impact, the team began documenting the process and then pushing its implementation across a wider area. As the pandemic dragged on, EPL allowed Agastya to continue doing what it did best – at a reduced level of intensity, perhaps, but nonetheless offering a glowing example of the determination and the drive to do whatever it takes to remain relevant in a time fraught with limitations.

Over the next several months it became clear that the EPL programme was helping to stem the learning losses suffered by most children. The children that were able to access EPL claimed that their learning had gone up because they had the freedom to learn on their own. Agastya's proactive instructors will claim that the foundation's culture of rapid innovation allowed them to quickly and seamlessly implement EPL. However, the transition from physical to EPL was not an easy one;

something Ramji recognizes and holds with both appreciation and amazement: "Long working hours from home strained women instructors even more, as they now had to look after their families and teach from home with limited materials. Faulty internet connections meant disruptions to classes. Pandurang, an instructor in Maharashtra, got around this by carrying out his online classes from a converted cowshed on a hill!"

More than anything the children were confused. In such uncertain times, they were witnessing hardships on their own families like never before. Many had lost their confidence and self-esteem, and needed to feel that there was someone that they could lean on, someone who cared for their learning and wellbeing.

Ramji describes a call with a YIL in Kancheepuram. When asked how she was coping with the learning loss she responded that her father, an auto rickshaw driver, had lost his income and that the family had stopped eating rice and vegetables. Another girl in north Karnataka said she had lost her scholarship to go to college. Fortunately, a few friends pooled in money to fund her scholarship.

Agastya began distributing food to villages near its campus. The Agastya staff even delivered food packets to the home of an elderly blind woman who could not come to the Agastya van to collect her food packet. On being told that Agastya staff had brought her food she said with a grateful smile and tears in her eyes: "You have been sent by God."

In their online EPL sessions the Agastya teachers began including jokes and stories into their lessons to humanize their interactions. To get children's contact numbers Agastya instructors would drive to their homes, sometimes travelling 200 or 300 km in their own vehicles to get there. These quick front-line micro innovations, some of which became national programmes, characterized Agastya's response to COVID. Ramji calls this "bottom-up visioning."

Agastya's resilience during a time of unparalleled adversity is lauded by Phanish Puranam, Professor of Strategy and Organization Design at INSEAD. "A culture of constant experimentation, of problem-solving, of creativity... that's what you need to adapt to the new normal, that's what every company is struggling to do, to cope with the post-pandemic world. For Agastya, that's a little bit easier because that's what they've been doing all their lives. We don't know the shape of the next shock. What we do know is that if you build a culture where management makes employees feel safe and respected, then the employees are more willing to experiment without a fear of failure. That's the lesson that one can draw from Agastya far beyond the boundaries of a non-profit and corporation."

The effects of Agastya's adaptability were going even beyond EPL. Battlefield innovations were springing up across the organization, as the synergy of purpose and survival catalyzed creativity in a manner that left even Agastya's most ardent flag-bearers pleasantly surprised

A Smart TV project, which was piloted in about two dozen villages, projected live-streamed sessions to a smart TV that children would gather around to watch. A volunteer from the village was entrusted with ensuring COVID protocols were followed and was also connected by phone to the instructor on the screen so that children could ask their questions and get answers.

At one point, Ramji called Manju for an update and asked what more Agastya could do to make the remote learning methods of EPL more effective. Manju suggested that if the children could be given some materials, it would be helpful.

Agastya already had the Maja Box – a collection of curated experiments that children could take home. However, this was expensive to make, so Manju modified the box into a more abridged Home Lab Kit, which cost only 500 rupees (US$6) and was distributed to some 20,000 children. Along with the kit, children were provided with experiments and a booklet of instructions that they could refer to.

Eventually, once physical classes resumed, EPL would formally wind down. However, the success of EPL was a catalyst for ideas for the foundation both during and after the pandemic.

As the crisis worsened, pressure grew on Ramji to address the organization. He sent out an audio message in which he frankly laid out the severity of the crisis facing Agastya and asked what the organization might do in this situation. He answered his question by saying that the crisis, great as it was, was nevertheless to be seen as an unique opportunity for Agastya. Throughout this period, Agastya was frantically back in 'sandbox' mode, trying to apply the constraints placed upon its model against the foundation's strengths to see what long-term opportunities might spill out. The results would set the stage for Agastya's next leap forward. For a while, Agastya had used origami as a way of explaining ideas and helping children to make paper versions of its models. The Agastya campus had welcomed origami experts such as V. S. S. Sastry in the past and paper modelling had been featured in Sarga Samvad workshops as well. The success of the Home Lab Kit, designed by Manju, led Ramji to ask whether it was possible to make the kit for within 100 rupees. However, the cost of even the most basic materials exceeded this target. Not to be daunted, Manju suggested that the handbook that was provided with the Home Lab Kit could be re-engineered to be broader and richer.

The Agastya team, including Shrishail Dhanawade, Subramanya Shastry (Subbu) and Vagisha Thakur, began testing whether a low-cost, origami-inspired book filled with foldable experiments and concise instructions could be used to adequately illustrate scientific concepts.

ActiLearn 1.0, as it is called, costs only about $1 and is brimming with over 50 experiments that children can work on at home, either alone or in small groups. These experiments range from making a model of the human lungs to cutting out a 'brain map,' which can be worn like a cap showing different parts of the human brain. The book is available in English and in different regional languages.

The synergy between content, cost and ease of access due to Agastya's physical reach into rural India makes ActiLearn (available in both physical and digital form) one of the most exciting programmes to have been developed in recent years. ActiLearn is expanding Agastya's radius by reaching children unserved by Agastya's physical and digital interventions. In 2022, industrialist and philanthropist Kiran Mazumdar-Shaw provided the funding for 25,000 ActiLearn books to be distributed. The numbers grew quickly and by mid-2023 over 400,000 in children in 25 states were enjoying the experience of ActiLearn. Agastya's aim is to have 1 million ActiLearn books in the hands of children each year and to grow that number as the book itself evolves. True to the culture of obsessive iteration, the Agastya team began working on *ActiLearn 2.0* almost as soon as the first version was released.

Another result of Agastya's obsession with staying relevant during COVID was the WeLearn app. Taking a leaf out of the EPL's book, WeLearn was Agastya's formal push into the online learning space. The app allows children to select subjects and topics that are of interest to them. Before seeing a video, children are asked a few questions to gauge their understanding. The same questions are then posed after the video to assess whether there has been an improvement in their understanding.

The melding of physical and digital learning – what the foundation decided to term its 'phygital' revolution – is one of Agastya's cornerstones in scaling up further. For some, this may seem like a divergence from the original hands-on methods, which endeared Agastya to so many. However, others believe that with the right balance, Agastya could preserve the fundamental value of its offering while experiencing explosive growth.

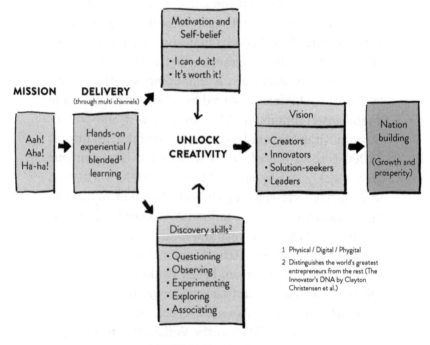

**AGASTYA CHANGE MODEL
– UNLOCKING CREATIVITY FOR NATION BUILDING**

As Ramji recalls, "In terms of reach we were seen as one of the largest organizations offering in-person creativity-based learning in the world. I told the organization that the pandemic had given us a singular opportunity to blend our strengths in physical learning (which few, if any others, have at scale) with digital learning to become an unmatched player in "phygital" learning."

Narayana Murthy is one such proponent of the digital revolution that Agastya is attempting to bring about: "I believe that using digitization, using the power of the metaverse, of augmented reality and other such phenomena, Agastya teachers sitting in one place can communicate to children in a distant place. By creating a mechanism whereby questions are quickly incorporated with answers in the next session, the drawback of digitization that you and I see in not being able to satisfy the curiosity of children can be overcome to some extent. Therefore, digitization will offer very helpful tools to scale up the extraordinary value that gems like Agastya can bring to the table."

The worry is always that physical concepts, if taken online, will become less relatable and lose their impact. But this is not necessarily true. There exist many examples of highly physical activities that organizations have managed to transmit as learnings via the digital medium.

"Boston University had people teaching physiotherapy in Bulgaria," says Sushil Vachani. "They would train the trainer, but the lessons are beamed centrally, so it is possible to do a very hands-on activity remotely."

Sri Jagannathan works pro bono for Agastya in the US (Agastya USA is a registered non-profit run by Venkat Ketineni in the Bay Area) and seconds this philosophy. An ocean engineer, Sri has a PhD in naval architecture from the University of California, Berkeley. Having happened

to visit an Agastya science fair while on a trip to Bangalore in 2009, he connected immediately with Ramji and
sought to build on Agastya's success.

"My focus has been to bring Silicon Valley approaches
and technology to Agastya," he explains. "What the US
has shown us is that you have to constantly do experiments and have a strong propelling vision. When you
keep doing these experiments, certain nuggets fall out
and you get breakthroughs. These breakthroughs can
drive an organization forward. What I saw in Agastya
was linear scaling. It is important, but when you look at
the scale at which India needs intervention, linear scaling may no longer work after a point. You may need a
different approach."

Sri is of the view that while hands-on approaches have
numerous benefits, the ultimate goal needs to be that
they offer an impactful intervention to a child. So, while
touch and feel are remarkable, the ability to transmit
understanding need not be diminished when you move
to a more virtual experience. Couple this with the idea
that the scope to play with parameters, alter materials
and change environments is far greater in a virtual interaction, and a case could be made for significant impact
even with a digital delivery model.

"We can look at macro-scaling," Sri adds, "but there
is also micro-scaling, which happens within one's own
mind. Letting the child's imagination take flight is a powerful thing. It is about arriving at the correct balance."

Finding this balance will be critical as Agastya seeks
to regroup in a post-COVID world and continues along
its mission to spark curiosity in India's furthest corners.

———————

As a co-founder of the technology-centric think-tank iSPIRT, Sharad Sharma has had a front row seat in India's growth in the information and technology space.

"The idea of a digital public infrastructure is gaining traction in India," he says, describing India's recent burst in online digital activity as having had a Roger Bannister-type effect on digitization in the rest of the world. "Before Bannister ran the four-minute mile, it was deemed impossible. After he did it, others started following suit. Globally, digital transformation is happening because India has shown that it can be done effectively even at immense scale."

According to Sharma, Agastya's work is creating a platform upon which India's digital revolution will depend.

"I feel that what Agastya is doing is going to be very critical for the future," he states. "We have to turn Indian technology into a source of competitive advantage. India is at a cusp. If we must build an economy based on science and technology, then the conversation shifts from 'Can you be a call-centre worker or an Uber driver?' to asking 'Can you innovate?' This is what Agastya is doing. It is creating the base that can help India start asking whether it can be an innovation-based economy."

Sunand Bhattacharya of Boston College sees the path ahead as one that needs to build on Agastya's immense knowledge capital. "The problem that Agastya has is that is has done all this great work and no one seems to really know how important it is. There is an awakening even in India that if we don't invest in our human capital, we're going to be left behind. Agastya has done all the work to show that its methods are relevant, and now it's time to project and let others invest in replicating the methods."

Phanish Puranam echoes this viewpoint, observing that Agastya currently sits on a gold mine of knowledge

and data that it should mine through using more formal R&D methods. With the proper funding, Agastya
could create a truly world-class R&D centre yielding new
insights on teaching methods and learning impact. This
in turn will allow Agastya to build strong co-creation
capabilities with children, teachers and more partners
around the world.

In 2021, the Agastya team formally registered a new
entity: Navam. The new company was initially meant
to complement the work of Agastya, but with a deeper
focus on locating and supporting exceptionally gifted
children across India. Registered in the relatively newly
formed state of Telangan, Navam's progress – whose
name means 'new' or 'novel' – initially stalled for lack of
adequate funding. Seeing this as an opportunity to pivot
once more, Agastya began mulling over how Navam
might better serve the larger cause of education. As a Sec-
tion 8 company, Navam – unlike Agastya – was allowed
to generate revenue. In contrast, all of Agastya's inflows
had to come from donations and there was never the
possibility of charging a fee, even for programmes where
Agastya was offering a service to another party.

The proposal to somehow monetize Agastya's vast
reservoir of intellectual property had come up nearly a
decade previously. At that time, the board had decided
against it, choosing instead to focus on the foundation's
core offerings and philanthropic ethos. However, with
Navam, the possibility arose again, and the time finally
seemed right. The mandate was simple: Navam would
have access to Agastya's models, methods and knowledge
capital and would use this to build a revenue model and
push Agastya's learnings into the private education space.

To captain this initiative, the management turned
again to Nitin Desai.

Nitin's wealth of experience with different aspects of Agastya's operations meant he was well placed for the role. His aim is to take Navam to the extensive private school network, offering access to models and teacher training, but at a cost. Schools that were so inclined could even have an Agastya science centre in-house, staffed by a trained instructor and with models that rotate so that fresh new concepts are always on offer.

As Navam began curating the models that it believed would most engage with private schoolchildren, the company approached the Telangana government with an interesting proposal. The government's T-SAT programme, which beams videos directly to screens located in government school classrooms, was looking for unique content. Seizing this opportunity, Navam realized that it already had high-quality content that fitted perfectly with what the T-SAT programme was looking for.

A series of 24 episodes each lasting 45 minutes were taped and are broadcast across the state and into schools once a week. Initial numbers around this initiative suggest that a total of 5 million children are reached with each session. It is a staggering achievement when you consider Agastya's total reach was 2 million just before the pandemic struck.

In 2022, shrugging off the effects of COVID, Agastya would resume its march to reach the furthest corners of India once more. With support from the Infosys Foundation, Agastya launched its first initiatives in the north-east of India, in the Bodoland Territorial Region of Assam. The target involves the deployment of nine mobile science units to reach 29,000 children and 200 teachers over the next three years.

The veritable barrage of new innovations that arose out of the COVID crisis has allowed Agastya to recalibrate its trajectory once again. What seemed to be a clearly losing cause at the beginning of 2020 instead resulted in a rich period of inquiry, problem-solving and ideation. Solutions that emerged not only helped Agastya to survive the pandemic but also projected a roadmap for a phygital revolution that the team calls Agastya 2.0.

Agastya 2.0 once again illustrates the foundation's staggering appetite for scale. Despite appreciable reach and an enviable track record, Agastya decided to aim higher. The new target suggested by Sri Jagannathan: 100 million children, 1 million YILs and 1 million teachers by 2032.

The methods that will be used to achieve these numbers rest on blended learning, an expansion of the teacher training network to have more teachers in each school, using digital learning to grow the peer-to-peer teaching ratios, and creating a 'data backbone' for learning. There will also be a host of other measures that have yet to be thought up, but their genesis is all but guaranteed considering Agastya now functions as an irrepressible ideas factory.[3]

The 100 million target is so astoundingly large that when Agastya was celebrated by the Clinton Global Initiative in 2022, the team – supported by Nish Acharya – scaled it back to 37 million in five years to avoid generating undue scepticism. Even when this seemingly more sedate number was announced by Chelsea Clinton, she paused, asking the audience, "Do I hear any gasps?"

Despite this, if you speak with Agastya employees, even 100 million seems to be digested rather easily, with most fairly certain that it will be achieved.

Among the benefactors who have bought into the Agastya 2.0 vision is Los Angeles based entrepreneur Mahesh Naithani. "My objective is not just to give money, but to create something emblematic," says Naithani, whose present goal is to have a Gudupalle-like campus in his home state of Uttarakhand, in North India. "It must be mission oriented, and within that, it should be legacy oriented."

Naithani connected with Ramji in 2013 through his childhood friend Dhirender Singh. Singh had served in both the education and the defence ministry.

"I understood that to simultaneously build science labs around India would not be possible. What Agastya was doing was filling a gap that all schools had," Singh says of his early impressions of Agastya. "The vision that attracted me was that people would see Agastya and try and replicate their labs and programmes in their own schools."

While in the government, Singh, as the Union Home Secretary, was instrumental in helping Agastya to cut through red tape and policy bottlenecks. After he retired, he committed to helping Ramji get funds for Agastya from abroad and consequently connected him with Naithani.

Naithani's vision for Agastya is as bold as Ramji's.

"In the next ten years, I'm hoping that Agastya will be able to produce at least 100,000 brilliant scientists. I think Agastya can do that as it goes further," he says. He is a firm believer that without the proper level of marketing and PR, Agastya will not be able to harness the power of the public.

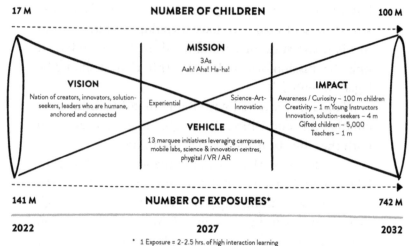

AGASTYA VISION 2.0

Above graphic adapted from Choose Possibility: Take Risks and Thrive (Even When You Fail) by Sukhinder Singh Cassidy

"If the public understands that there is a value to this, then even though they may not contribute, they will become your secondary salespeople. That is a starting point. The value of promotion is to remind and create a curiosity that something is happening and that maybe we should all participate."

How does an organization scale exponentially in a space like education?

In a 2004 paper for *Harvard Business Review*, V. Kasturi Rangan of Harvard Business School offers an interesting viewpoint: "Most of the nonprofits operating today make programme decisions based on a mission rather than on a strategy. In fact, many nonprofits don't have a strategy at all. They rally under the banner of a particular cause, be it 'Fight homelessness' or 'End hunger.' And then, since that cause is so worthwhile, nonprofits support any pro-gramme that's related to it – even if only tangentially.

While it's hard to fault people for trying to improve the state of the world, this approach is misguided. Acting without a clear long-term strategy can stretch an agency's core capabilities and push it in unintended directions."[2]

In carving its path ahead, Agastya needs to be mindful of such pitfalls. Education is a broad palette, and it may be tempting to assume that as long as a programme has a sliver of connection to education, it is sufficiently contributing to the cause. By remaining critical of any new programme, Agastya has always forced extreme scrutiny of its own offerings before deeming them worthy of dissemination. In order to generate volume while keeping these filters in place, the foundation will need to dig far deeper to innovate within the blended learning space. Considering the already crowded digital education landscape, it remains to be seen how Agastya will create impact without merely replicating what others are doing or otherwise simply waving a digital brush over its existing offerings.

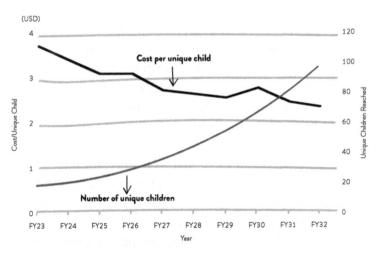

RAPID SCALING TO COME AT REDUCED AVERAGE COSTS THROUGH DIGITAL DISSEMINATION

As Jerry Garcia is often quoted to have said: "You don't want to be the best of the best. You want to be the only one who does what you do."

Agastya may not have been the first to explore the impact of hands-on experiential education, but in many ways, it perfected its model and evolved it into something so unique that it truly was the only player in its field. Whether it can do this once more will define its success, and maybe survival, in an increasingly digital-centric world. Challenges Agastya will face in evolving from a scaled organization to a movement include finding and motivating replicators and future change makers from outside the organization, ceding control and ownership of Agastya's unique brand of teaching-learning to an ever-expanding cadre of volunteers, monitoring impact, creating new partnerships and building synergies between the core organization and the larger movement.

The introduction of the National Education Policy in 2020 also brought some new challenges and opportunities for Agastya. After aligning itself with the NCERT thus far, Agastya will need to find its place within the new policy if it is to successfully create private–public partnerships to emulate the successes seen in North Karnataka.

As the team gets older, there is also the fear that Agastya will not grow beyond its founders.

"The problem I have found with some NGOs is their inability to cut the umbilical cord and create an organization," observes Bhaskar Bhat. "They become like family businesses. 'The founder's way or the highway' doesn't do the organization any good. Particularly in this sector it is even more intense because most founders are intimately involved with the stakeholders, and they are carried away by the business model that delivered the first impact, and they think that is the only model."

For the most part, Agastya's installation of a professionally managed system – complete with enterprise resource planning, customer relationship management software, and extensive and rigorously implemented human resources policies – has already pushed the foundation beyond the whims of any founding members. However, Agastya's intention to become a movement will be driven, in no small part, by its ability to introduce, promote and encourage a new generation of altruists. Effective succession planning – which is already underway at Agastya – will be vital to ensure that, when the time comes, the baton is passed seamlessly. New ideas may clash with the old, but provided the culture of frank, honest dialogue pervades, they will find common ground.

Indian history has seen numerous 'golden ages'; times during which science, culture, and society advanced in bursts of untrammeled flourish. It would be fair to say that these periods were successful because the leaders of the times encouraged curiosity, creativity and allowed questions to be freely asked without fear of retribution.

Ramji emphasizes the importance of building the 'absorptive capacity' of a nation. Much like spongy soil rich in nutrients readily absorbs water to create a flourishing eco system, communities that are questioning, observant and willing to experiment (qualities that nourish the mind) are spongy and absorbent and can more readily utilize capital and technology (rain and sunshine) to create prosperity. "Agastya's role as a socially innovative, transformative, and responsible enterprise rested on its ability to create connections both at the level of the mind and the heart among people and ideas across the social spectrum. We have catalyzed and created new and unexpected opportunity spaces.

We have striven to inspire by demonstrating the possibility of great and positive change in the most challenging of circumstances."

Indeed, Agastya's vision and story coincide with an emerging and confident India, which seeks to play a vital role as a creative power on the world stage once more. It is perhaps fitting that for both Agastya and India, a long but exciting journey lies ahead. India's 'Chandrayaan moment' is expected to lead to a massive increase in demand for science and technology education and more broadly creative learning across India and Agastya is brilliantly positioned to leverage this opportunity.

Ultimately, however, when the numbers have been crunched, the reports studied and the books balanced, it is the stakeholder – the child – that resides at the centre of it all.

Mounika, a village girl from an indigent farming family, was an underachieving student with little interest in studies. Her father had decided to marry her off at a young age. One day, an Agastya teacher persuaded Mounika to visit his session. The teacher asked for volunteers to give a tiny sample of blood. Without asking why, Mounika extended her finger, which the teacher pricked with a sanitized needle. He took a small sample of her blood and after analysing it, he told her what her blood group was. Mounika recalls her world changing in an instant. She suddenly realized the power of science and glimpsed a whole new world of knowledge to be discovered. Mounika's grades in school began to move up, but her father was insistent that he would get her married. She offered her father a deal. If she came first in school, would he agree to postpone her marriage and send her to college instead? Perhaps thinking there was little chance that Mounika would rank first in her class, her father agreed.

Mounika achieved the top rank in her school exams and entered the well-known Sri Venkateswara University, where besides earning a BSc degree, she became a student leader. Mounika's story highlights the inestimable value of an igniting moment, in this case one caused by a simple prick on her finger.

Agastya's main role is to provide an endless stream of such 'pinprick' moments to as many children as it possibly can. To this end, Ramji speaks of the three Rs – reach, richness and rupee. As Agastya moves ahead, each needs to improve without compromising the other two. Only then can the overall purpose be adequately served.

Within its mandate, its mission, and even its determination to reach across the nation and spread its message, there exists the purest purpose.

Reach the child. Spark curiosity. Nurture creativity. Instil confidence.

It's as simple as Aah! Aha! Ha-ha!

And yet, bringing this simplicity to a nation of hungry, eager children requires nothing less than the strength to move mountains.

1. https://www.nature.com/articles/nature06589

2. V. Kasturi Rangan, "Lofty Missions, Down-to-Earth Plans," *Harvard Business Review*, last modified March 2004, https://hbr.org/2004/03/lofty-missions-down-to-earth-plans.

3. The development of customized local language tech modules for Agastya 2.0 was led by Aarthy Parthasarathy under the guidance of Thiagu.

AFTERWORD

1. **A DEFINING VISION IS WHAT DRIVES SUCCESS.**
The difference between those who truly succeed and those who only attain middling success is that the former often have a clear vision from the beginning on what they were setting out to achieve.

   An inspiring vision or magnetic mission can be simple, unexpected and must touch both the heart and mind. "Many organizations suffer an exponential decay of vision over time," says Ramji, stressing that communicating the vision and mission constantly is imperative to keep it alive.

   Agastya's great strength was that it very early on identified the issue it was trying to solve and set this at the core of its philosophy. They made sure that this was then communicated vertically and horizontally both within and outside the organization. Articulating the vision again and again – through speeches and internal team discussions – only reinforced and honed the message further.

Says Ramji: "A village boy, a young Agastya Young Instructor Leader, once asked me how I had come up with the idea of the campus. I was about to reply 'on autopilot' when it hit me suddenly that the visual image of the campus had been stoked by my vision of Shangri La from James Hilton's *Lost Horizon*. I hadn't thought this thought for a decade or more. It took a young boy's curiosity to make me pull out a hidden picture of the mythical Shangri La from the recesses of my mind. So, make sure that your vision is alive and burning within you, that you live it not mechanically but with energy and passion. Even when you think you are lost or wayward, it is amazing how reconnecting with your vision can drive you and your team towards the right path. By some wonderful intelligence peculiar to humans, when you dream and feel something deeply in your mind and heart, you stand a great chance of realizing it."

2. **ONCE THE VISION IS DEFINED, NEVER BE HESITANT TO PIVOT SHAMELESSLY AROUND IT. BE FLUID AND FLEXIBLE, NOT RIGID.**
   An unbroken chain of cause and effect constantly buffets human beings, adding uncertainty and complexity to life. There are only so many things that you can control, and they aren't many. So, adapt and go with the flow. If you can't reach your goal directly, don't worry. Being open to possibilities will help you to see and seize opportunities as they emerge. It will help you to find new insights and create more powerful and meaningful goals and innovations. In their book *Whiplash*, Joi Ito of MIT's Media Lab and Jeff Howe of *Wired*, distinguish between compasses and maps. Maps might give you a detailed path to reach your destination. Compasses are

directional and rely on your creativity and capacity to explore and discover your own path. Agastya has followed the path of the compass and frequently "danced in the white spaces" between government and business, science and art, and formal and informal education. It's a path that has offered Agastya freedom to explore, innovate and create. The journey has been richer for it.

3. BALANCE DISCOVERY SKILLS WITH DELIVERY SKILLS AND ENCOURAGE CONSTANT MOTION

Discovery skills are the ability to question, observe, discover, experiment, associate and network. By developing them, we embrace obliqueness and uncertainty as opportunities, not obstacles. This will make your organization more agile, fluid, and adaptive. At the same time, delivery skills build a bias for action because action energizes, clarifies, and encourages constant experimentation leading to new solutions. In *The Innovator's DNA*, Christensen et al suggest that discovery skills are more common among founders while delivery skills are stronger among CEOs.

Finding a balance between the two creates a feedback loop of ideation and implementation that pushes the organization into a self-sustainable cycle of innovation.

Ensure you are constantly forging ahead, reinforcing the idea of a permanent but tempered revolution. The Mobile Science Lab and The Lab on a Bike are physical manifestations of the idea of continuous movement. Agastya's relentless innovation and focus on "the next project" helped it build the innovation agility, capacity and stamina it needed to turn the COVID crisis into an opportunity.

4. BE PATIENT AND STAY THE COURSE.

"I was frustrated with the slow pace of fundraising, which prevented Agastya from building its dream school," Ramji recalls, "In hindsight, it almost feels like divine powers willed it so Mahavir and I might acquire the patience to pursue deeper and broader objectives."

What at first appeared to be a disaster was the catalyst for Agastya's mobile lab and outreach programs. The obverse might also be true. Today's quick success might lead to complacency and sow the seed for tomorrow's failure.

Not everyone will move at the same speed as you. In socially rich and complex contexts, the interests of different stakeholders need to meld and synchronize before the wagon can move forward. When things don't move at the pace we wish them to, we become frustrated. The fault might lie in our limited perspective. So, cultivate the wisdom to be patient, and the patience to gain wisdom. Stay in the fray and wait for your moment because learning to play the long game delivers rich rewards.

5. WELCOME UNCERTAINTY OR, IF THAT'S NOT POSSIBLE, ACCEPT IT AS AN INEVITABLE PART OF LIFE.

"In the early years of Agastya, I used to spend considerable time mentally adjusting to the constant and, sometimes nerve-racking, uncertainty that I faced – and continue to face." Ramji recollects. "The pain of uncertainty was acute when I transitioned from my job as a banker in London to become a social entrepreneur in India. The fear of the unknown was a new and unsettling experience. I asked Dr. Balasundaram what J. Krishnamurti had said about uncertainty.

'He might have said that life is uncertainty,' Balasundaram replied."

Seeing that uncertainty is inevitable and ever present, learn to accept it as one of life's certitudes. Uncertainty comes with open possibilities, which can develop into new paths. Building Agastya's ability to deal with uncertainty has made it a more resilient organization. The decisions to buy barren wasteland in a remote rural area, to shift away from a school to a school for schools, to launch the mobile science lab and create the discovery centre were made during periods of high uncertainty and low resources. They have proved to be among the best decisions taken by Agastya.

6. CONSULT A WIDE SPECTRUM OF PEOPLE.

"Whenever an entrepreneur or executive has complained to me about the lack of a mentor or the absence of an enabling network, I have advised them to pick up the phone and ask for a meeting with the most important or accomplished person they know of that could potentially help them." Ramji declares.

Most people, however important they might be, love to talk about their lives, and share their views and opinions. Seek and meet them, take notes, and grow immeasurably. There's a deep and vast sea of knowledge, expertise, and wisdom among the old and young, great and ordinary that you can tap into for little to no cost. Listen carefully to what they say, and often *do not* say.

The probability of connecting the dots to create a new insight, idea, or course of action increases as you meet and interact with people from a wide spectrum of backgrounds and interests.

Says Ramji: "I have learnt as much from talking and listening to India's former president A.P.J. Abdul Kalam, the father of India's green revolution M.S. Swaminathan, former atomic energy commission chairman P.K. Iyengar, my father and mother, my friend Gopi Warrier, Agastya board members, educators, scientists, academics, artists, executives, entrepreneurs, bureaucrats, and politicians in India and abroad as I have from talking to and interviewing both privileged and underprivileged children, parents, and schoolteachers.

I have benefitted equally from reading books on education, cognitive science, social science, creativity and history, among others. I have particularly enjoyed validating the findings and assumptions of formal research through personal observations and interactions with people in cities, towns, and villages. Connecting with people at the human level has given me both great joy and insights."

7. CURIOSITY MUST BE LIVED AND BREATHED. ASK QUESTIONS CONSTANTLY.

The world's economic, social and spiritual progress often has been the consequence of periods of deep and persistent questioning and enquiry. In contrast, most of us are trained and conditioned to know the right answer. Looking for an immediate answer is almost our instinctive response to any problem or challenge that we face. The inordinate emphasis that we place on tests and exam grades to measure our progress through school and university has played no small part in encouraging such behaviour. We are taught that the bright kid is the one who knows all the answers; the one without the answers is stupid or ignorant. However, unlike in a test or exam, the real world rarely offers one right answer. The right answer depends on the context as well as our aims and objectives. Above all, it depends on the question that is being asked. By learning to pose and formulate a wide range of questions, you can develop the ability to unfold new possibilities and eventually find new and better answers that a kneejerk or quick answer might have pre-empted you from doing. So, learn how to question.

Ramji recalls a visit to a school in Jaipur in Rajasthan: "I was impressed with the way the Agastya teacher had engaged the children who responded enthusiastically to his questions with a flurry of answers. This was no small achievement in an environment where children were shy to speak up. I was equally surprised by the fact that the children did not ask any questions. I asked the children who they would consider to be the more intelligent: the one who knew all the answers or the one who asked questions. 'The one who asks questions,' a girl said. 'Why so?' I asked. 'Because there is no end to how many questions you can ask!' the girl replied to general laughter. I asked the students why they did not ask questions. 'Fear,' a boy said."

A rigid environment that discouraged questioning at home, in the community and at school was limiting the children's ability to grow into adults that could create, innovate and better their lives. Agastya's mission, as much as anything else it set out to do, was to crush this fear completely and allow children to question everything.

8. STAY CLOSE TO THE ACTION.

There is a thrill in building something from the ground up. As Agastya's chairperson, Ramji always believed that he had a special responsibility to demonstrate and communicate his passion and commitment to advancing Agastya's mission.

"For this, I have found visiting and being in the frontline to be indispensable," he states (Always and especially in a crisis or challenging situation, as a leader you should be prepared to say, "follow me," not "attack" – this builds your credibility and raises the organization's motivation and morale more than anything else you might say or do). It is on the frontline, in thousands of classrooms across India, that Agastya's work gets done every day. Being there means observing teachers conduct classes in remote rural schools and villages, interviewing children, parents, and schoolteachers in their homes, talking to and interviewing educators and academics or presenting Agastya's case for money to fund its operations to donors and partners. The more I have done this, the more I have found that newer ideas and thoughts have entered my consciousness and the more empathy, understanding, and competence I have gained to advance Agastya's mission."

9. BUILD CAPACITY TO INNOVATE AND CREATE IN THE FACE OF COMPLEXITY

Ramji recalls Dr. Iyengar's advice to him, "Don't be a copycat. Do something that makes others want to learn from you." Innovation and creativity is not the preserve of the gifted or a select few. You must believe that you can create and innovate, a point that might seem obvious to those in the thick of innovative cultures.

To those whose work environments are characterized by an absence of innovation Ramji says, "Don't lose hope."

Driving innovation is perhaps the most important 21st century skill. It can happen if you create an attitude of "open minded curiosity" coupled with "tippe top thinking" (simplicity, counterintuitive, unexpected, upending conventional wisdom). The quote from the French Romanian artist Brancusi is one Ramji has used extensively across the globe in his speeches, namely "simplicity is complexity resolved." The tippe top idea is a great example of this as it embodies the entire Agastya mission and can be a talisman for not just the education, but for any system looking to infuse wonder and inquiry into its DNA.

10. DO SOMETHING BECAUSE YOU BELIEVE IT IS THE RIGHT THING TO DO.

"Whenever you are in doubt, or when the self becomes too much with you, apply the following test. '*Recall the face* of the poorest and the weakest man whom you may have seen and ask yourself if the step you contemplate is going to be of any use to him.' I have found these stirring words of Mahatma Gandhi to be of immeasurable value in giving clarity and purpose to my actions," Ramji relates.

It might help to ask yourself why you are doing what you do, who you are working for, and what impact it is having, and might leave behind, after you are gone.

11. MONEY MIGHT BE OVERRATED AS A SOLUTION TO PROBLEMS

Most of us believe we need money to achieve our aims and dreams. We spend a lot of 'what if' moments thinking how more money will liberate us. Money is important but overrated as a solution to many problems. If you view the absence of money not as a disaster but as an opportunity to create and innovate, you might build things that might surprise you. There is much truth to the saying "abundance makes you poor." Even if you are not short of money, it might help to practice thinking poor. "What would I do differently or better if I didn't have money?" is a question worth pondering. Lack of money might free you from the limitation of resource dependent mental models. Raising money can become an inexorable treadmill occupying most of your mental space and time. It is worth stopping and asking the question, "Would less money actually help me better achieve my goals? Or "How can I achieve more with fewer resources?" You will be surprised how much more innovative and inventive you might become when you are forced to rethink and readjust to living and acting without the money, fame or relationships that you and your enterprise have become dependent on.

12. WHILE KEEPING YOUR END GOAL(S) IN MIND, THOROUGHLY ENJOY THE PROCESS OF GETTING THERE.

The great tennis player Arthur Ashe said, "Success is a journey, not a destination. The doing is often more important than the outcome." Nothing you do will feel like time wasted or a disappointment if you enjoy the process of living and growing through your journey. Your drive, energy and ability to raise your sights can make your journey an endlessly exciting and fulfilling process. Your dreams and goals might feel at times distant and unattainable, but as you focus and apply yourself wholeheartedly to reach them, some goals might no longer seem so grand, uplifting or fulfilling anymore. Some others, added by circumstances unexpectedly, might, to your surprise, turn out to be more relevant and fulfilling.

As described in this book, Uma, an Agastya Young Instructor Leader, responded to the question, "What impact has Agastya had on you?" with "I am not afraid to speak any more." Her answer persuaded Agastya to add the words "instilling confidence" to its mission. This was seen time and again when scores of case stories of children impacted by Agastya showed that its interventions had not only enhanced the science knowledge of the children but had given them the skill and confidence to apply their creativity to solve problems in their communities, which led Agastya to invest in project-based learning.

Finally, understand that failures and disappointments have their own return and should be welcomed as opportunities to reflect, learn and move forward. Agastya's serendipitous journey is replete equally with false starts and disappointments that sparked successful innovations.

13. DEVELOP STRONG NERVES.

As often as you can handle it, subject yourself (and your organization) to a difficult challenge or situation. This will build your resilience to deal with the increasingly difficult challenges that an expanding endeavour will invariably throw at you. When you act to create something new and different, you will inevitably rock the equilibrium. This will throw up new challenges and obstacles for you to overcome. View these as welcome signs, indicating that you are on the road to making something happen. Purposeful action leads to obstacles, overcoming which builds character and resilience, which are essential for success.

14. THINK BIG

'Big' could be in terms of scale (how can I reach 100x more customers?), quality (substantially raise the quality to a level no one has experienced or dreamed of?), economics (can I do 10x more at the same or lower cost?), legacy (what will people say 50, 100 years from now?), which means think and act long term, don't be tempted by short-term gains. This does not mean that you will not need to balance the need to score short-term hits, to quickly attract customers for example, with the ultimate goal of creating a sustainable legacy.

"The idea of Agastya – and what it stands for – is more important even than the physical organization," says Ramji. "This idea, if it is of value, should live in the hearts and minds of millions, hence bringing about a movement whose momentum can vastly surpass that of the original mission."

Julius Caesar famously said of his rival Pompei "Pompei has merely done something, I stand for something." Before envisioning greatness, it is vital to ask: 'What do we, as an organization, stand for?'

15. EMBRACE DIVERSITY AND "STRANGENESS"

Agastya's strange workforce combined different perspectives, backgrounds and personalities to create an organization with greater plasticity, fluidity, adaptive intelligence and resilience.

Phil Jackson, the coach of the Chicago Bulls, was always questioned over why he put up with Dennis Rodman, the flashy, rule-touting, bad boy of basketball who so clearly contrasted with the rest of the championship winning team. Jackson defended Rodman, calling him the team's 'heyoka' – a title usually conferred to a certain member of a native American tribe. "The heyoka was a cross-dresser, a unique person who walked backwards. He was respected because he brought a reality change when you saw him." (*The Essential Bennis* by Warren G. Bennis and Patricia Ward Biederman)

Welcome the 'strange,' because anyone bold enough to be different will almost certainly help you think different.

16. LEARN TO BECOME A GOOD COMMUNICATOR / PUBLIC SPEAKER

This will widen your canvas and impact and build your reputation. A lot of what Agastya was able to achieve came from Ramji's ability to effectively sell his vision. Whether addressing halls in the Indian Institute of Science, Harvard, MIT, or Beijing University, or speaking with a rag-tag group of village students, he always ensured the purity and intensity of the message remained uncompromised. It was this communication that allowed Agastya's vision to endure, even when there were but a few takers.

17. HARNESS TRUST TO BUILD AN ORGANIZATION OF CARING, CHANGE MAKERS

Agastya's ability to look beyond marks and qualifications to find employees was a matter of necessity at the beginning. But the resulting army of BEEs (bachelors of energy and enthusiasm) – who had something they want to prove or set right – became a force of nature unto itself that took Agastya to otherwise unconquered peaks. (Central to Agastya's organizational strategy is the idea of getting people with ordinary backgrounds to achieve extraordinary results).

Instilling confidence in the team and exhibiting genuine caring is the bedrock to creating a self-motivating, internally energised team. Freedom and autonomy, combined with the systems to track and monitor progress was central to implementing this.

That Agastya was able to maintain this even as it scaled up was truly remarkable. It would have been impossible to keep functioning in the 'mezzo zone' without a team that, although spread out across the country, had a common love for the cause and a steadfast belief that they had the unwavering trust of their seniors backing them.

18. WRITE YOUR OWN STORY AND LIVE WITH THE CONSEQUENCES OF WHAT YOU BELIEVE

As a wise yogi once remarked: for millions of us, a 40-year career is nothing but the same year repeated 40 times. It is surprising how many of us can indeed write our own stories, be our own authors and go on to lead infinitely more fulfilling and meaningful lives. All it takes is introspection, energy and the courage to confront your own conditioning.

The shackles that society – and our own acquies-
cience – impose on us are usually false and illusory
in nature. They need to be broken free. There is, of
course, risk, uncertainty and some getting used to,
but the rewards of a life of agency and purpose can
be infinitely greater than of one that blindly follows
the herd.

19. SECRETS OF AGASTYA'S INNOVATION SUCCESS:

a. Emphasis on fostering discovery skills, namely
   questioning, observing (especially looking for
   asymmetry in situations), experimenting (without
   fear of failure), and associating (connecting uncon-
   nected dots)

b. Talking to/learning from customers

c. Democratizing innovation across the organization

d. Bias for action and staying close to it ("act your way
   to thinking")

e. Going where others have not gone or chosen not to
   go (counter-intuitive thinking and actions)

f. Articulating big goals in the midst of constraints,
   even creating constraints when needed, to motivate innovation

g. Desire to be a trailblazer, not a copycat

h. Tying financial and psychic rewards to innovation

i. Mindset of welcoming crises/challenges as potential (breakthrough) opportunities

ACKNOWLEDGEMENTS

A special thanks to the numerous people who gave their time to be interviewed for this book.

Alok Oberoi
Executive Chairman, Everstone Group;
Board Member, Agastya International Foundation

A.M. Naik
Chairman Emeritus, L&T Group

Amit Chandra
Partner and Chairman, Bain Capital India

Antonio Riera
Senior Advisor, The Boston Consulting Group

Bala Warrier
Former CEO, The Manipal Foundation

Bhaskar Bhat
Former Managing Director, Titan Industries

Dhirendra Singh
Former Union Home Secretary, Government of India

Dirk Smit
Vice President Research Strategy, Chief Scientist at Shell

Dr. Anil Kakodkar
Former Chairman, The Atomic Energy Commission of India

Dr. Baluragi
Author, Former Professor of Physics, Gulbarga University

Dr. K. VijayRaghavan
Former Principal Scientific Adviser to the Government of India;
Emeritus professor and former director,
The National Centre for Biological Sciences

Dr. K. G. Narayanan
Former Chief Advisor, DRDO; Director,
Aeronautical Development Establishment

Dr. V. K. Aatre
Former Director, DRDO; Advisor to the Minister of Defence;
Board Member, Agastya International Foundation

Dr. R. Mashelkar
Former Director General, The Council of Scientific and
Industrial Research

Dr. Vinay Dabholkar
Author; President, Catalign Innovation Consulting

Dr. Kota Harinarayana
Former Programme Director and Chief Designer,
Light Combat Aircraft

Erin Guzman
Senior Director, ESG (Environmental, Social and Governance),
Synopsys

Ganu Subramanian
Former Vice President, Hewlett-Packard

Gavin Dykes
Programme Director, Education World Forum

Gururaj "Desh" Deshpande
Founder and Chairman, Sycamore Networks;
Founder and Trustee, The Deshpande Foundation

Harsh Mariwala
Chairman, Marico

Hayagreeva "Huggy" Rao
Atholl McBean Professor of Organizational Behaviour and
Human Resources, The Stanford Graduate School of Business

H.N. Srihari
Board Member, Agastya International Foundation

Jaishree Deshpande
Founder, The Deshpande Foundation

Jonak Das
Discipline Lead, Exhibition Design,
The National Institute of Design

M. Shivkumar
Author, Science Model Designer

Mahesh Naithani
Chief Executive Officer, PRISM.science

Manish Gupta
Founder and Chief Investment Officer, Solidarity Advisors

Manu Prakash
Associate Professor of Bioengineering, Stanford University;
Co-founder, Foldscope Instruments

M.R. Rangaswami
Founder at Indiaspora, CEF & Sand Hill Group; Philanthropist

N.R. Narayana Murthy
Founder and Chairman Emeritus, Infosys

Nish Acharya
CEO, Equal Innovation;
Senior Fellow, Clinton Foundation

Pankaj Talwar
Founder and Director, Talwar Equity Management

Paul Glick
Executive Director, Rural India Supporting Trust (RIST)

Paula Golden
President, Broadcom Foundation

Peter Patch
President and Founder, Patch & Associates LLC

Phanish Puranam
Roland Berger Chair Professor of Strategy & Organization
Design, INSEAD.

Ram Shriram
Board Member, Alphabet; Managing Partner, Sherpalo Ventures

Rekha Jhunjhunwala
Director, Rare Enterprises; Director, Rare Family Foundation

Rishi Krishnan
Director, Indian Institute of Management, Bangalore

Ron Berger
Author; Chief Academic Officer, EL Education

Sharukh Mistry
Founder Partner, Mistry Architects

Sharad Sharma
Co-founder, iSPIRT Foundation

Sharon Kumar
COO, Exstemplar Education Linkers Foundation;
Director, IRIS National Fair

Sri Jagannathan
CEO, YoGeo

Sunand Bhattacharya
Associate Vice Provost for Design and Innovation Strategies,
Boston College

Sushil Vachani
Former Director, Indian Institute of Management, Bangalore

S. V. Ranganath
Former Chief Secretary of Karnataka

Tadashi Tokieda
Professor of Mathematics, Stanford University

Vasanth Nayak
Co-founder, MurthyNAYAK Foundation

Vidya Shah
Executive Chairperson, EdelGive Foundation;
Board Member, Agastya International Foundation

Vishal Gupta
Investor, Rare Enterprises

Also, to the amazing team at Agastya for lending their memories and learnings so this story could be told:

Ajith Basu	Mukesh Kumar
Babitha Rajashekhar	Nimesh Patel
C. K. Rao	Nitin Desai
Chayya Devi	Rakhi Advani Gautham
Dilip Kumar Gowda	Ramji Raghavan
Dr. Shibu Sankaran	Rashmi Jejurikar
Geeta Patil	Revathi Narayanan
Hamsalatha K	Sai Chandrasekhar
Hariharan Ganesan	Sheetal Kataria
Jayamma P. S.	Shiv Kumar Chaudhary
Koppala Balaram	Shrishail Dhanawade
K. R. Ranganathan	Sridevi M.
Padmanabhan Kumar	Subramanya Shastry
Laksh Kumar	Suresh T.S.
M. Sandhyapriya	Syed Mohammed
Mahavir Kataria	Thiagarajan K.
Manjunath Prakash	Vagisha Thakur

And a very special additional thank you to Alok Oberoi, whose generosity made available the funds to bring this project to life.

ABOUT THE AUTHOR

Adhirath Sethi is a businessman and author, based in Bangalore. He is also a trustee for the Agastya International Foundation.

He is an alumnus of The Rishi Valley School, Eton College, and the London School of Economics.

A former management consultant with The Boston Consulting Group, he took an all too eager plunge into entrepreneurship in 2008. As the Director and CEO of Poly Fluoro Ltd, he has worked to grow the company over ten-fold and establish its reputation as one of the leading manufacturers in the field of high-performance polymers.

His first book, *The Debt Collector's Due*, was published by HarperCollins in 2015 and draws on his own experiences with hiring debt collectors to recover funds for his business. The book has been optioned for being made into a TV mini-series.

His second book, *Where the Hills Hide their Secrets*, published in 2019, is set in post-colonial India, where the murder of a local woman sends secrets and scandals spilling out of the woodwork across the fictitious hill-station town of Nalanoor.

He has recently finished a third work of fiction – Searching for Saanvi. It is a love story, wrapped in an adventure, wrapped in the coming of age saga of a young man, who falls in love with a girl when he is 10 years old, only to spend the next 15 years looking for her after she mysteriously disappears.

In 2019, to commemorate Agastya's two decades since inception, a proposal was put forth to capture the story of the foundation's remarkable journey. The advent of COVID meant that this plan was temporarily put on hold. However, in 2021, the idea was revived and Adhi-rath offered his time to bring the book to life. He spent the first half of 2022 interviewing anyone that might have insights into Agastya. Speaking with everyone from front-line workers, to donors, to board members, and senior management, the inside story of Agastya began to emerge. *The Moving of Mountains* is thus infused with the distilled learnings from thought leaders, captains of industry, staff and the founders themselves.

As a board member of the Agastya International Foundation, and as Chairman of the Navam Foundation, Adhirath's involvement in the NGO space spans over 10 years and includes contributions to fundraising, operations management and strategy.